THE RECOVERY OF MEANING

An Essay on the Good Life

THE
RECOVERY
OF
MEANING

An Essay on the Good Life

C. DOUGLAS McGEE

RANDOM HOUSE

New York

*The author wishes to thank the following for permission
to reprint material included in this volume:*

J. M. Dent & Sons Ltd. and the Trustees of the Joseph Conrad Estate
for excerpts from *Victory* by Joseph Conrad.

Dover Publications, Inc. for excerpts from *Mind and the World Order*
by C. I. Lewis.

Faber and Faber Ltd. and Harcourt, Brace & World for an excerpt from
"The Hollow Men" by T. S. Eliot in *Collected Poems 1909–1962*.

Harper & Row, Publishers, for excerpts from *The Web and the Rock* by
Thomas Wolfe.

The Macmillan Company, Macmillan & Company Ltd., and Mr. M. B.
Yeats for eight lines from "A Prayer for My Daughter" by W. B. Yeats,
from *The Collected Poems of W. B. Yeats*. Copyright 1924 The Macmillan
Company, renewed 1952 by Berta Georgie Yeats.

The Macmillan Company and Rupert Hart-Davis Limited for an excerpt
from *The Letters of W. B. Yeats*, edited by Allan Wade. Copyright 1953
and 1954 by Anne Butler Yeats.

The Nonesuch Press for excerpts from *The Complete Works of William
Blake*.

G. P. Putnam's Sons for an excerpt from *Art as Experience* by John Dewey.
Copyright 1934 by John Dewey.

Charles Scribner's Sons for excerpts from *Look Homeward, Angel* by
Thomas Wolfe.

The University of Chicago Press for an excerpt from the Richard Lattimore
translation of *The Iliad* by Homer. Copyright 1951 by The University of
Chicago Press.

First Printing

© Copyright, 1966, by Random House, Inc.

Library of Congress Catalog Card Number: 66-26072

Manufactured in the United States of America
by The Hadden Craftsmen, Inc., Scranton, Pa.

For M. B. M. *and* D. R. M.

ACKNOWLEDGMENTS

Years of unsystematic reading have left me with intellectual debts so extensive that I cannot even remember the names of my creditors. Thus, while I claim no originality for this book, and would mistrust a work in normative moral philosophy for which such a claim were made, I am embarrassed by the suspicion that I have taken the ideas of other men for my own, and am now unable to give credit where credit is due.

I can acknowledge what I feel to be my principal debts. C. I. Lewis, Baker Brownell, and Paul Henle in their lives as well as through their teaching showed me what philosophy at its best can be. Thanks are due to the students and auditors in my courses in ethics, aesthetics, and philosophy in literature; many of the themes developed in this book I first made explicit in class or seminar, and student response and criticism was almost always useful. In teaching aesthetics I have found the work of Monroe Beardsley especially helpful, and that help has carried over into this book. David A. Dushkin and Sylvia S. Moss of Random House have provided editorial aid and comfort for which I am deeply grateful. I am also indebted to Professor Vere C. Chappell, Consulting Editor in Philosophy for Random House and Alfred A. Knopf, and to Professors Morris Weitz and Peter J. Caws for encouragement and advice.

The typing was done by Mrs. Mildred Tubby and Mrs. Maria J. Parker, and I thank them for their patience and good work. I should like to acknowledge a grant for secretarial assistance awarded me by the Faculty Research Committee of Bowdoin College acting on behalf of the Shell Companies Foundation.

C. D. M.

South Freeport, Maine
23 April 1966

CONTENTS

ix

THE RECOVERY OF MEANING

An Essay on the Good Life

INTRODUCTION

The end of all moral speculation is . . . by proper representations of the deformity of vice and the beauty of virtue, [to] beget corresponding habits, and engage us to avoid the one and to embrace the other. But is this ever to be expected from inferences and conclusions of the understanding, which of themselves have no hold of the affections or set in motion the active powers of men? They discover truths: but where the truths which they discover are indifferent, and beget no desire or aversion, they can have no influence on conduct and behavior. What is honorable, what is fair, what is becoming, what is noble, what is generous, takes possession of the heart, and animates us to embrace and maintain it. What is intelligible, what is evident, what is probable, what is true, procures only the cool assent of the understanding; and gratifying a speculative curiosity, puts an end to our researches. Extinguish all the warm feelings and prepossessions in favor of virtue, and all disgust or aversion to vice: render man totally indifferent toward these distinctions; and morality is no longer a practical study, nor has any tendency to regulate our lives and actions.[1]

DAVID HUME, *An Inquiry Concerning the Principles of Morals*

There is such a thing as ethical analysis, and there used to be such a thing as moral philosophy. The business of ethical analysis is to determine the meanings or to clarify the use of the moral terms that occur in our judgments of good and bad, right and wrong, obligation and prohibition; such analysis also tries to discover whether or how moral argument can be rational. The analysis of moral discourse has been the chief concern of ethical philosophers in England and America for more than fifty years, and their occupation has a clear claim to the title "ethics." Their investigations have not provided final answers to any questions, which proves against the philosophers only that they have been doing philosophy. Results need not be conclusive to be useful; one can learn care and caution at this school, can learn to look to his meaning and his evidence before venturing to pronounce on right and wrong.

Although this is not a book in analytic ethics, it has not been thought or written as it might have been if there were no such discipline as analytic ethics. It uses some of the tools and appropriates some of the insights of contemporary analytic philosophy. However, its purpose is only incidentally the analysis of moral language. For this reason it is not a book written for the professional philosopher—at least not for the philosopher in his professional role.

"Moral philosophy" is often used as a synonym for "ethics," and even for "analytic ethics," but that is not how "moral philosophy" will be used here. The term will be taken in one of its old-fashioned senses and will be used to mean the attempt to develop and defend a substantive view of the good life and of what it is that makes the good life good. The object of the book is to criticize, to argue, and to persuade; to speak to the reader who (it must be assumed) feels that he wants a life in some sense "good" and is willing to listen to discussion of what that sense might be. The assumption is essential: such a discussion must take for granted at least a generalized desire for a good life. Lacking that desire, the reader has no reason to read, and this lack—though certainly rare, since it would amount to not caring whether one's life was in *any* sense good—cannot be remedied by reading. What is more usual is an uneasy sense that one's experience of life ought to be found better or more meaningful than it is, and that it could and would be if one knew a direction or a pattern to give it. Given this much the moralist has all he needs to ensure the possible usefulness of his work.

One further limitation of the use of the word "moral": the morality to be discussed is as limited as it can be to questions concerning the personal lives of individual men and women. So far as issues of social or political philosophy arise, they are peripheral. Traditional moralists usually talk about how man ought and ought not to deal with his fellow creatures; this is useful and sensible and we shall do so too, but our primary focus is so far from social that it could even be called "intra-personal." This is not to say that man can or should live untouched by the world around him—our argument will be that he should not and cannot—but only to make clear that our central concern is with the individual's experience of life, with that accumulating and summated experience which when we survey it we judge to be as a whole worthwhile, or a waste of time. Each of us is first of all responsible for himself, and one good place for morality to begin is at home. What is to be argued is that there are ways of informing one's life, possible patterns of feeling, attainable attitudes toward expression and order, that conduce to a life found meaningful and good by the person who lives it.

There is nothing new in the idea of attempting to give form to life and character; its inspiration is as old as the Greeks and animates traditional Christianity. (It has recently fallen on hard times: the professors adapted it as "humanism" and made it nostalgic and priggish, while the coffee-house existentialists transformed the ideal into self-creation out of nothing, making it at once incredible and melodramatic.) Moral philosophy that bears directly on the individual life is not absent from Aristotle or Santayana, and echoes of both are audible in what follows. But despite these elective affinities there is inevitable divergence. Most humanists, from Aristotle to Santayana, have been able to speak to man as citizen, have even thought it possible to address themselves only to the man essentially involved in a clear social structure. Now that each of us is accidentally involved in any number of unclear and shifting social situations, but essentially involved in almost none, it is no longer useful to speak to the single moral agent as if he were essentially a political creature.[2]

If, for historical reasons, it is inopportune to take as moral subject man as citizen, for intellectual reasons it is impossible for many to accept the Aristotelian doctrine that man has a fixed, metaphysically grounded nature, essentially distinguishable from all his other natural characteristics, and that moral theory can be built on this essential nature. This doctrine cannot successfully be defended, but rather than argue against it we will try to see how much can be done without it. The same can be said of religious belief that man has a guaranteed cosmic place and an immortal career. This is not to endorse the quick positivistic dismissal of metaphysics and religion as "mere nonsense," for there are affective lessons to be learned from them, and it is worth asking whether these lessons can be saved after the cognitive claims have been dismissed. Much that any sensible person could say on the good life will be compatible with a whole range of theories of reality and religion. So much the better; but it must be made clear that our recommendations rest on no such foundation. The compatibility can be accepted as a consonance between our views and the affective bearing of less agnostic positions, but the appearance of support must in honesty be rejected. The appearance turns out to be an illusion, to be no more than appearance. To say this is not to be quixotically candid, for candor in this context may discover common ground. The unwillingness to take at face value the claims of metaphysics or the language of religion, the suspicion that it makes no sense to say that their statements could be true or false, are characteristic both of this book and of those by whom a book of this sort will be read.

We must also accept our mutual liabilities. Most philosophers who have advanced views of the good life have done so on what seemed to them firm, metaphysical foundations. If we disallow the claim that certain standards of rightness or goodness are sanctioned by the structure or nature of reality itself, but try to do justice to the moral insights some such systems have embalmed, we have a difficult way to go. Part of it leads through a corner of the theory of knowledge: to discriminate what is morally pertinent and useful in various traditional and modern views, man's moral situation can be looked at in the light of his attempt to *know,* and of some radical criticisms of cognitive endeavor. This sifting starts with the problem of "the meaning of life," discovers the affective or emotional crux of the question, and tries to show how the needed senses of "meaning" and "justification" resolve themselves into awareness of activities and experiences as themselves self-justifying. If our felt situation arises from apprehension of an ultimate and lonely responsibility for ourselves, our hope can be to establish in the will and emotions of the single self a pattern of awareness felt as an inherent sense of meaning and purpose.

Although they come with various cognitive credentials—some honest, some forged—it is for our affections that philosophies, religions, and ideologies compete. To examine their claims is more often than not to learn how not to live. Most represent extremes of one sort or another, exaggerating some partial insight until it becomes perverse; we can use Aristotle's technique of showing how the extremes must prove abortive and letting the viable means show themselves before we have to show them. Positive argument will come, but if the ground and motive of the good life are affective, effective argument must reach that ground. If personal morality had a compelling rational basis, the moralist could rest his case on rational demonstration and deduce the certain canons of moral rationality. In fact no ultimately rational ground is available, and to insist on its necessity is one road to moral disaster. Not rationality but reasonableness is what we can reasonably hope. Because this species of reasonableness is itself an aspect of affective life—often absent in very rational men—it would be misleading to speak of one strain that must concern us in terms of conflict between emotion and reason, between the affective and the cognitive. Order and pattern are indispensable to the life found good, but the most appropriate models of order are not to be found in mathematics or in science, although the importance of these paradigms of rationality is never minimized in all that follows, but is taken for granted. If we are to use any cognate of the honorific "reason," then "reasonableness" in the sense of affective order must be understood. "Affective order," in turn, must be seen to mean not just a pattern of experience, but a pattern that, lived through, is *felt* as order and as its own sufficient reason for being.

Models for such order can be found, objects and experiences felt to exemplify an optimum balance of affective qualities, to combine intensity, complexity, and form in a whole that brings not merely immediate satisfaction but a sense of completion and of realized purpose. We cannot literally and seriously say that to lead a good life one must become an artist; nor is it suggested that we give our lives to the contemplation of works of art. What will be argued is that we can look to an ideal of aesthetic order —the achieved integration of intense immediacy and strict control, of unified difference, rhythmic diversity—as a model for the ordering of our affective lives. We can do this because we are not wholly passive to experience, because our vision of our lives is a constantly reinterpreted reconstruction, and because "intensity," "diversity," and "discipline" seem perfectly to characterize the affective desiderata of the good life. It is true that to find the specific forms most appropriately human we must look beyond the idea of order itself, must try to discover patterns of experience that peculiarly express and satisfy the human shape, but before this difficult attempt we can state the most general conclusion of our argument. It is that the life found good by the person who lives it will be a life felt to embody an integration of the power of immediate experience and the constraint of an appropriately human order, the tension between lyrical intensity and firm and formal control. Exclusively to emphasize intensity is the way of romantic anarchy; exclusively to emphasize diversity is to recommend frivolity; to speak only of order is to be a pedant and to praise pedantry. What Adrian Leverkühn said of music can be said of the good life: it represents "the highest and profoundest claim of feeling to a stage of intellectuality and formal strictness."[3]

I

CLEARING THE GROUND

Man can embody truth but he cannot know it.[1]
WILLIAM BUTLER YEATS, *Letter to Lady Elizabeth Pelham*

Contemporary English and American philosophy is often censured for neglecting "The Big Questions": questions about the meaning of life, the justification of life, man's place in nature, goodness, truth, and beauty. This charge is only partially just. The philosopher can answer the imputation of frivolousness or evasion of responsibility by showing The Big Questions to be unclear. He can, by reference to a defensible and useful standard of meaning—a criterion for distinguishing meaningful questions and answers from meaningless questions and answers—argue that questions about the meaning or purpose of life are literally, or scientifically, or "strictly speaking," senseless. He will be aware that just such questions *feel* to many people most important, but he can plausibly claim that his specialized philosophic work has been done in showing that the questions are at best unclear. His analysis of the questions shows that what they really ask for is not fresh facts or scientific knowledge, but emotional or affective consolation. There are specialists whose business it is to cope with emotional problems, but this, it may be said, is not the special business of philosophy. The philosopher has a just claim to specialization in intellectual or conceptual clarification and is entitled to restrict himself to conceptual or linguistic analysis as the best means toward that end. Such analysis does show that there is something odd and elusive about questions like "What is the meaning of life?" That oddity will be exposed in this chapter, and can be put in the form of a dilemma: the clear answers that can be given to such questions never seem to satisfy those who ask them, while the answers felt to satisfy the questioners are never very clear.

This far analysis of the questions can take us, and this far we shall find it useful to go. Beyond analysis things become less clear, and the moral charge against modern philosophy is that it will not go beyond analysis. When in later chapters we see where every step away from analysis takes us, we may understand and sympathize with those who confine their philosophic practice to the diagnosis of linguistic confusion.

A. MEANING

What, exactly, is one asking for when one asks for the meaning of life? Unless we take the trouble to understand the question, we will never know whether it has really been answered. What sort of answer would answer this question?

The clearest kind of answer is near at hand: when in contexts less charged with emotion we ask questions about meaning, it is generally because we have failed to understand a sentence or a word. If we suppose our questioner to be unclear about the meaning of "life," the four-letter English word, we can easily answer his question. We can point to various living things and say that they have life; in one clear sense of "meaning" a term means what it stands for or denotes. We can give instances of the denotation of "life" by pointing to objects characterized by metabolism, growth, reproduction, and internal power of adaption to environment. We can go on to give the connotation or intension of the word "life"; the meaning of "life" in this sense is to be found in the dictionary. Or we can say that the meaning of "life" is its role or use in English, and describe the meaning of "life" in terms of its use.

At least three things must be said about this answer: it is clear, it is correct, and it is dissatisfying. If we were to claim that a question had been answered, we should have to recognize that the question pedantically answered was not the question poignantly asked. If we argue that language alone has meaning, strictly speaking we are right: to ask for the meaning of "life" is either to ask about a word or to trade on some ambiguity in the notion of "meaning." But the most extreme pedant could not be so insensitive as to believe this question to be a request for the definition of "life." The questioner already knows what the word means; he feels his question to have far deeper import. We must suppose that "meaning" is here being used in a broad sense. To please the purists we can allow that, strictly speaking, it is misused. So be it. If we would uncover the real intent of the question, we must try to follow the sense of those who ask it.

B. EXPLANATION

It conduces to clarity to distinguish questions of definition from questions of explanation. The former have to do with words and send us back to language; the latter refer to extra-linguistic things and send us for their answer to the world of objects. Useful though this distinction is, it is often neglected, and questions about the meaning of life can be obscured by this negligence. Since it is unlikely that our questioner wants a definition of "life," it is possible that what he wants is some kind of explanation—an explanation of the phenomenon of life, or of his life, that he can understand. Again we shall have to clarify the question. We shall have to become at least as clear about "explanation" and "understanding" as we did about meaning.

Let X be an object or event to be explained. There are two general kinds of answer to the question "Why X?" or "Why did X happen?" or "Why does X happen?" These kinds of answers are called (1) "causal explanation," and (2) "teleological explanation." We need only broadly characterize these categories; more can be said about them than we need to say.

1. *Causal Explanation*

Aristotle called the causal kind of answer to the question "Why X?" explanation in terms of "efficient causes." Much later, during the seventeenth, eighteenth, and nineteenth centuries, when the image or metaphor of the machine dominated speculation about the natural world, one spoke of "mechanistic explanation." Today the mechanical model is obsolete, and if one wants to speak about scientific explanation he is faced with the problem that no simple model is adequate to convey its complexity.

Even so, it is possible to state in a rough way the most general aspects of causal or scientific answers to the question "Why X?" Any such answer will involve a minute description of events and classes of events; the determination, according to some guiding hypothesis, of increasingly refined correlations among more and more determined classes of events; and the formation of increasingly general hypotheses on the basis of which particular events or hitherto unobserved correlations among events can be predicted. These three phases of inquiry are not separate and distinct. Description, correlation, and the formation of explanatory or predictive hypotheses go on concurrently and are altogether interdependent. This complexity forbids easy exposition, but we shall not go far wrong if we take the key notion involved in causal explanation to be *prediction*.

One has explained an event causally when he has shown how

it can be predicted. A class of events is scientifically understood when there is some reliable general hypothesis that correlates the events in question with a variety of other events. This much is grossly accurate to scientific practice, and more than this need not be argued since it is sufficient to show that one who asks for an explanation of life can be given it. This is the kind of understanding biologists, psychologists, and social scientists provide. Nor is there good reason to believe that scientific explanations of the complex phenomena of human life are in principle impossible; whether we find the prospect exhilarating or appalling is another matter. Such explanations will of course be complicated and unsure—the number of variables involved will be tremendous —but in principle they are available.

Suppose we come with this good news to the man who would understand the meaning of life. Suppose we tell him that if he is willing to wait some few years an answer will come from the laboratories of physicists, physiologists, and psychologists; suppose we construe his question in a scientific way—and answer it! The chances are good that he will be as little satisfied with this empirical or scientific answer as he was with our earlier linguistic or analytic answer. He might acknowledge that our explanation of the origin and development of life was accurate; he might allow that our description of the causes of his own action was convincing; and he might still insist that this was not what he meant at all.

If we, having provided clear answers to his confused and tormenting questions, are again tempted to break off discussion, we should allow two considerations to qualify our impatience: to stop here might be to dismiss the question, but it would not dismiss the dissatisfaction the question tries to express. That dissatisfaction and the rejection of scientific attempts to meet it are in a tradition as old and respectable as Socrates, Plato, and Aristotle. We cannot simply declare that all the sensible answers are in. This would be by definition to dismiss as senseless all teleological explanation.

2. *Teleological Explanation*

The teleological answer to the question "Why X?" was called by Aristotle explanation in terms of "final cause"; its central place in his system virtually determined the course of science for two thousand years. To explain X teleologically is to show that some purpose is met or fostered by X, to show that the existence or occurrence of X serves an end, and to discover the end it serves. (The vine, said Aristotle, puts forth its leaves to shade the grape.) To understand a thing in this sense is to see its place in an order of interlocking goals, in a structured hierarchy of ends. (The end of the grape is to make glad the heart of man.)

The key notion involved in teleological explanation is *familiarity*. Beneath all complication what the purposive question finally asks is this: "Why—to what end, for what purpose, to accomplish what goal, to satisfy what motive—would I have done X?" Understanding in this sense is an exercise in empathy. For the questioner to "see" the place of X, for him to "understand the meaning" of an event, is for him to recognize the end to which he or someone somewhat like him would have brought the thing about or how he would use it. It is not essential for his feeling of understanding that he sympathize with the end achieved by X; this helps, but it is enough that he is able to imagine using X as an instrument or artifact.

The attempt to understand all nature in telic terms, to use purpose as one's most general category of explanation, tends to speculation about God's purposes or to the speculation that God is the end of all ends. It seems that the chain of events must have its end, the system of purposes must culminate in some final purpose. Since nothing in nature can be the goal toward which all of nature tends, the final purpose of man in nature must lie beyond nature and man.

This recourse has its attractions. The vision of the universe presented to the imagination feels immediately, intuitively "intelligible." We feel that we see why it should all be just this way, and within the broad and general picture there is room for the play of intellect, for demonstration of the propriety of just this or that relation of means to ends. Although the teleological picture as a whole may be the product of highly rationalized wishful thinking and have no warrant other than the comfort it can give us, it is nonetheless true that powerful thought can go into the establishment of connections within the whole and into the details of its internal architecture.

Insofar as scientific explanation means empirical description, prediction, and control, it is a platitude to say that reference to final causes does not contribute to scientific understanding. Detailed criticism of teleological explanation is unnecesary. The best argument against its scientific usefulness can be put in one phrase: science has not found it useful. For what, then, is it useful?

To be lost in the dark is a terrible thing. It is a terrible and inevitable thing to leave home, to be alone, to be a stranger and afraid. Each of us has had to leave home, and even if not all there was customary and ceremonious, at least it was to a degree dependable and familiar. Even when it was not good, it was familiar. Imagine the child lost in the forest, in the city, in the desert, and you will begin to see the virtue of explanation in terms of purpose, of explanation that has as *its* purpose the establishment of a peculiarly human rapport between man and nature.

If causal explanation serves to show us the predictable regularities of things, even allows us to some extent to control their flow, it still seems to leave them, in essence, alien and inhuman—as, of course, they are. Thus there are those who say that science does not tell us *why* things happen; that science does not explain, but only describes; that science does not give us understanding. Their "Why?" is openly or secretly teleological. The questioners will be satisfied only with an answer that assures them that the universe behaves as they do, that it has purposes, that it uses one thing to accomplish another. Thus, however well established the law of gravity, whatever its utility in prediction, it tells us only that things behave in such and such a way, and it may feel far more deeply illuminating to hear that water flows downhill in order to reach its proper place. We have our errands, and we can understand this. We build things, and we can understand that had we built birds, we should have given them hollow bones and short intestines because their purpose is to fly,[2] and had we made men, we should have given them thick bones and long intestines as it is the end of man to contemplate. "To understand" in this sense is to recognize why someone like you (perhaps your parents, except that they were much stronger than you, much wiser, and moved in mysterious ways) should have designed these things to the accomplishment of these ends. And things thus understood seem far less foreign, seem, after all, homely—perhaps, finally, benign.

This is not merely one sort of answer that satisfies those who ask for the meaning of life; it is the most usual sort, a usual genus of which other answers are species. The general end of teleological explanation is to render events human and familiar, and this quiets those who question the meaning of life. It gives an answer in terms of purposes they can imagine having, or by reference to motives in some way familiar to them. If one can sympathize with the motives, the events imagined to follow from them will seem not only natural but right and just. Even when nature seems most conformable to the spirit of man—at the coming of spring, perhaps, or in the light air after a summer storm—no one is ingenuous enough to say, "Yes, I should have done it just so, if I knew how!" Only some poets, close as poets can come to the childlike human heart, come close to saying this. Most of us are less honest and conceal the simplicity of our feelings even from ourselves, freeze our first warm intimations into a cosmology, colder, but with a respectable air of rationality.

When sympathy is not possible, empathy can serve. The mild

and gentle questioner may feel that *he* would never send a storm to blast the crops or a plague to blight the people who had failed to do him honor; but he can imagine what it might be like to be more stern or jealous than he is—and if he were, and if he had the power, so he might act. The patterns a man can feel himself into, the sequences he can imagine someone like himself bringing about, will feel intelligible. Even when the events are untoward or tragic, even when we would not have willed them if we could, if we can imagine what it would be like to use them for some end, we will feel we understand them. And yet, flexible as is this standard of "understanding," there are occasions empathy cannot reach, and we find ourselves about to lose touch with any model recognizably human, with any saving image of justice, utility, or rage. Then one of two things can happen: we may save our feeling of understanding by the invocation of mystery, or the line may break, leaving us in apathy or terror.

The consolation that can be achieved by reference to the mysteriousness of God's ways is, when viewed without sympathy, astounding. This reference gives no fresh information, explains nothing not equally explicable without it, predicts nothing, and often lightens an otherwise intolerable burden of grief. It is perhaps the plainest example of pseudo-explanation, but it is not so plain how it saves a rapport between man and all that is less or more than human. But this, too, becomes clear when we remember the desperateness of the situation and the awfulness of the alternative. What is altogether unfamiliar is not even thinkable, cannot be entertained, is less a possibility to be envisaged than a wordless gesture toward the horror. Try to imagine that nothing should be recognizably anything, a flux in which no things could be known by shape or function, in which all analogy should be altogether drowned; even in nightmare we recognize ghosts of recognizable things, and we hold on to ourselves. Try to imagine almost losing yourself, keeping only the realization that chaos has come again. But such terrible formlessness, being beyond the possibility of description, can only loom up as an obscenity, as a name to shudder away from, as worse than death and hell, although resembling the latter.

Words can at best suggest the presence of chaos; the feeling escapes them. And as desperate diseases call for desperate cures, when all ordinary analogies fail, we call on the dangerous name of mystery, refer to mysterious means and mysterious ends. This amounts to a faith or hope that there operates through inscrutable events some motive we would feel as human if we knew it. We want to believe that behind the opaque screen of things there works a will remotely like our own: at least a will that acts toward ends, that molds and moves, that brings all things in its own good time, though its ways are known only to itself. To think of the child's relation to his father, be his father cruel or kind—the relation of dependence on uncomprehended power and inscrutable motives—is to touch the ground of the saying that we must become again as little children. To be at last at home again, that is the answer.

It is unnecessary to press the pathos of this position, though it can bear a considerable weight. The present point is this: all that is central to such "explanation"—sympathy, empathy, familiarity, return—all speak most directly to our affective nature. Their appeal is to emotion, feeling, or will. What is answered is not a question, but a need. This centrality of sentiment tends to confirm what we may in any case suspect: that to ask for the meaning of life is not to ask for any kind of information. One reason why the problem feels so deep and so hopelessly puzzling is that it seems to be the kind of question that must be answered in one of the ways that a question of fact or of definition can be answered, while no such answers are ever satisfying. If those who ask the question remain dissatisfied with definitions, descriptions, or predictions this does not mean that their problem has a cognitive answer, but one that is impossibly deep and difficult. It may seem so, especially to them, but in truth no information is wanted, and the whole sum of scientific information would not serve.

When all the questions of fact and definition have been answered, what remains is the need to feel a certain way or to get over feeling a certain way. The seeker wants to feel significant, purposeful, properly placed, or at home. He would escape the sense that he is lost and that his loss is unimportant, that he has no ends or none that justifies effort, that he is placeless, uncared for, and alone. No answer will satisfy unless it restores the sense of a place in an order of things humanly conceived. The terms of the answer must be those of will and purpose; there must at least be analogies in which the questioner can rest. That the answers that speak to his feelings are without scientific sense, that they give no information about matters of fact, that they express nothing which could be true or false—this cognitive meaninglessness of them may seem unimportant when measured against the affective resolution they sometimes bring.

The problem of "the meaning of life" is affective; it does not follow that it is uninteresting or unreal.[3] But to say that to ask for the meaning of life is to express an emotional need may still seem too deflationary to some, and before accepting it we can try the analysis of a closely related question.

C. JUSTIFICATION

It is difficult to express the common feeling that one's life stands in need of vindication. Even when we think we can give good reasons for our particular acts, we may feel forced to bafflement or despair if we ever try to justify the sum and pattern of events that is our life. It is true that we need not and should not be forever summing up. It is true that there tend to be certain times of day or year or life when we feel most liable to account for ourselves to ourselves. It is also true that the time never comes when our lives feel wholly beyond question. "What have I done with what I have been given?" One seems for a moment to stand at the end of his life, knowing that life is ending at every moment, and feeling that the word he must speak is a word of vindication. "I must answer at least to myself for my life and my talents, and what answer shall I give?"

If we can never know ourselves finally exempt from the felt need to justify our course of life to its most knowing judge, we should be as clear as we can about the justice of the question. Can we ever reasonably ask for a justification of human life in general, or of our own? Does it ever make sense to try to justify one's life? Once more we must cope with a term as strong in force as it is weak in sense. We must try to make clear the kind of thing that calls for justification, or to which the demand for justification appropriately applies. We must ask exactly what it is to justify any X.

The clearest course will be to show what "justification" means in one specific context: the world of nature. More complex settings could be considered, but none can be specified with equal clarity and economy or without the use of language essentially equivocal or obscure. This specification begs no questions: by starting with the natural world we can see one point at which naturalism is likely to be rejected, and also see why the modern supernaturalist rejects it at just this point. There are other reasons for beginning with what we all take to be our common and public world. For one, we do so take it; it is the natural world in which most of us naturally believe and on which we base our practical calculations. Also, while it may well be an implicit definition of "evidence" to say that we have no good evidence for the existence of any other world, this definition not only conforms to our usual weekday feelings, but properly leaves the burden of providing a different definition to those who think they should have one. ("The evidence of things unseen" is a beautiful phrase, but its force arises from our sense that it expresses a paradox.)

Scientific understanding of the world can be stated in physical, biological, psychological, and sociological terms. These categories overlap, combine, and subdivide. Man, feeling, thinking, speaking, and acting, can be understood in these several ways. In his use of symbols man entertains his past, figures to himself what is future or absent, imitates the miracle of action at a distance, turns his thinking back on itself and, as an aspect of the peculiar advantage of explicit language, incurs the peculiar liability of linguistic confusion. The abstractness, perspicuity, and reflexivity of language are at the heart of its utility, and their nature can be explained in terms of its use; it is when their pragmatic ground is disregarded that they seem gratuitous and unnatural. Our reason and its language are inseparable aspects of a suitably complicated response to a complicated world; their origin, nature, and utility are grounded in the matter of the psyche and its needs. The same can be said of all those events that are categorized as "mental." If the category is to be useful in explanation, it will group together according to some criterion a range of publicly or privately observable happenings, or at the furthest stretch of meaning will postulate unobserved natural events in attempting explanations of observable behavior. "The spiritual," if used, will be an honorific name for aspects of the mental.

1. *Of Means*

The clearest sense that can be given "justification" is one it seldom has in ordinary use. We can say we have justified an empirical or scientific prediction when we have shown it to be based on the best evidence available at the time it is made. The better the evidential ground, the more justified the prediction and the better its chance of confirmation. A variant on this sense is that in which we justify the existence of something, say X. To justify the existence or occurrence of X is to show its relation to some Y and Z and to demonstrate how, given Y and Z, X can be predicted. Insofar as justification consists in showing external relations, the notion of justifying everything is senseless.[4]

A more usual sense of "justification" is that in which we speak of justifying or vindicating a course of action. ("Why did you do that?") Justification in this sense is a combination of the two kinds just described: it is to show that given a course of action, A, a certain result, R, can be predicted; it is to explain that A and R stand in certain regular and predictable relations. Given the end (R), health, the doctor can tell you the means: taking the pill (A) is justified by its causal connection with better health. Given the desired end of political power (R), Machiavelli will tell you the means. Given as R "the greatest happiness of the greatest number," the followers of Mill and Dewey will try to prescribe the means. Given the end of inflicting sexually satisfying pain, the Marquis de Sade can perhaps suggest the means.

The compelling thing about the end to be achieved is that it *is* given. By and large we simply find ourselves wanting what we want, valuing what we value, and all our effort of thought is bent to the achievement of an end beyond question. "Reason is, and ought to be the slave of the passions, and can never pretend to any other office than to serve and obey them."[5] If this is the case, if our goals and desires are part of the personality we find ourselves with at any given time, we can accept this neither as an ideal nor as a program, but as a fact to be understood. Like other natural facts, human ends and aspirations can be explained naturally. Whatever the R you want—fame, love, death, or a house in the suburbs—it is in principle possible to explain, causally, why you want R. If you have chosen it from among several alternatives, it is possible to explain why you have chosen as you have. This does not mean that ends are simple or that they are necessarily fixed once for all. They blend and change and they can be changed, seldom by ratiocination alone, but by influences and arguments which touch the conative-affective springs of our lives. These changes too can be explained.[6]

It is possible to justify means by showing that they lead to predictable ends. It is possible to explain why a person has the ends or goals he has. And it is unlikely that the man whose means and ends had been thus explained would feel that they had thereby been justified. Neither the fact that we find ourselves with the goals or values we have nor the fact that having them can be causally explained seems enough to free us from the feeling that the ends which give direction to our lives need vindication. Whether or not it is available, what may be wanted is a sense of justification in which we could justify our most general goals.

2. *Of Ends*

We know that particular actions can be justified as means, justified by reference to the ends that lie beyond them. If justification in this sense is taken as the only model for all justification of action, one can justify an end only by showing it to be a means to some further end. All ends become proximate, all justification is of means, and nothing can be considered an end in itself. This solves the problem of justifying ends by denying that ends as such can be justified.

Leaving aside for one moment the inadequacy of arguments against ends-in-themselves, we can allow that *if* vindication of ends is construed on the model of justification of means, the justification of any act or activity must always refer to something beyond the action itself. From this follows one of two possible consequences: (*a*) either it makes no sense whatever to speak of justifying the sum of all one's acts, one's life; or (*b*) one must justify his life or human life in general by reference to something that lies beyond it, to something transcendental. Fortunately there is a third way of making sense of the felt need for justification, a way that depends on rejecting the inadequacies of this model. But it will be useful first to consider the morally consequential ways in which this mode of justification is misleading.

a. BEYOND NONSENSE

It is not inconceivable that the seeker after justification might accept an analysis that showed all ends to be proximate, admit that it was on this analysis impossible to justify the whole of life, and find his felt need for a sense of justification as strong as ever. Perhaps if men were perfectly rational such things could not happen; but we are not so, and they do happen. It is unreasonable to think that man is wholly accessible to reason and to expect that a problem philosophically condemned as "meaningless" is finally removed to where it can do no further harm and there can be safely ignored. Such hopes are not merely illusory, they are dangerous, for the affective ground of philosophical puzzlement often remains unaltered after the problems in their would-be cognitive form have been solved or dismissed. The unquiet, insistent feelings from which many philosophically formulated questions grow—problems about meaning and justification, about other minds and the external world, about alienation and communication, about good and evil—not only affect far wider populations than professional philosophy does, but often (and often in secret) successfully appeal their conviction by analytic philosophy or go underground to escape the rational consequences of having been found to depend on misuses of language. "Off with his head. So much for Buckingham." And in silence and darkness the root of the problem grows on.

This should not be taken as a denigration of linguistic or analytic philosophy. The analysis of The Big Questions and their answers is an almost indispensable propaedeutic; it serves to discover their ground in feeling. Although we need neither accept imperialistic claims made in behalf of linguistic analysis, nor refuse to consider questions beyond its reach, we can allow that such analysis has shown the futility of spinning further and thinner metaphysical systems—spider webs to do the work of rock—and has cleared the way to approaching The Big Questions as the affective problems they are.

b. THE UNNECESSARY LEAP

Suppose the dissatisfied questioner will not recognize his problem as affective, clings to the model of justification already described, and refuses to accept the answer it entails: that there is no sense in asking a justification for the whole of life. This situation sounds complicated, but it is common: it is from this crisis that many are tempted to leap to the supernatural. For what is one to do if he insists that the whole of life must have a cognitive justification and that whatever justifies life must lie beyond it? He will be driven—intellectually driven, as it seems to him—to postulate a transcendental justification.

What really drives him is the combination of a conceptual model and an emotional need. The model leads him to think that the justification of life requires reference to an object or goal beyond life, and the need will not let him rest until he believes that the object or goal is there. Since this apparent crisis can be exploited by melodramatic forms of theology, its pattern should be made clear. If one accepts the view that all human ends must be justified in the same way one justifies means, one must accept one of two alternatives: either life as a whole must be without justification or naturalism must be rejected. To many souls acceptance of the former is equivalent to intolerable despair, and any supernaturalism will seem preferable.

If the first of these alternatives is emotionally distressing (which does not prove it false, but only distressing), the second is worse than intellectually feeble. It is not simply invalid, it is dishonest to argue that because we need something we have it, or because we want something we are entitled to it. Such sentimental sophistries were never thought of so long as faith in the supernatural was habitual and strong and was supported by an

27

unquestioned revelation and by what seemed to be cogent argument and the necessities of explanation. But since it would be as useless to condemn the need itself for existing as it is sophistical to pretend that—since the need exists—there must also exist a supernatural justification for it, we may seem to be at an impasse. Fortunately, the supposed dilemma is false. It disappears when we discard the means-model of justification.

C. THE APPROPRIATE MODEL

Sometimes if we try to say why we have done a thing, or why we act in some way or another, we are able to say only that this was something that we wanted to do. We may, at an understandable loss for better words, say that the activity is fun. This is a legitimate justification, one species of the most basic genus of the justification of acts. It marks the fact that we do numbers of things for the sake of the doing, not for the sake of anything that lies beyond them. Walking, talking, reading, working, serving, making love, playing games, looking at pictures, or listening to music—any of these or almost anything else can be taken as an end-in-itself, as a self-justifying activity. Any of them can also be used as a means—of transportation or for the sake of health, of gaining information or giving it, of extending influence or making money, of begetting children or rising in the world, of acquiring an impressive culture. Sometimes when we are asked or ask ourselves why we are doing this thing, we justify our activity by reference to something beyond: then we are saying that our activity is a means to that further end. Sometimes, startled by the question and feeling that activity can be justified only as a means, we lie, inventing ends we hope may satisfy and quiet the questioner. But at other times the demand for justification will properly seem to us puzzling and strange. If asked why you are smoking a cigar or listening to a Mozart concerto or playing with your children or donating a pint of blood, you may feel abashed and not know what to say. You may say "Because I enjoy this" or "Because this is what I want to do"; you may be trying in some way to say that you find what you are doing to be intrinsically worthwhile.[7]

A traditional mistake is easily made at this point. It consists in supposing that the words "for pleasure" add something to what would be told by a full description of the activity found good. Pleasure is not a separate thing or event to be found apart from pleasant activities, and it is an error that can lead to moral disaster to believe that playing or working or loving ought all to be paid at the end with the same kind of coin.

The idea of pleasure per se is an empty abstraction; one reason why it is foolish to give oneself to the pursuit of pleasure as such is that there is no such thing to pursue. (Perhaps this turns out after all to be another instance of our fascination by the means-end model. It is easier to talk in its terms than in terms of intrinsic goods, and so we try by words to separate or to detach in fact what only words distinguish—the pleasure, say, of a pleasant walk from the fact that the walking was pleasant—just so we can call the activity a means to an extrinsic end.) To say "I did it for fun" or "It gave me pleasure" is to emphasize an immanent aspect of some activity, a felt quality that does not exist apart from the experience it qualifies. There are things we do for the sake of the doing, activities that are their own excuse for their exercise, experiences we find intrinsically satisfying. The pleasures of memory or daydreaming do not exist apart from their occasions. The fun of playing tennis is not a thing separable from playing tennis, not an end that can be felt or enjoyed or possessed apart from the game; it is just playing tennis and enjoying it. The pleasure of making love is not a separate experience beyond making love, not something further or later for the sake of which we make love. The satisfaction of a good day's work is not paid us as our wages are, as a reward anterior to the work or exchangeable at a market value for some other good; the satisfaction, where it exists, is inherent in the work, and is felt as an aspect of the work itself.

"Satisfaction" is a less appealing but less misleading word than "pleasure." That all acts are done with some satisfaction in view is a trivial truth, equivalent to saying that by "action" we mean behavior which proceeds from motives to ends, but it is at best misleading to say that the end of all acts is pleasure. Pleasure is only one species of the genus satisfaction. It may be the kind of satisfaction that strikes us most strongly, but many acts are done because they are qualified by other kinds. To say that no act can be done except to increase the pleasure of the actor is either a disguised tautology or a false psychological statement. If it stretches and thins the meaning of "pleasure" until that terms covers the end of every conceivable motive, from those of Heliogabalus or Al Capone to those of Brutus or Flaubert or Schweitzer, then it is an empirically empty tautology: it has no significant contrary, makes no distinctions, and gives no information. Misusing "pleasure" as a synonym for "end" or "satisfaction," it repeats the verbal connections of "motive," "action," and "end" in a pseudo-factual mode. If, on the other hand, our regular and limited meaning of "pleasure" is retained —a meaning according to which we can make distinctions in experience, applying "pleasant" at some times but not at others —then the assertion that no one acts except to maximize his pleasure is genuinely empirical, and is false. An equivocation on these meanings of "pleasure," (and the fact that it tends to make us feel cynically penetrating and worldly-wise) accounts for the plausibility of philosophical hedonism.

Some activities are felt to require no justification beyond themselves and, except by representing them as means, can be given none. It is such inherently satisfying activities that can provide a suitable model for the justification of life. To meet the felt need to justify one's life will not be to demonstrate some relation of it to a transcendental end. No such demonstration is necessary, which is fortunate since none is valid. The kind of justification appropriate here is inherent and affective. One can come to have the sense that the experience of life is its own excuse for being. We can live through forms of life in which we find an immanent justification of the whole.

D. THE AFFECTIVE PROBLEM

The problems of the meaning and the justification of life are finally affective problems. As such they survive the demonstration that they are, "strictly speaking," senseless; they survive the recognition that their old, would-be cognitive answers cannot stand. There is no guarantee that they have any satisfactory "answer" at all, but if we are to attempt one we must try to express it in terms appropriate to the nature of the problem— in terms of volition, of emotional satisfaction, of affective arrangement. The problematic feelings are those of deracination and meaninglessness, futility and the failure of significant purpose, affectlessness, isolation, and the loss of a home in the world. We sense the lack of an understanding more to our human purpose than the understanding we have, and in our loss we do not know how to direct and dispose our lives. What we need is not so clear to us as its absence. We have our work and our days and feel the insignificance of endlessness. We are given our assignments and try to lose in busyness our sensed lack of purpose. We talk and talk about lack of communication. We apprehend that we are alone in a largely indifferent world. Our sense is the sense of guilty exile, drifting, and unnoticed annihilation. Allow for rhetorical exaggeration, and the question still remains: how can we honestly cope with these problems after we recognize their affective nature and the inanity of all but affective answers?

In trying to answer this question we must first try to show some reasons why our common situation appears to each of us as a personal problem. We can then go on to speak of various attempted solutions and escapes: of returns to self-delusion, of the attempt to lose the burden of separate consciousness by absorption in immediate experience, of flights to other worlds and the building of walls, of love, and even of little escapes for the slightly concerned—basement workshops, Elks and Eagles, the innocent distractions of education, and the solemn titivation of keeping abreast of the news. There is much to be learned from abortive, fantastic, or violent extremes, more than emerges from their obvious failure to sustain a life found good. The characteristic mistake of practicing moralists is to take some cherished and partial insight for a comprehensive prospect of the good life, to warp to its focus all other considerations that can be bent to the appearance of support, and to reject as impertinent or immoral whatever limits or contradicts their intense and one-eyed perception. Often they have seen what they have seen, and if we can discover and discount the distortions of their various and partial visions, we may be able to interpolate to a more just and truly viable moral position.

But after all this what must be presented is a way of living that requires acceptance of those felt problems that trouble our deeper lives, a pattern of life that holds in itself a reasonable hope that the experience of life can be found justified and meaningful in its appropriate way. "Man can embody truth but he cannot know it." The sentence is ambiguous, and we must do our best to understand what it affirms and what it denies. It is possible for us to learn to do without the dream of transcendental references or ends, and then to find true and appropriate satisfaction in the attempt to make life itself embody a sense of significance, wholeness, and form. Life must justify itself in the sense that a work of art does—there is no honest alternative. And to whom? First to its one immediate spectator, who is at once the artist and his work.

II

THE EGOCENTRIC PREDICAMENT

*The saying of Protagoras is like the views we have mentioned;
he said that man is the measure of all things, meaning simply
that that which seems to each man also assuredly is. If this is so,
it follows that the same thing both is and is not and is bad and
good and that the contents of all other opposite statements are
true because often a particular thing appears beautiful to some
and the contrary to beautiful to others and that which appears
to each man is the measure.*[1]

ARISTOTLE, *Metaphysics*

*Which of us has known his brother? Which of us has looked
into his father's heart? Which of us has not remained forever
prison-pent? Which of us is not forever a stranger and alone?*[2]

THOMAS WOLFE, *Look Homeward, Angel*

There is nothing new in the recognition that there are influential connections between theories about human knowledge
and theories about man's moral situation. There may be no
necessary logical connection between a man's notion of what he

knows and how he knows it and his sense of the meaning of life, but the relation between these is neither arbitrary, erratic, nor weak. The correlations between particular theories of knowledge and particular moral-affective outlooks are too regular to be wholly accidental and too important to be left unexamined. One difficulty is that while we are all philosophers, we are the sort of philosophers whose theories are held too deeply down to be clear or explicit. Even so, some systematic relation between our ideas of knowledge and reality and our attitudes toward life in the world can be elicited from most of us. An epistemology or metaphysics that many people implicitly accept is likely to have some consequential bearing on the rest of their implicit philosophy.

The purpose of this chapter is to make one such relation explicit. In the background of the moral visions with which we are concerned lies an implicit theory of the ground and scope and limits of human knowledge, a modern theory more than two thousand years old.[3]

A. PROTAGOREAN CRITICISM

We have heard that "Plato is philosophy, and philosophy is Plato," and that all of Western philosophy is a footnote to Plato. There can be no simple explanation of Plato's greatness or importance, but it is possible to gesture broadly toward two grounds of his influence. He expressed in dramatic and beautiful form certain attitudes and aspirations that are characteristically human, and he did this in the course of argument against philosophic doctrines that threatened man's confidence in a set of beliefs designed to justify those attitudes and support those aspirations.

These subversionary doctrines are represented in the Platonic dialogues, as they were in the life of Athens, by a group of philosophers and teachers known as "sophists"—Protagoras,

Thrasymachus, Gorgias, Critias. Plato's work is a long and eloquent defense against the sophists, and that work has made his academic and literary fame, while the names of his opponents would be almost unknown if they did not occur in Plato's writings against them. One may therefore find it paradoxical that the philosophic mood most characteristic of literate people in our time and place is not Platonic but Protagorean. It is in the sophists that we find our original ancestors, the articulate spokesmen for our unspoken philosophy.

The connections between theory of knowledge, metaphysics, and moral philosophy were never far from the minds of the sophists, and are a principal theme of Socrates, Plato, and Aristotle. To start, as Protagoras and Gorgias did, with criticisms of ordinarily uncriticized notions of knowing is often to end by rejecting the uncriticized reasons we ordinarily give for our actions. It was not simply because they were epistemological and moral critics that the sophists were attacked by Plato. Plato was the shrewdest of critics and half sophist himself, but Plato was a critic because he thought he could demonstrate better reasons for conduct than the good but thoughtless man can ever give, while the sophists held that all such reasons were inadequate or a sham. The sophists stopped with criticism, with rejection, with relativism. For Plato their skeptical conclusions pointed to a standard of moral reason beyond their grasp—because it was beyond the scope they allowed to human knowledge.

It would be fruitless to reopen this debate except for illustrative ends. Most of us have implicitly settled the issue between absolutism and relativism in metaphysics and morals. That our settlement against absolutism is probably correct is in a moral context no more important than the fact that we have made it. Very few of us figure among our premises absolute and universal standards of goodness and beauty, knowable through the agency of pure reason. But among the rest of us there may not be many who fully understand and emotionally accept the consequences of this brave rejection. We must see not merely how our notions of knowledge condition our apprehension of life, but more particularly we must try to see the relation between the empiricism, relativism, or subjectivism we sophisticatedly profess and our vision or lack of vision of the good life. We can begin by showing that one of the perennial problems of the theory of knowledge, that which modern philosophers call "the egocentric predicament," has its perfect moral correlate. Although the phrase is modern, the problem in all of its forms— epistemological, metaphysical, ethical, cultural—was opened most acutely by the sophists, and neither Plato nor anyone after has been able to close it again.

If we leave aside guesses about the character of the experience of unborn children, we will probably be close to the truth in supposing that each of us starts his conscious cognitive life as a naïve realist. We take our senses to be like open windows; we cannot help believing that we are directly aware of the physical world around us. We say that we are aware of the rose itself in the rose garden; the real physical rose is present to our minds; the redness of the rose is on its petals and we believe we see what is out there to be seen, what is there independently of our seeing of it, what does not in any way depend for its being on ours. In supposing that our awareness somehow contains the physical thing, or is a direct and unconditioned apprehension of its surface, we are supposing also that we have a world in common. If, when each of us looks at the tree in the quad, the same tree is in your mind and in my mind, at least that item of reality is common to us both and furnishes an objective and impersonal ground on which we can meet. When you say "The tree is in the quad" and when I say it, our words are taken to refer to a reality genuinely shared, and communication thus presents few problems.

Trouble begins with the recognition that there are appearances that no one believes truly to represent the existence of independent things, but that are, as appearances, not distinguishable from those believed to be identical with the surface of things "out there." Who believes that the railroad tracks really converge a hundred yards down the line? The "surfaces" that appear do converge. Who supposes that when he presses his fingers to his eye and sees two roses, he is aware of two physical flowers? Who believes that the stone puts on a pound or two of weight when he takes it from his right hand into his left? Yet all of these are real appearances, as are those in a vivid dream. What appears to the mildly unfortunate man who sees red as green and to the madman who sees and feels insects creeping and stinging all over his body—this is seeing and feeling of the same sort as our own. Each of us sees what he sees, and those who wish to dispute correctness will have to do so on some ground other than vivacity or immediacy of apprehension.

The unreflective notion that in perception one is in immediate contact with the surfaces of physical things is naïve just in being unreflective or pre-critical. What is sometimes called "realism" need not be naïve, but naïve realism cannot withstand criticism. The occurrence of sense-illusion and hallucination, of dreams, of seeing things that turn out not to be there, is too common to leave our naïveté undisturbed; we begin to distinguish our immediate and personal experience from the world of objects. To generalize, it becomes obvious that much of what we see and how we see it depends on us. Appearance is sense-dependent, and to recognize this destroys the simple belief that experience directly or transparently delivers to each of us a common and shareable world of objective things.

Related to this point is another that philosophers have called "the incompatibility of data": two or more characteristics that could not objectively qualify the same thing nonetheless appear to do so. We should not willingly suppose that the same penny was at once round and elliptical, but at this moment the penny that you are looking at straight on appears as round to you as to me—looking from a different angle, as one always does— it looks elliptical. So the surface that from a distance looks smooth, looks rougher the closer you come, and the round gray tower seen after sunset is square and almost pink in the morning light. Qualities appear from one perspective that are incompatible with those that appear from another, and yet it is arbitrary to fix any one vantage point as *the* correct place to stand. We do fix such points for the purpose of making particular observations, but we could as well have chosen some different point and made a different observation. For the purpose of some particular measurement, some perspectives and techniques will be more convenient than others, but it would be odd to argue that from one of these convenient points and only from there was one directly aware of the surface of physical things.

For criticism of this sort there is no good stopping place. What was accepted as a common world for sense and science may seem to lose its objectivity and dissolve into a private world of sensation. Rightly or wrongly I may reason that since things are known only in my awareness, and since my awareness is and can only be *mine,* I can know nothing that is not a part of myself. To speak of what is not an aspect of my awareness is to gesture toward the unknown; to speak of what could not be in my mind is to talk without meaning or to invoke the unknowable. What experience could I have that was other than mine? And what can be in my mind other than my own sensations and thoughts? All I know, all I can ever know, is myself. I am caught in the charmed circle of myself. Otherness will seem an illusion, will seem at most to be self-alienation.

Most poignant, perhaps, will be the lost otherness of other human beings, but here we have affective trouble either way. Before criticism, the real life of others may feel impossibly distant, but after criticism it can seem no life is real that lies beyond one's own. If I suppose that you are an opaque and independent object with a being apart from my mind, I shall believe that there is a distance between us that can never be bridged. You are irrevocably other, and I am irredeemably alone. I cannot have your experience, feel your love or pain, share your sensations or thoughts. Words are what we can exchange and I can touch your hand, but the thoughts for which your words are counters—so it may seem—are and can only be yours. I may have like thoughts, but in the nature of our case I cannot have your thoughts. And however you may respond to my touch, however deep we suppose our affinities of sense, we feel, at closest, beside each other, always different feelings. Our selves may touch at their borders, but the heart of the matter must always be mutually hidden.[4]

But suppose, on the contrary, a kind of solipsism, a belief supporting a feeling that the world is real only as your idea and can be known as nothing more. Then from isolation you fall to deeper isolation, for if all the world is your idea, you are utterly alone in it. There is no other to know, only some set of phantoms or projections of the self. If "to know" is to know a thing that exists independently of one's knowledge, if "to love" is to be in some relation to another self, neither knowledge nor love will be possible in this universe of the solitary ego. It will be small comfort in this world to feel that whatever is has its significance only in relation to you; this would be to say that one aspect of the self is related to another. One could speak of self-love, meaning a kind of metaphysical narcissism, but such a love is not likely to lessen loneliness.

The notion that only one's own mind and ideas are truly knowable is a possible outcome of Protagorean empiricism. If knowledge is *identified* with sense-experience (and Plato charges that Protagoras reduces all knowledge to the mere having of immediate experience), it does end in radical subjectivism and skepticism. That a theory which bases knowledge on experience must identify knowledge with experience is fortunately untrue. The empiricist need not accept an extreme Protagorean position (it is doubtful that Protagoras did), and we can still ask after the consequences of an empirical and critical theory of knowledge without pushing to the extremes of skepticism. The Protagorean position is uncomfortable even short of the extreme; its discomforts are those that we know, they are our own.

"Of all things the measure is Man, of things that are, that they are, and of the things that are not, that they are not."[5] That man is the measure of all things is a doctrine and an attitude that openly or secretly influences our views of knowledge, of the nature of reality, of goodness, and of culture.

1. *Knowledge*

Perhaps the Protagorean, ancient or modern, means to say that each man is the sole measure of knowledge and truth. Appearances occur to every man, and appearance is completely democratic. For each of us each appearance as such is as real as every other, and none of us is entitled to say that what immediately presents itself to his mind more truly *appears* than another man's presentations do to him. If to speak the truth is just to report appearance, then truth is, as appearance is, relative to each man. The word "true" thus interpreted can no longer do the jobs for which we need and successfully use it. We use the word to label, assert, or accept particular statements about the world, and we need to make the objective distinction it supposedly marks. If "true" means no more than "it seems so to me," then to call sentence *"P"* true is merely to report that you happen to believe it. This may express something about your mental state, but it tells us nothing about the rest of the world.

Under this dispensation, "truth" names a psychological relation between some believing subject and his belief, but "true" in its ordinary and useful sense distinguishes a relation between a belief or statement and its evidence or object. The oddity of extreme subjectivism becomes more obvious when we see that on this interpretation of "true," either no one could ever contradict anyone else or contradictory statements could both be true. If, when I say " *'P'* is true," I mean only " *'P'* seems true to me," and when you say " '*P*' is false," you mean no more than " '*P*' seems false to me," our statements can both be true and yet not contradictory. Each of us is making an autobiographical statement and neither of us succeeds in talking about "*P*." If such statements are "about" anything, each is about the person who makes it. An even more extreme interpretation might argue that not even autobiographical truth was involved. " '*P*' is true" could be considered merely expressive, like "Hurrah for '*P*'," and no exclamation as such can contradict any other. There is no contradiction between my smile and your frown, and hence no purported statement of truth could ever be contradicted. If, on the other hand, we claim to be neither reporting our beliefs and feelings about "*P*" nor expressing ourselves toward "*P*," but really to be talking about "*P*" and its relation to the world, and go on to say that "*P*" and "not-*P*" are both true, we are using "true" in a way that denies the distinction we are using "true" to make. If anything can, without bias, be called "nonsensical," this can be.

In its extreme form the doctrine that each man is the measure of all things is not only odd, but self-defeating. In the *Theaetetus* Plato demonstrates this self-defeat and destroys the doctrine. So, defeated as an explicit doctrine two thousand years ago, it persists as an attitude, with a rationale that is seldom explicit. Consider the common phrase " (Sentence) '*P*' is *true to me*." What "to me" is supposed to subtract from "true" is not clear —it is probably intended to express open-mindedness or diffidence. In fact it changes the subject. When we hear the word "true" we prepare for a claim about the relation of "*P*" to the world, but the "to me" steals away the ostensible claim. " '*P*' is true to me or for me" means at most "I believe '*P*'." Although disguised as a genuine and genuinely arguable claim about the truth or falsity of "*P*," and thus about the state of affairs "*P*" is supposed to describe, it is no more than a profession of belief.

The "true to me" way of talking is sophistical. The speaker

pretends to himself and to others to be making a responsible claim about the truth of "*P*" (and thus about the falsity of "not-*P*"). He seems to claim that reality is as "*P*" describes it. He is, as his evasions and disclaimers may show, talking about himself and his state of mind. Such sophistry will never go out of fashion. It enables a man to hold beliefs while escaping responsibility for supporting them with evidence, to express predilections disguised as facts, to escape the burden of cogent argument, and in general to evade the recognition that he believes what he believes without evidence, argument, or reason.

Fortunately we can take *homo mensura* to mean not that each man is the measure, but that mankind or humanity is the measure. A sensible theory of knowledge can be worked out in these terms; in fact, most modern theories of knowledge have been. Such theories do not fantastically and irrefutably place each man at the center of the universe, nor do they make each of us the sole and irresponsible standard of truth. Even so, no sensible theory of knowledge can circumvent the sharpest Protagorean point: that each man is the center of *his* universe. Whether or not he knows it, each man is at the center of all he knows. No man has knowledge that is not grounded, finally, in his own senses and his own mind. Much, indeed, of what we know, we know by report. We take the word of travelers, scientists, and poets, but these words must be heard by each of us, must be made part of us, must be tested on our pulses, for the final locus of all knowledge and culture can be nowhere but in the minds and lives of each individual knower.

Here we can see one ground in cognition for one affective paradox. Each of us knows the occasional feeling, sometimes settling into mood, that our lives and all our little times are beneath seriousness or significance, are trivial and fruitless episodes in a process unthinkably vast and, finally, beside any conceivable point. Then, in the same moment, or in the next, we sense that the real significance of all this vastness is given it by ourselves—a little agitation of matter, the briefest flash of light, and this brief light we feel to be the center of all, the conscious moment that gives whatever importance it has to whatever it is that exists. This all but simultaneous sense of insignificance and centrality is grounded partly here: in our unromantic moments we reject the fantasy that we *are* the universe, but we also sense that the only universe we can know is the universe *we* can know.

So let us doubt that each man is the sole measure; we cannot doubt that each man must measure. However often our committee meets, however public our conversation and our records, everything of knowledge in them must come to rest in you, must be judged, finally, by you. Not the measure, then, but a measurer, and this presents problems enough. Protagorean criticism at least makes clear that no man can escape making judgments he alone must make. The responsibility is there, personal and lonely, like all genuine responsibility. The great virtue of the Protagorean criticism of knowledge is that it reminds us of our responsibility and keeps it, even painfully, before us.

To define reasonable limits of responsibility in knowing and judging, and thus to specify the class of questions we can sensibly require ourselves to answer, is one job of analytic philosophy. We merely accept one of its obvious conclusions in saying that it does make sense to ask whether particular items of purported knowledge are true, and according to which criteria of "truth." These are questions answerable within limits set by experience and reflection on experience—but the problematic feelings can persist after the sensible questions have been answered. Although we are likely to wonder in ignorance, we can know the strangeness of our question and still find ourselves asking if we are sure that any sensation or idea of ours is like its object. (As if we could climb outside our minds to catch and check a resemblance to some altogether unexperienced thing.) We may wonder whether the thoughts behind our words are like those that go through the minds of other people. (As if we could literally think their thoughts, and know that we had accurately compared them with our own.) The situation may seem even worse when we brood on the singularity of our own sensations and feelings. Nothing seems closer to us, more ourselves, than does immediate, personal experience, and what seems closest seems least communicable. The sadness is that there are times when we know that no clear questions remain unasked, no sensible word unspoken, no further account of experience to be given, and feel nonetheless accountable.

Let us agree, at least provisionally, that the analysis of knowledge and of language has shown a whole range of disquieting questions to be in a strictly cognitive sense unreal, has shown some traditional problems of knowledge to have their most accessible cause in linguistic confusions, in applications of inappropriate criteria, or in the use of misleading models. The problems we may feel about the correspondence of our "ideas" with their objects, about the likeness of those sensations and thoughts that are so indefeasibly *ours* to the mysterious mental lives of other people, about our solitariness and responsibility, so far as they are epistemological questions, can be given appropriate answers or can be dismissed. The egocentric predicament, as a felt problem, remains. The cure of intellectual confusion is itself worthwhile, but it also allows us clearly to see the problems that remain unassuaged.[6]

What stands clear is first our genuine responsibility in knowledge and judgment, and to see and accept this is the beginning of honesty. But our responsibility and loneliness can remain surrounded by an atmosphere, an air, in which they look larger than life, loom in the exaggerated shapes of responsibility without standards and loneliness without hope. These feelings can survive, and that is why philosophic analysis is only the beginning of honesty, perhaps at the very best the beginning of wisdom, but not the end of either. What can honestly follow is not an attempt to translate emotional malaise into cosmic speculation, but an attempt to deal with the post-rational problems in their own affective terms.

44

2. *Reality*

While the special sciences describe particular kinds of things—matter and energy, plants and animals, motivation and thought—and try to explain their causes and behavior, traditional metaphysics purports to give information about the character of reality as such; its province is being qua being. It may be that all men are metaphysicians in their bones, that the urge to speculate on what is really real is an ineradicable human instinct, but even if this were true it would not follow that the metaphysical need could be met except in dreams. (One reason metaphysics is so vulnerable to criticism and so persistent is that it is easy to recognize the fantasies of other people.) The sophists, however, were no more skeptical about metaphysics than they were about less recondite realms of knowledge, and for that reason it would be wrong to read too much of positivism into their denials. It is rather that each man is the measure of *all* things, and hence of the real. The questions of what it is to be real and what is real must be answered for each of us by each of us. For the extreme Protagorean skeptic the answer is terribly simple: what is to each man, is; reality is whatever appears to each individual. There is no being, only seeming. No argument is possible, for all are equally right and equally wrong. Above and beyond the unsteady light of each consciousness stands no impersonal criterion of the real.

We may well stick at this radical subjectivism—after all, most of us do successfully distinguish among appearances, holding some to be reliable clues at least to future experience—but we must again acknowledge its grain of truth. It is up to each man to judge, and this takes us back to the problems of knowledge. Whether we claim knowledge of this or that real thing, or of reality per se, the beginning and terminal points of knowledge are personal. Gorgias said that even if there were one reality it could be neither known nor communicated, since the apprehension of the real would still be peculiar to each. Stop short of the irrefutable fantasy that there is one reality for each knower and a different reality for each knower at each moment. What remains is that each of us must, according to *some* criteria, distinguish between the less and the more real, the merely apparent and the more fully existent, the inconsequential happening and the significant event.

If by "metaphysics" were meant the understanding, clarification, and improvement of vague criteria and categories like these, the practice of metaphysics would be not merely unobjectionable, but of great utility. Allowing that its results will be abstract, formal, and categorial, reflection on the modes we use to order our lives is an almost necessary first step toward their better formation.[7]

In practice each of us acts as if some organization of experience were better than others, and our notion of "better" is likely to be pragmatic. Our active lives do not disprove extreme Protagorean skepticism, they only render it practically useless or misleading. "Real" (with its range of opposites—"illusory," "sham," "counterfeit," "trivial," "ephemeral," "merely mental," "merely physical," "fictional," "inartistic," "insubstantial," "dead or stuffed," *et cetera*—each used to make a different distinction and each qualifying the use of "real" in its context) marks one range of distinctions we make within experience, and make according to criteria that reflect human circumstances and ends. In our situation and in our organization of it we have much in common, but if this tends to the practical nullity of extreme subjectivism or skepticism, it does not relieve each man of responsibility for criteria and judgment or give responsibility to some impersonal all. Even if you believe that it makes clear cognitive sense to speak of reality in general, you do not escape the fact that your concept of what this reality is and your assertion that it is reality itself you know are functions of criteria and of judgment that you have had to decide were acceptable.

Put aside for the moment its doubtful extreme, and the heart of the Protagorean lesson remains: *however* you construe the concept "real," whether as marking a set of distinctions made within experience or as distinguishing something which transcends all experience, it is you alone who must judge what it is to be real and which things are real. You can evade recognition that you are deciding and judging, but this ensures only that your commitments are made in the dark. To relinquish judgment to another is to judge at second hand. Help and support are not unavailable, but the final responsibility is your own.

3. *Ethics and Morals*

The basis and expression of sophistic morality will by now be obvious. What is right is right to me or for me; the only standard of goodness lies in my will. No moral truth is possible, and there can be no formal contradiction between moral judgments. When you say that X is right and I call it wrong, the closest thing to fact that is conveyed is that you want or like X and that I do not, and between these statements there is no disagreement. Or "X is good" may mean "Hurrah for X!" while "X is bad" expresses (rather than reports) the speaker's revulsion from X. Expressions of this sort are neither true nor false, and no contradiction between them is possible. There can be the kind of disagreement that comes to blows, but we are not asserting opposite truths when I am expressing my emotions and you are expressing yours.

If a disagreement that can come to blows is serious, then not all serious disagreements concern the truth or falsity of statements. In such cases the sophist Thrasymachus (who appears in the first book of Plato's *Republic*), despite what appears to be an inconsistency, is willing to make judgments of right and wrong. Right, he says, is the interest of the stronger; might makes right. If there are no extra-personal standards of rightness, how can we settle moral disputes except by coming to blows? And how are we then to know who is right except by waiting to see who wins the battle? The inconsistency is that if each man's opinion is as good as every other man's, the defeated are no less right than the conquerors. The fact is that no one listens to the losers.

A radical ethical subjectivism is one possible outcome of Protagorean criticism; that it is the only possible outcome is not as clear. It is possible to interpret "man is the measure" as meaning that mankind is the only judge, that it must be the human voice that speaks the final moral word. That word we shall see to be not wholly equivocal. We need not accept the extremism that holds the whole content of goodness to depend on individual acceptance. We need not believe that each judgment must be without precedent or guidance. But we cannot deny that each of us must judge. Only one person can make your decisions and your judgments of right and wrong; no one else can take the responsibility for the life you intend. To accept the judgment of others is to judge their opinion worth accepting or their displeasure worth avoiding, and this judgment of worth is one's own. To drift is to decide by abstention or to decide to trust to circumstance.[8]

Indolence and ignorance effect a kind of anesthetized decision. It would be wrong to pretend that all the advantages lay with being fully conscious, but few can choose and successfully maintain a deliberate and blissful unconsciousness. The rest of us must evaluate, rank, weigh, and decide with some degree of awareness, and the only question is whether we do these things well. However untheoretical we may be, our conduct will display some order of values, some pattern of flights and pursuits, some notions of better and worse and good and evil. The structure may be grotesque or irregular almost to chaos, and if it is, our lives will evidence this, showing that deliberate choice is a necessary but not a sufficient condition of reasonableness.

Much in our lives must be accepted as we find it, and it may be peculiar to speak of decision where so much is decided for us, but to recognize the very possibility of a conscious choice of a moral order is to take one step toward a life that will be found good. There will be the more reason for making the step in consciousness when it is seen that the only alternative is an unconscious stumble, leap, or sprawl. If we go deliberately we can have the help that we choose, but the final responsibility for our judgments and ways must rest on each of us alone. To this there is no alternative.

4. *Culture*

Sophistical criticism and skepticism were, in their original explicit occurrence, both cause and consequence of the social situation in which they arose. Criticism by the original sophists came at a time when the traditions that supported Athenian civilization had begun to lose their hold on the most civilized Athenians. The arguments of the sophists might not have been heard in a more stable social and political environment, but the weakness of tradition invited criticism, and criticism further weakened traditional beliefs. Social antecedents and cultural consequences do not bear on the validity of argument. The hard core of the Protagorean position, its emphasis on the ultimate first-personality of all judgment, cannot be softened by reference to the Peloponnesian War. Nor need this emphasis be taken as occasion for either enthusiasm or nostalgic reaction; it can be understood as a sober reminder of something we would often prefer to forget.

As long as there is little awareness of personal responsibility in epistemological, metaphysical, and ethical judgment, as long as acceptance of traditional standards is not explicitly questioned and the nearest thing to decision is a quick surrender of responsibility, only so long can a culture remain fixed and stable in its old beliefs. But that dissatisfied and skeptical spirit of inquiry of which we are often so proud, which we rightly see as the cutting edge of all conscious improvement, will be confined by no cherished boundaries, and tends inevitably to touch the unthought ties that bind. There is danger in thinking too long, or in beginning to think at all: a man may discover that he is free on his own recognizance. A good skeptic, like Protagoras, will think it best that few men ever think enough to endanger the innocence of their captivity. Both fear and attraction are in the prospect. The awareness of individuality and of responsibility not infrequently come together, and if both can be felt as great values, neither is sensed as an unmixed blessing. Among the consequences of this sense when it becomes widespread may be the fragmentation of what had been felt by its members to be a well-poised, ordered, and organic pattern of culture.

Protagoras said, "I know not whether the gods exist, but I know that they should be worshipped."

It would show a guilty arrogance if the intellectual were to claim the influence of his kind to be responsible for the atomized state of our society. The philosophy of the schools influences us less directly than the philosophy in the air, and the latter in turn arises from many places other than the academic chairs of philosophy. It is not possible to weigh the effect of philosophic criticism on society and culture and then measure this influence against the effects of science, technology, industrialization, urbanization, increasing population, international tensions. Attempts to reduce all these to some essential one prove only the bias of the school that does the reducing. Each influence has influenced the others, and all together have borne on the evolution of a society that exists as an organization of splintered functions. The functions are integrated with impressive mechanical efficiency, but the men have disintegrated into their functions. It seems easier this way. It seems an efficient alternative to responsibility.

The criticism that can force an explicit awareness of individuality on us can be given a more technical formulation than has been given here, and the refinements of professional philosophy are not wholly without popular influence. It is not the listening to lectures that makes us Protagorean, but the professors do sometimes make clear to us how Protagorean we are, and the effect can be to make us more Protagorean than ever. It is not surprising that this should be resented, since our situation is felt more intensely as we grow more conscious of it, and one would not want to insist that sharp pains were always preferable to dull aches. Nor should we optimistically discount the possibility that awareness of individuality may contribute to loss of personal as well as social integration and to recoil from responsibility. Protagorean criticism, deliberate or half-unconscious, professional or amateur, can make it too clear that in every decision of final moment each man is finally alone. It can make us aware of doubts and visions the affective significance of which overflows their philosophic formulation: a sense of unattachment and loneliness, a feeling that there once was a supporting structure of extra-personal standards of judgment and conduct that has disappeared, the thought that somewhere one pattern must exist from which each life might take its shape, a pattern that would give its meaning to the whole. We feel that our grandfathers must have had something we have lost, and of course they had; but the self-assurance of innocence once lost is hardly regained.

Often it is easier to try to run away, and the same analytic intelligence that makes us see our singularity has contributed to a social organization in which this insight can be in part evaded. It is still possible to surrender to groups that are glad to do all the thinking and deciding for us and forbid us to think at all. But there is more flattery in the temptation to find relief in a peculiarly modern form of work: functioning as a not unconscious part of some machine, more or less living in and for an organization that accepts the gift of selves and absolves responsibility by dilution. Also, to avoid pain, we can cut ourselves to bits, operating by reference to our several social roles and presenting each piece of ourselves to the care of someone else until everyone has a collection of pieces and no one owns a whole self. It is already likely that we know others only as their roles. The chances are great that none of us has ever met a person who was all there. What is worse is that most of the few who see that there are alternatives think that these are exhausted by escape to the garret, the road, or the graduate school, to a contrary world in which definition is accomplished by saying "No!" A society composed of functional fragments, hitchhikers, and hermits is too fragmented to lend useful structure to personal integration. It is a society in which individualism has either committed suicide, been frightened to death, or degenerated into those parasitic forms of rejection that take their life from the sick body on which they depend. Yet it must be a society that has gone through individualism and the recognition of responsibility and come out on some bad other side. If we look in this direction for help, all we will see is our personal problem writ large.

The cogency of epistemological criticism is not qualified by its moral consequences or by whether its social context encourages its hearing and acceptance; the balance of real gold in the treasury is not altered by the needs of the bankrupt state, although some situations encourage counterfeiting. Protagorean criticism is likely to be heard in and help to create a certain kind of social world, and both its valid critical points and its exaggerations combine with some social situations to create an awareness of self so keen that it cannot be borne by most men. The awareness feels like a problem that must be solved, an account that must be settled, a word that must be spoken. In fear that there are neither answers nor auditors, we begin to ask to be told the meaning of life. The sense of aloneness transforms the trivial truth that I cannot be you into nothing less than torment. From such solitariness we think there must be an escape. We wake up to the aloneness of the immediate self, then passionately seek to sleep again. This we must now see is a crisis in feeling, a crisis that has its roots and must have its resolution in the life of the individual soul. This is a problem that is neither narrowly epistemological, metaphysical, nor psychological. It would be best to call it "moral." (Suppose that it were, as we know it is not, a respectably cognitive question: we should then be responsible for assessing the truth of its answer in final aloneness.)

This aspect of our moral situation sets its limits, and circumscribes the ground on which we must try to build an honest and appropriate answer. The ground itself and its limits must be explored still further since much philosophy has offered itself as a ladder over the wall or a rope let down from above, an engine to smash or a key to unlock the gates, a highly respectable disguise under which the self could escape from itself.

B. ESCAPES AND RETURNS

To understand the ways of would-be escape we shall continue through this chapter to consider the centrally problematic sense of aloneness, the sense that one is cut off by his individuality from all light and warmth not his own. This crisis can be thought of as having two dimensions: (1) the problem of community, and (2) the problem of communication. We can think this way—although we do not *feel* these problems as distinct. Their artificial distinction is pedagogically useful, since some attempted escapes from isolation emphasize one of these aspects of feeling and some emphasize the other. By "the problem of community" we can mean the attempt to achieve a real and full community of being, to *be* not alone, to be one with, to be ultimately indistinguishable from something not one's self. By "the problem of communication" we can mean the attempt to convey one's experience or to transmit what feels like information from one isolated knower to another without loss of content or of truth.

It is possible in the name of honesty to forswear important truths. We would reject illusion, but we should not despise the advantages illusion has sustained. It is doctrinaire to deny the

moral benefits that can come of belief that some myth is literally true; it shows thinness of understanding to think that advantages so supported ought casually to be discarded. If our
problem is to learn the latest word in chemistry, we sensibly go
to the newest laboratory and listen to the youngest professor;
it would be eccentric to base chemical theory on a historical consensus. It is said that in analytic philosophy history begins with
G. E. Moore; the psychiatrists scarcely go beyond Freud; in physics the journal that appeared today was out of date last week;
in the realm of moral attitude the oldest and deepest traditions
are the best guides. We can rationally reject pseudo-science and
much of the metaphysical support of traditional values has pretended to the character of science, but there is no inconsistency
in rejecting the pretensions of metaphysics while admitting and
even trying to preserve some portion of the affective benefits of
metaphysical belief. Such spoiling of the Egyptians would be
dishonest if the connection of doctrine and attitude were logically necessary or inevitable, but we shall see that it is neither.

The affective advantages of metaphysical belief are not rooted
in the truth of the doctrine believed, but in the believer's vision
of a structure of criteria, an ordered hierarchy of goods or values
independent of him or any single human, existing in the nature
of reality as such. Metaphysical commitment carries the conviction that there are supra-personal entities, exemplars, or principles available to man's rational or intuitive mind. These archetypes, essences, axioms, truths, or meanings are at the same time
objectively subsistent standards of value to which men must
conform to be rational and good. It is not just the belief that
reality itself has an intrinsically intelligible structure, but the
belief that this structure incorporates or sanctions standards of
meaning, evaluation, and conduct that gives the believer his
sense of cosmic rationale. In all metaphysical systems there is,
however obscurely or esoterically defined, an essential relationship supposed between the macrocosm and the microcosm; the
structure of the universe is or ought to be approximated by the

texture of men's lives. (We have before this encountered a double sense of being a small and peripheral part that is central to the whole.) Man's position in this light is that of the soldier who knows his station and its duties. The burdens of responsibility are lightened by belief in an external order that sets the conditions of goodness at conformity and is an authoritative source of discipline, form, and support. This objective organization of values is at the same time an objective order of meanings. The metaphysician feels that he has discovered a suprapersonal currency for conceptual exchange and an invariant and objective system of referents for general terms. This means more than communication among philosophers who agree; if minds meet on a truly common ground, there is an end to isolation.

1. *Platonism*

It is against the background of Protagorean criticism, relativism, and skepticism that the drama of metaphysics is played out. Discussions of subject, object, the nature of reality, and the connection of reality with meaning, are perennially post-Protagorean, are always constructed in the face of disaster, have always the nature of a defense. Historically this is most obviously true of the classical defense, the rescue operation launched by Plato.[9]

For Plato the physical and apparent world is hopelessly Protagorean. In the physical world reflected in our senses, and even more in immediate sense itself, all is flux and change. Plato and Protagoras agree with Heraclitus that one cannot step into the same river twice. Words which refer to particular things—this circle, that flame, this person—constantly shift and change their meanings as particular things shift and change. The apparent world slides away from the words we would use to name it, unreal and unstable as shadows are, not to be caught in any conceptual nets. Clear communication is not possible. The chaotic world of things and sense is beneath the possibility of knowledge. The spirit in this ugly, imperfect world is a stranger and alone, always trying to remember some better home.

Solitary confinement to the flesh is the common human lot; in our physicality, in our senses, we are condemned to solitude, particularly, and change; one's body is "an envelope of flesh and blood in which a spirit happens to be sheathed." The philosopher alone can truly escape, for his spirit, as pure reason, is capable of reaching the supra-mundane world of subsistent forms, or universals. Plato's solution to the problem of communication spurns the world of sense, touches it only as the lowest step on a ladder that leads to a realm of perfect, changeless paradigms: circularity, straightness, humanity, beauty, justice. These forms are far too good to exist in time and space. The worldly surveyor may deal with cords pulled taut and the fleshly lover long for some beautiful love, but only the philosopher knows universal Straightness and Beauty. Such perfection as *he* knows cannot be learned from gross and imperfect physical copies, nor can it be these imitations he refers to with general terms: perfect whiteness or exact equality have never been seen on earth, and "whiteness" and "equality" must refer to their perfect, and hence other-worldly, exemplars.

The character of the philosopher's knowledge means that he must have access to the originals of things, and this access cannot be through the particularizing and deceitful senses. It is his reason that goes beyond this patch of snow and that white wall to reach the idea of whiteness itself, the universal that things of a white appearance more or less exemplify. Through the senses we have our fleeting impressions of particular men, but with our reason we can grasp the single, perfect essence of humanity, that universal characteristic that each human imitates. As human animals we will fall in love with particular beautiful things, but our final dissatisfaction with them proves that our human reason always longs for beauty itself, for the absolute beauty that beautiful things partly show but largely conceal. What is eternal, immutable, divine escapes the senses, which can at best hint at what lies beyond. (If we believe that perfection must exist, the fact that it cannot be found in this world will be taken as evidence that it must exist in another.) Only through rational apprehension of pure forms can we transcend the tyranny of sense, escape individuality and the conditions of individual judgment. There being only one essence of beauty, the form of beauty that you and I know is numerically identical. We mean the same thing by "beauty." The problem of communication is solved.

From its solution follows the transcendence of the problem of communion, for in our apprehension of the universal there is nothing idiosyncratic: it is the universal reason in us that rises to the idea. Plato does waver on this point, but however much of personality remains in pure knowing, all that separates us, all that isolates us, perhaps even all that individuates us, is left behind. It is the separateness of flesh that creates the problem of communion, and the philosopher is always dying to the body. The changing, deceitful, relative world, the world of particularity and isolation, of sensation and lust, falls beneath reason, giving way to the vision of Goodness, Truth, and Beauty.

What can be said? It is beautiful and false.

2. *Appearance Again*

The philosophic distinction between reality and appearance, being and becoming, the one and the many, has a long and impressive history. The notion that beyond the painted, changing veils of sense, beyond all that particularly appears, there is a reality more stable and far more knowable—this feeling grown into doctrine is a cultural commonplace. (Specific doctrines are as various as climates, and the affections they would rationalize as common as our natural situation, grown-up and frightened as we are, abandoned in India, or Greece, or Concord, Massachusetts.) In Platonic or neo-Platonic form, the doctrine survived the Middle Ages, Aristotle's ages, only as a rationale for mystics and poets. It enters modern philosophy upside down, or so Plato would think, as metaphysical materialism.

To Descartes it is the physical and material world that our God-given reason shows us to be the common object of rational knowledge. What is immediately knowable is one's own knowing mind; "I think, therefore I am" is itself intended to prove the existence of nothing but the singular mind that thinks it. The only directly knowable thing is the conscious self, but the existence of God is supposed to follow as the conclusion of a compelling argument, and the goodness of God is a guarantee that a common and accurately knowable material world exists, that machine-like world that seemed on the point of complete surrender to geometry: filled space, pure extension, all that is quantitatively measurable.

There is the difficulty that our senses are more impressed with qualities—taste and color, smell and touch—but science based on qualities had earned a justly bad reputation, and it is easy to show that the senses are great deceivers. Given the goodness of God the senses might be trusted for gross and practical purposes, but it could not be the business of knowledge to deal with mere appearance. The objects of knowledge must be knowable with certainty; the terms of science must refer to hard, clear, calculable, common reality. It is extension and weight that are calculable, and they are grasped by mathematical reason.

And so the external world, our real environment, was seen as a great material machine that was, when most real, most rational. A perfect consonance, underwritten by God's good will, existed between its principles and those of the rational mind. Not on the pragmatic senses, but only on the rational grasp of extension could objective knowledge find its real foundation.

Gilbert Ryle has said that Descartes pictures the mind as a ghost haunting a slot machine. The technically philosophic difficulties of Descartes' position are internal: having wholly separated mind from body, he can give no consistent account of their relation and apparent interaction. Having built his sole bridge from the singular mind to all that lies beyond it on an argument for God's existence and goodness, the collapse of this notoriously flimsy argument leaves each isolated mind with only itself to know, and objective knowledge, defined as correspondence between the mind and the materially real, becomes impossible or inexplicable. His failure as a philosopher is found here: he has not succeeded in exposing a ground of certain knowledge of objective reality, and this is what he set out to do. From our moral point of view this failure would be bad enough if it were no worse than this, but his picture of the encapsulated consciousness, essentially detached from everything else, reinforces the sense of alienation from our own bodies, other people, and all things.

If one grants Descartes the initial theoretical isolation of mind, he is not on his own ground truly entitled to assert the existence of anything other than that; the rest of the world recedes, leaving the mind alone with itself. Common sense in some of its moods agrees with this notion of a ghostly and wholly detached mind, and some philosophers, not thinking to re-examine the terms of separation, have seen in Descartes' unreconciled dualism a cognitive confirmation of their feelings of singularity and isolation. Without stopping to criticize the absolute distinction he draws between a self-enclosed mind and the rest of reality, it is clear that the philosophy of Descartes cannot offer itself as a theoretical solution for a set of affective problems that the theory reformulates in extreme and hopeless terms.

With the exception of Marxism and existentialism, contemporary secular philosophy finds its ancestors not on the Continent, but in Great Britain and in the eighteenth century. Whether you would go through Kant or, as William James suggested, around him, it is Locke, Berkeley, and Hume who are the modern progenitors of empirical philosophy, and each of them can be understood as taking a further step away from Cartesian materialism. This is not the only way to understand them, but it is a way that illustrates our particular problem.

John Locke's intentions were anti-Cartesian and he thought himself an empiricist, but these good intentions failed him when he came to consider the reality of material substance. It was his program not to accept any sentence as true unless the senses gave some evidence for it. He recognized the absence of such evidence for the existence of a substance independent of but standing beneath its attributes, but then was overwhelmed by incredulity when he tried to think that the redness, sweetness, and juiciness of the apple might exist apart from a material substratum. It seemed to him that there must be an underlying but unobservable "it" that was the apple in reality and to which all the sensed qualities of the apple belonged. Hemmed in, like Descartes, by the demand of grammar that whole sentences have subjects, he found himself forced to the assertion that the real object of predication was independent of its sensed predicates, that it must be an entity in which attributes inhere and predicates qualify. In honest vacillation he felt he could neither dispense with the notion of material substance nor say what he took it to be. He said it was "a something, I know not what." He knew he could say no more, but felt he could say no less. He must have known of sentences like "It is raining," and he did know that no one could be aware of or even conceive the substance of a stone as something distinct from "its" shape, color, impenetrability, and the pain in the toe that can be had by imitating Dr. Johnson. But it seems difficult to do without the picture of underlying material substance, especially since it is reinforced by subject-predicate grammar, and it is not surprising that common sense still follows Locke, and by kicking thinks to refute Berkeley.

Berkeley and Hume were less tolerant of inconsistency than Locke was, and neither was willing to cling to a would-be hypothesis for which there could be no evidence. Berkeley had an additional animus that was also a limitation: in the name of religion he wanted to refute the materialism of Descartes and Locke and the tendencies toward materialism he saw in Newtonian physics. That it did not turn out as he wanted was not just a piece of bad luck: criticism is not easy to start but it is even harder to stop.

It was Berkeley's proposal that we abstract from our concept of a material thing all those sense-qualities that depend on our perception and then try to see what is left. We are left with nothing to see. Take away the visible redness, the visible and tactile roundness, the felt resistance, and the tasteable sweetness of the apple, and nothing is left at all. But sense-qualities are functions of senses, and sense-experience depends on mind: without sense and mind there would be no sense-qualities. Thus Berkeley was led to say that "to be is to be perceived," to exist is to be present to a perceiving mind, man's mind or God's. In this way the idea of a physical thing dissolves into ideas of its attributes, and these, Berkeley argued, depend on mind. But Bishop Berkeley exempted the mind itself from this dissolution. The mind or soul was an independent mental substance underlying particular ideas, a spiritual substratum.

It was left for Hume to show that the mind itself, the last refuge of substantial stability, is knowable only as a collection of qualities and tendencies. Just as we cannot find a substratum behind the appearance of physical things, so there is no mental substance to be found behind sensations, thoughts, and feelings.

For my part, when I enter most intimately into what I call myself, I always stumble on some particular perception or other, of heat or cold, light or shade, love or hatred, pain or pleasure. I never can catch myself at any time without a perception, and never can observe anything but the perception. . . . If anyone upon serious and unprejudiced reflection thinks he has a different notion of himself, I must confess I can no longer reason with him. All I can allow him is, that he may be in the right as well as I, and that we are essentially different in this particular. He may, perhaps, perceive something simple and continued, which he calls himself; *though I am certain there is no such principle in me.*[10]

It is a complicated line that leads from Plato and Aristotle to Descartes and Locke, to Berkeley, Hume, and Kant, and to the theory that holds all knowledge of existence to be grounded in appearance. All philosophy is a criticism of previous philosophy, and what is important for us is the difficulty of going backward. Philosophy is not cumulative as science is. The philosopher cannot take for granted the positive work of previous philosophers, but we may assume that previous criticism is valid unless it has been decisively refuted. It is not impossible to take the long road back to Plato or to Locke, but it is difficult for those who would be rational, since step by step they must refute the criticisms of the generations between. Small wonder that the few secular metaphysicians who survive in our time can scarcely rise to this and succeed in talking only to each other. Whether we like it or not, for most of us transcendental metaphysics is no longer a live option. We know and we feel that that way out is closed.[11]

3. *Catholic Christianity*

It is probably the Christian solution to the felt problems of aloneness, purposelessness, and the fear of death with which most of us are most familiar. Our historical and personal situation is in part a function of two thousand years of Christian culture. To talk about the moral life of modern man in accidental or deliberate ignorance of this massive conditioning of the Western world, to speak as if the world that is our situation had no past, is to ensure a shallow picture of the present and baseless visions of the future.

Traditionally Christian solutions are both metaphysical and valuational: they have told the believer what was real and how he ought to value things, the structure of the universe and his place in the structure. There has been an emphasis not only on communion but on community: all Christians are members of one system, the mystical body of Christ. In these terms one can be assured that he is not alone, for God is not only with each Christian, God is in His Church. Catholic Christianity thus has had an individual and an institutional dimension, both cooperating to convince the individual that his life has an inner order and an established place. For generations this felt certainty was reinforced by a hierarchical order of Church and society that seemed universally binding, a relatively clear-cut order with clear divisions of responsibility, an order that proceeded from Pope to Emperor to nobles and commons and bound all together (if only in accepted theory) into one organized and organic whole. In this society there was a place for everyone and everyone knew his place. In this society each depended on all. Given relatively stable lines of subordination and expectation each man could feel at home in the social world. Even the oppressed generally conceded the right of their oppressors.

Santayana pictures the society thus organized as a kind of Jacob's ladder, with the orders ascending and descending in regular and colorful patterns. The tableau was not without gratifications, aesthetic and moral, even to its lowliest participants. In our time it takes a kind of unimaginative dryness to cant against churchly pomp, while the least of the faithful are quick in its defense. A vicarious glory moves men more, gives more color and a greater sense of significance to their lives than intimate and democratic drabness ever can. Magnificence can uplift us all, and no honest man begrudges a glory he thinks deserved. In fact, most men are so constituted that, if they have nothing to look up to, they will not look up at all.

In a hierarchically organized society, especially if its principles are theocratic, each man can know what he is entitled to expect, what is expected of him, and why his place has the rewards and duties it has. One knows not only where he stands, but why he stands just there, and what he must do to maintain his stance. When the structure is porous or flexible enough to permit striving after enhanced status and greater position, the rungs to be climbed are clearly and publicly marked, the techniques not mysterious. As long as such a society remains vital, outward and visible signs will be taken to signify inward and spiritual grace. There is more than an accidental touch of Plato and Aristotle in the idea of its advocates that the hierarchical orders of Church and state were the city of God on earth. In principle the bases of hierarchy were form and value, organization and spirituality, definable merit. In fact merit was not infrequently despised and neglected—there was precedent for this—but a man could have a clear idea of why he was dissatisfied. There were abuses of power—wherever there is authority there will be abuses of authority—but the dramatic circumstances of their expression should not lead us to exaggerate their scope in comparison with the consequences of dull and theoretical modern cruelty. In *The Red Badge of Courage,* Stephen Crane speaks of the passing of that pageantry of war which put heart into a man even as it killed him.

Now no one stands or falls on ceremony, and death and life are equally drab. Now we feel that there are eminences neither to storm, to look up to, nor to stand upon. Most of us rest on the featureless and democratic plain; a few climb up on piles of money, envied for what they have, seldom respected for what they are. When all accept that things and money alone confer distinction—that is, when there is no distinction, only glamour and naked bribery—then nothing seems worth living for but money. Perhaps this is inevitable when all people, rich and poor, feel that their lives are caught in the either/or of myth and meaninglessness and lose confidence in their myths. While that confidence held it was not so easy to separate social considerations from those bearing more particularly on the individual life. A man fulfilled himself by filling his place in the natural and supernatural orders, by becoming carpenter, counselor, warrior, or priest. A man did not become merely a piece of a man, other pieces shattered into a jumble of detached and alien fields. Each was a necessary human voice singing just his essential part in the chorus of praise to God.

The acceptance of a common myth not only unified society, it defined each man's place in society and the role of society in the life of every man. Even so, it is possible to speak of the individual as well as the social dimension of the Christian cure for the pain of individuality. No man was ultimately alone; the Kingdom of God was imperfectly visible in the world, invisible and perfect above it, and most nearly found in the soul of every believer. The Incarnation was not merely a profound and unintelligible event, part of the history of a minor province of Rome, it was a moment perpetually renewed: God was made incarnate in the ceremony of the Mass and in the heart of every Christian man. To believe that the Kingdom of God is found within can be to find an escape from loneliness. The aspiration toward the unity of perfect communion, toward loss of self, the surpassing desire for the beatific vision, the desire for salvation and the conviction that its means are available in the world and in the self may produce a spirituality so profound that singularity is despised and for the time forgotten, apparently transcended. Personality and pride of self are but the last and most insidious snares in the flight of the alone to the alone.

As has often happened historically, we have been carried away, have flown away from the Church toward mysticism. This precipitate haste to be out of the world carries one past the best human part of Catholic Christianity. It is in its sacraments that the Church is most truly and beautifully human, for in the sacraments the Church recognizes, celebrates, and cherishes the themes and moments that most fully define the life of man in the world. It is a fact of the deepest simplicity that some things are more important than others, but men are easily distracted and liable to forget. By fixing the human themes in ceremony—Baptism, Communion, Confirmation, Penance, Marriage, Holy Orders, Extreme Unction—the Church does its best to ensure their proper emphasis. The sacraments can be understood as celebrations of man's fate, as expressions of the structuring events in the lives of each of us. The man who orders his affective life around recognition of these things—births and children, a clear relation to his society, personal commitment, the importance of corrigibility and choice, love, vocation, the awareness of death—this man enacts, and feels that he enacts in his own life the lives of all men. In giving these themes his rapt attention, in spending on them his greatest intensity, he can achieve the sense of universal humanity.

We must in time return to this possibility of feeling the universal in the particular; even detached from the institutional setting that has surrounded and sustained it, it remains a potent suggestion for the ordering of life. The idea of creating a sense of form by a certain distribution of intensity, of making an immanent order by the selective emphasis of affective values, is not an especially religious idea; it is more like an aesthetic ideal. If we here signal the first convergence of two sources of all that follows in this book, we should also enter an admission and a warning. The admission is that any belief has greater moral potency when taken to be literally true; the warning is that moral potency is no test of literal truth.

Of course we know these things. In our more rational moments, or in thinking on subjects on which we allow our reason to function, most of us would agree that the truth of a statement cannot be judged by the degree of our pleasure in hearing it. All of us are adept in believing what pleases, but considering abstractly we should probably say that the truth or falsity of a story does not depend on the affective consequences of its acceptance. The unblemished belief in the continuing redaction of the city of God on earth, the vision of Jacob's ladder, helped to produce and sustain an order of society that was brutal and beautiful, oppressive and magnificent, irrecoverable, inimitable, and fertile in suggestions for new departures. But we cannot without terrible confusion identify truth with affective or political consequences. We cannot claim that the Christian myth is more or less than a myth. We cannot validly argue that the story is true on the ground that belief in it is found to have good emotional effects. The story may be true or it may not be, it may be neither true nor false; this question must be decided not by reference to the personal and social order that belief in the story sustained, nor by our dislike or admiration for that order, but by reference to the evidence its supporters have adduced in behalf of the truth of the story itself. None of the would-be evidence advanced is capable of convincing a person who is not, on other grounds, already convinced.

The moralist who finds material for admiration in the vision of Jacob's ladder but who is not thereby seduced into taking its supporting myths as true must be prepared to recommend those aspects he would preserve on some less fanciful metaphysical or moral basis. This amounts to defending without recourse to myth, or with the recognition of myths as myths, aspects of affective orientation that have always depended for their strength on the belief that myths were literally true. It also ensures that one's recommendations will come with diminished force. When clarity makes persuasion difficult, it is easier to argue from a position of obscurity. Yet, if morality is to be rational and honest, we must accept the liabilities entailed in attempts to be clear. It is not honest enough merely to state the source and nature of the ideals for which one argues. It is also necessary to distinguish truth from myth and demonstration from persuasion.

4. *Mysticism and Protestantism*

The Church has always mistrusted her mystics, and with good reason. Mysticism is the purest form of personal religion and can never fit with perfect comfort the confines of any particular organization; as Emerson said, all mystics belong to one country and speak the same language. Each mystical experience—that incommunicable, breathless vision of God; that vision which surpasses seeing; that rapture in which the spirit dissolves in the presence of God—is the unsharable possession of a peculiar soul, and in its luminous singularity leaves community behind. To speak of, or publicly to celebrate this vision is to change its essence, or rather to substitute something that can be sung and spoken of for something that cannot.

It is only the successors of mystics who can found religions, so few men being mystics. A religion that is to work and to save in this world must have its organizers, politicians, and soldiers. To spread its good word, it must have clear channels of communication. To maintain the unity and intelligibility of the faith, it must have those who can in part translate unspeakable visions and mysteries into intellectual systems for the curious and sermons for the devout. Such talents for organization, administration, and systematization are seldom found in the rare soul that feels the full and immediate presence of God. However deep his institutional commitment, the mystic is at bottom an anarchist of God. His relation to God is a relation of one to One; it cannot be socially mediated. Its whole and perfect passion paradoxically rises from singularity to loss of all distinction; its passion rises to passionless perfection only when the single soul is totally lost, abandoned, absorbed without remnant into the luminous all and nothing of its very God. Some last shudder of the self one fears to lose, the death of some last distraction, and then nothing to hold, nothing to keep, past fear and past desire, sinking into the unspeakable absence, the darkness beyond color which is the living presence of what can only be named God.

The mystic loses himself in God and, to continue Emerson's figure, is cut off from all his fellow men by his nationality and by the difficulty of its language. He moves like an alien through the grosser community to which, as sometimes less than God, he is condemned. The Church, as a human community under Divine auspices, requires acceptance of the publicly communicable word of God, conformity to a code that must, in the nature of the worldly case, mold and maintain the piety and hope of the multitude of simple, sophisticated, and unmystical lovers of God. The Church is organized and exoteric, as it must be, to save souls; the Church must channel the waters of life to bring at least one saving drop to each ready to receive it. But the mystic claims to have transcended the need for translation and mediation, to have returned to the original source, to have bathed and drowned in the very spring of light; for this reason, mysticism is never far from heresy. The Church in the world does not object to the inwardness of the Kingdom of God, but it may object to the mystic's claim that he has a peculiar relation to its King. The mystic, unlike the ordinary saint, makes claims that cannot be confirmed. Not only the incorrigible first-personality of his experience, but its insistence on ineffability and the consequently contradictory and figurative language by which the experience is at best only signaled, place him beyond the pale of human judgment, even if the judges speak in the name of God Himself. At the depth of his spiritual life the mystic is the most dangerous kind of outlaw: he makes no attempt to break the law, but claims to be above it.

The mystic loses his loneliness when he fully loses himself, but in achieving what he takes to be perfect communion with God, he may leave behind the lawful community of his fellow-believers, and in matters of profoundest importance—in fact, precisely in matters of profoundest importance—he speaks an ecstatically contradictory language of his own, and insists that communication is finally impossible. Such rapt and holy outlaws must be watched. If in their confident oneness with the source of life they sometimes bring fresh life to ancient forms, they can in the same divine irresponsibility and human isolation destroy those outward forms that sanctify the lives, assuage the isolation, and make hopeful the deaths of ordinary men. The soul of the mystic is exposed to special dangers, but it is the mischief he may work in the community that turns his personal affliction into a public menace, for here is the recipe and germ of chaos: when to the deepest and most consequential spiritual claims is added the condition that only the claimant can judge their validity.

It is the mark of the mystic to be utterly convinced of his calling. It is in his unshakable conviction that he is one with God, a conviction itself a function of the intensity of personal experience, that his loneliness is lost. Take away that perfect confidence, remove or weaken the assurance of unmistakable communion, and into the terrible gap will rush self-inquisition, anxiety, and the permanent presence of fear. So far as the mystic has, in his reliance on God, let go his hold on authoritative personal and social forms, so far as he has ventured out beyond the bounds of received and public words, that far is any weakening of faith a prelude to spiritual agony.

To take oneself alone to God is a recourse no religion can neglect, but it is a dangerous recourse when taken alone. From a fortunate encounter new life can seem to come; to some it has seemed to come abundantly, overflowing all forms to bring refreshment and hope to a whole congregation—the enthusiasm of a Wesley is the great and ambiguous gift brought back from such vivid meetings. But the meetings are always at hazard, the forms of recognition not settled, and the manner of greeting so dependent on persons that few can be perfectly sure what exactly has been met. Enthusiasm, like love, can subside, leaving one to recognize that nothing has been encountered beyond a figment of the self.

At its best and at its worst, Protestantism is mysticism for Everyman. The visible Protestant churches are seen as social or, at best, spiritual conveniences: each man must stand without essential mediation in the presence of his God. The word of God was given once for all in His Book; in personal communications to each believer, God continues its exegesis. Some claim to have heard the voice of God speaking with special clarity and strength, but there can be no support of such claims beyond reference to the Book, which is to say beyond reference to the acuity of one's own apprehension of the voice of God. The attempt to justify some interpretation of Scripture by reference to the Book (that is, by reference to what can only be some interpretation of it), at once represents bad reasoning and suggests the invaluable contribution that Protestantism has made to the growth of individual freedom.

If every man were a perfect mystic, Protestantism would be an ideal religion. If no man could doubt the accuracy of his hearing of the voice of God, if every man were always convinced of his oneness with God, traditional and institutional mediation between man and God would be, at best, unnecessary. If every man were always convinced of the real and immediate presence of God, loneliness would be unthinkable and anxiety unknown. Nothing like this is the case. Utter conviction of a special relation to God is granted to only a few; to the many doubt is always possible. To the mystic *manqué*—a characterization that, in this world of less than saints, unhappily applies to most religious Protestants—there is between utter conviction and utter loneliness no solid place to stand. Protestantism as a saving way unrealistically relies too much on the hope of assured communion. It is less an answer to man's aloneness than a restatement of the question.

It is likely that the majority of Protestants are saved from loneliness by thoughtlessness, as a majority of Catholics may be saved from thought by their sense of a place in a structure of things they need not understand. Protestantism will come to life again and again in its revivals—revivals are its life and its best mission. But Protestantism grown genteel, Protestantism without enthusiasm, loses significance as a religious force, even when its churches continue to perform a useful role in social service. For the individual who would save his soul, the emphasis on man's aloneness in the presence of God adds anxiety to isolation and aggravates what it may have come to cure. Whether we call it grace or election, and whether we regard it as evidence of the presence of God or the presence of malfunction in the nervous system, we must recognize that the sense of perfect union with God is a free and unpredictable gift one may hope for but not a condition one can rely on as a widely influential factor in the moral life.

For the well-behaved modern Protestant churches, this discouraging fact has pointed to inanition. The role they play in the lives of their people has declined to occasional homiletic exhortation, the provision of a place for marriages, funerals, and group singing, and the attempt to sell positive thinking as a substitute for spiritual life. None of this touches (except slightly to soothe) the insensitive crowds that pass through on Christmas and Easter; many of us are below the need for help. Those who think or feel are thrown back, more hopelessly lonely, into themselves. To the extent that they feel themselves somehow responsible, a burden of guilt, a sense of unfulfilled possibility is added to their isolation. Responsibility is a torment always renewed when the principles of its infliction cannot be clearly known and the conditions of its fulfillment cannot be clearly defined.

5. *Popular Existentialism*

The most pathetic effects of popular or literary existentialism are made by its playing on the problems of estrangement and lack of communication, on the feelings of responsibility and purposelessness. These are far from purely cognitive problems, yet an illusion of great profundity can be sustained by talking of such affective crises in pseudo-cognitive terms. Philosophers make popular reputations and their readers fall into the pit by taking these feelings to be questions demanding an answer addressed to the mind, problems to be solved by the manipulation of a recondite philosophical terminology. Then these questions seem uniquely deep, ineffably significant. They seem to be genuinely intellectual questions that nonetheless cannot be answered.

Whatever their intentions may be, the existentialists have been guilty of promoting a kind of half-conceptual hysteria by posing moral problems in a way that would permit them to be answered only in terms of Hegelian metaphysics and then declaring all such answers to be inapplicable. It is this gratuitous ambivalence that causes existentialists to oscillate between pride and petulance. How proudly and deliciously they shudder—the first men to discover mortality. And how obstinately petulant: first they burn their skein of metaphysical thread (Hegel is dead!), then plunge into the labyrinth, and then demand to be rescued with just that thread. From Kierkegaard to Sartre we have heard invocations of absurdity, intimations of anxiety, self-display in the face of responsibility. But if in reading the existentialists one manages to penetrate the barbarous terminology and the atmosphere of melodrama, one discovers that less is there than meets the eye. The "absurdity," which at one moment serves as a name for those feelings we have more simply noted, covertly changes its meaning and comes to signal the absence of what many non-Hegelian thinkers knew was never to be had: a rationally justifiable, all-justifying metaphysical scheme of things, a cosmic Dialectic in which all isolation and partiality are finally overcome. That "anxiety," which we think we recognize as our own, is in their case an aggressive querulousness at having lost a comforting notion of the arms beneath, the very particular notion being that of idealistic rationalism. The pain of responsibility that can itself be responsible and real is in their case that of philosophically spoiled children, coddled thinkers who have half let go of a fantastic metaphysical father-image—father made all the decisions—and who have been mourning flamboyantly ever since.

Much of what the existentialists *feel* about the human situation is justly felt—this is one potent source of their popularity—

but their reading of the significance of their feelings is too secretly sophisticated, too determined by unacknowledged metaphysical disillusion. They capture their audiences by appealing to half-thoughts and moods that genuinely exist, and then do not lay but exploit those feelings by picturesque and teasing verbal tricks, by terminological legerdemain. Their appeal (to adapt a phrase from Woodbridge Riley) is to the affectively afflicted who can recognize philosophical jargon when they see it but who cannot judge whether the jargon makes sense or not. In the face of a natural human situation that calls for sober analysis, steady understanding, and mature decision, they dabble like sly and perverse children in mock profundity, anxiety, and despair. For those who like this kind of thing it seems easy to slip back and forth among existentialism and other fashionable secular or religious diversions, to toy interminably with pseudo-cognitive "answers," perhaps just for the glum satisfaction of rejecting them. The harm in such intellectual self-abuse is that in prolonging the thrills it obscures the issues.

a. HEGEL'S CHILDREN

Because existentialism has been the modern movement that has made the strongest claim to speak to our affective situation, and because the feelings it exploits do exist and require honest treatment, it is needful, at some cost in technicality, to uncover premises often passed by in silence. In fairness it should be said that one reason for reticence is just that the matter is rather technical for popular discussion. The reader never captured by existentialism can without much loss skip over the technicalities. On the other hand, the reader who has accepted existentialism without quite knowing why might well read on and decide to accept its historical and technical presuppositions and to accept existentialism along with them. At least he will then be more clearly aware of what he is accepting.

It would go beyond the evidence to accuse any existentialist of intellectual dishonesty or bad faith, but it is possible to say that the rhetoric of existentialism rests on an insufficiently explicit base. What should be recognized by its lay readers is its deep dependence on the language and system of Hegel. We can show this most simply by considering how three of existentialism's nuclear terms, "absurdity," "anxiety," and "responsibility," depend for their meaning on their implicit relation to Hegelian metaphysics. After all, if a term like "absurd" means anything more than "alas!" it must make sense to ask what it would be like for things to be other than absurd. If it turns out that the only alternative to existential "absurdity" is that Hegel's peculiar system should be true, many will feel that "absurdity" in this sense names a real disease arising from an imaginary cure. If we can eliminate not only the illusion but the nostalgia for it, the disease in its specifically existentialist form will disappear, leaving a clearly affective problem, unconfused by metaphysical cant.

Fortunately, it is unnecessary to give a complete account of either Hegelianism or existentialism to make our particular point. It is *popular* existentialism that concerns us, that vague version that afflicts and influences the ideas and attitudes of the literate public, the amateurs of philosophy, the writers and critics, and even the many who without reading are susceptible to intellectual atmospheres. In another discussion we should have to note the differences among the thinkers generally called "existentialists"—Kierkegaard, Jaspers, Heidegger, Marcel, Sartre, Camus—but their differences in doctrine, however important, are less significant than the unanimity of their influence; nor should we be misled by their common fear of a common label.[12] Kierkegaard is not Camus; but on the issue at hand, the dependence of the existentialist anti-system on the system it stands against, they are alike enough to be lumped together. Even so, this dependence is especially clear in the case of Kierkegaard. The relation of his position to the Hegelian system is more explicit than that of later existentialists. When Kierkegaard says

"The System," he means the Hegelian philosophy. Hegel's System dominated speculation in the nineteenth century, seeming to many thinkers to provide a uniquely satisfying vision of the universe, of the totality of things in process, and of man's place in reality. Since the obscurity of The System resists explanation, we will try to explain only as much of it as is necessary to understand the background of existentialism.

i. The System. To say that Hegel was an idealist is to say that he held Reality to depend on mind: the structure and the content of the real universe are determined by the working of mind. Since mind works in dialectical ways, the structure of the Real is dialectical. For a system of thought-Reality (an unhappy term, but one must show that the two are really one) to be dialectical is for it to be rational; hence Reality is rational. Obviously the notion of the Dialectic is important. It determines rationality and Reality. Unfortunately it is somewhat obscure. Leaving aside the question of whether it makes any sense to say that Reality depends on mind, we can ask what it is for thought-Reality to be dialectical.

The first application of the term "dialectical" is to a relationship that holds between three notions. ("Notions," *begriffen*, are particular conjunctions of thought and Reality.) One notion, the "thesis," from the depths of its own meaning gives rise to a second notion, the "antithesis," which contradicts the first. Being, for instance, gives rise to Nothingness. The business of "giving rise to" is peculiar: the thesis itself somehow "contains" the germs of its own denial but this is *not* to say that it is a straightforward self-contradiction or a concealed contradiction from which a straightforward self-contradiction can be deduced. ("Contains" is obviously a metaphor, but in the Hegelian System such metaphors are accepted as explanations.) Even the thesis and the antithesis taken together, though their combination seems to the understanding to be contradictory and hence necessarily false, are seen by the higher faculty of Reason as a "dialectical opposition." It is the nature of such oppositions to be partly resolved and partly maintained in a third moment of the Dialectic, the "synthesis," a thought or thing that results from the "lifting up" of the thesis and antithesis. In this movement, whatever has been true in thesis and antithesis combines and emerges truer than ever; and whatever has been discordant, partial, and false is partially overcome or purged away.

But there is no resting place for the partial. The new synthesis itself turns out to be infected, unstable, and inevitably gives rise to a new antithesis. These combine to form a new synthesis, and so on and on until we reach the Absolute, the supreme synthesis, the whole System. It is the whole alone which is wholly rational, fully true, and really Real; anything less than the whole is only partially rational, partially true, partially real. This is not to say that every fragment of Reality is as rational, true, and Real as every other: the better any piece fits into The System, the more determinedly it is fixed in its proper place, the less absurd, the more rational and Real it is.

Man's moral task in this context is marvelously clear-cut. It is rationally to find his proper place in The System, to fit into his appointed rank in the on-moving dialectical march, to relate himself to the Absolute, which is at once the leader and the whole parade. At each of its dialectical moments the Absolute expresses itself in supra-personal, universal terms. It makes itself historically and socially manifest in society and in the State and presents itself to the individual in the majestic form of universal and rational law. The mere individual is in danger of unreality; to be out of step is a metaphysical solecism: it is to be absurd. The rational man is he who wills what the State wills, the State being the representation of Absolute Reason on earth, and who submits to the moral law as the Absolute expresses itself through society. To be thus rational is to be cosmically, universally justified; one's responsibility lies just in discovering the place in the world-historical Dialectic it has determined as his own. Fitting snugly there, one discovers that he is not alone.

He is supported by the Dialectic itself and by all those others who have also found shelter there. In compliance is rationality; in obedience is freedom; in conformity is peace. Outside there are only criminals, madmen, and strangers—metaphysical outlaws.

ii. Absurdity (fancy). The existentialist is a self-made and self-conscious outlaw, a defier of the Dialectic, a metaphysical Manfred. The curious thing is the way in which he must accept The System in order to defy it. What is the "absurdity" on which he insists with such anguish? It is "absurdity" as Hegel would define it. It is failure to be essentially determined by, cosmically justified by, some specified place in The System, failure to be a necessary moment in the dialectically, "rationally" necessary scheme of things. (A person never bemused by the hope of a Hegelian role should not find its absence absurd.) For the Hegelian the man who does not submit to definition by the Dialectic, who does not give over ultimate responsibility to The System, has forfeited his reality. He may merely *exist,* but he is not Real.[13] The mere existence of the outsider is of course absurd: rationality is the alternative to absurdity, and to be rational is to accept Hegel's definition of "rationality" and to fit into the universal thesis-antithesis-synthesis movement of thought and Reality.

Kierkegaard's Abraham illustrates the "absurd" position of the man who, to achieve an authentic or extra-Systemic relationship to the Absolute, dares to exist. Abraham's circumstance is especially absurd. God, a transcendent Absolute in this version, has ordered Abraham to kill Isaac, and seems thus to be contradicting Himself in two ways at once. Abraham must accept the contradiction that God requires him to stand outside a universal moral law which He has given—the commandment "Thou shalt not kill," a law in this case reinforced by the fact that the victim is the killer's son—and God seems bound at once to accomplish the sacrificial murder of Isaac and the literal fathering by Isaac of a mighty people. Abraham's faith is proved at least as much by his assertion of the latter contradiction as it is by his acceptance of the former responsibility.

Because the Hegelian takes contradictions as opportunities for dialectical ingenuity, Kierkegaard makes the assertion of impossibility the test and epitome of faith. The Hegelian will admit contradictions, but only to resolve them "objectively," "rationally"—that is, dialectically; he fits them into a wider whole, shows them to be lifted up and resolved in a higher synthesis. Kierkegaard therefore insists that the contradiction be accepted as unresolvably final, that anything other is less than faith. (If in degenerate, secular days "faith" has dwindled to "authenticity," the central meaning—that of radical rejection of The System—has stayed the same.)

To be in an authentic, unmediated relation to the Absolute, Abraham must assume a role not objectively different from that of a murderer, for the murderer likewise violates the universally applicable "Thou shalt not kill." No outward and visible sign distinguishes Abraham from the man who murders his son. Both the existential man and the criminal have left the shelter and support of The System. The criminal has fallen below the universal, has left The System, and is an outlaw; the religious existentialist who in faith asserts his naked existence has leaped above the universal to achieve an unmediated relation to God and is likewise an outlaw. The position of each is absurd; each in leaving The System has left rationality itself. Since The System is covertly accepted as the only possible source of reason, justification, or purpose, the man who chooses to exist leaps into a dreadful situation: he can be justified in his acts, in his very being, by nothing. The would-be outsider will make the dichotomy absolute. He will have supra-personal, metaphysical, Systematic justification, or he will have none at all. He insists that the former cannot be, and thus concludes that there is no such thing as rationality and justification, that he is wholly free, unhistoried, and responsible.

Why, then, is Abraham not a murderer? The only distinction

between Abraham and the murderer is subjective, hence not easy to describe. Fortunately it need not be described. Enough has been said to suggest that the terms nuclear to the rhetorical armory of popular existentialism derive such philosophic meaning as they have from the Hegelian concepts with which they correlate. The existentialist implicitly agrees with Hegel that the only rational life is one lived under the aegis of the Absolute—and then denies that this is possible, strikes a pose, and proclaims that life is absurd. He would believe with Hegel that man must and can locate his life in a universal, dialectical progress, must achieve his essential being by an integration with The System; then he cries that there is no System or ought to be none, and that this particular loss condemns man to anxious isolation and the pain of metaphysical freedom. Thus he exacerbates the poignancy of his problem and tickles his sense of despair by an implicit insistence that its unique "solution" is at once cognitive, real, uniquely satisfactory, and unavailable. He will be satisfied with nothing other than that which he rejects.

iii. Absurdity (plain). This hankering after Hegel is absurd, in the plain sense of "silly." The difference between the existentialist who thinks that there is a System, but that it is nobler or holier to exist outside it, and the existentialist who thinks that there is no System, so that we must despairingly exist without it, is a difference of detail. Both attitudes are reactions to a delusion. They are possible only to those who hold that Hegel's vision is the only "rationally" satisfying view of nature and man, who suppose that "reason" in any other than a dialectical sense is humanly irrelevant, who think without saying that since The System is lost, the human being is condemned to total and dreadful meaninglessness. These people have been so upset to discover that man and the world are as science and common sense describe man and the world, and not as Hegel imagined them, that they feel the rest of us should share their sense of shock. But if we were not on their debauch there is no reason why we should suffer their nausea. We will be the less inclined to when we see that it smacks of cheap melodrama: we almost expect to see Hegel descending through the ceiling on a rope crying, "All is not lost!" Or rather, that is the only ending that would satisfy our secret sentimentalists, and no doubt it makes them feel tough and grown-up to insist that happy endings never happen.

It is not necessary to review the analyses that have led to a general rejection of Hegelian metaphysics. Criticism does not show The System to be meaningful, desirable, and unattainable; it shows The System to be nonsensical. It does not suggest that once we had a cognitively meaningful rationale in Hegelianism and that now we must mourn its loss, but that there was never clear reason to think Hegelianism cogent or meaningful. There has been no loss except the loss of something we never had, or had only in whatever sense we have those waking dreams in which we assuage our actual anxieties by fantasies of a world in harmony with our will, or of a universe in which we combine in ourselves freedom, consciousness, and thinghood.[14] Perhaps it is not altogether childish to mourn the loss of daydreams when good sense dispels them, but neither is it altogether adult. What is completely irresponsible is to pretend that one's grief and pain, which may be genuinely felt, arise from a less factitious loss.

We may well hesitate to make accusations of bad faith, and we can refrain from further strictures on Hegel, but whatever we think of him it would seem no more than honest to make the dependence of existentialist terminology explicit. Why should this not be done? Perhaps because it would undermine the dramatic appeal of this popular philosophy. Existentialism would have far less appeal if it were generally recognized that the arms beneath, whose absence we are asked to view with despair, are those of a particular school of philosophy. This not only falsifies the ground of our situation—unhappy we may be, but not because Hegel is dead—it induces a kind of confused and unnecessary desperation. Existentialism appeals to uneasy people by a shrewd discernment of the phenomena of unease, and then pretends that there is only one alternative to this unease and that it is an impossible alternative. This is not merely a false dichotomy; it is vicious in its falsity.

b. THE AMBIGUITY OF "DECISION"

The issue that the existentialists obscure can after all be simply put: How is one to live in the natural world? Nor should we forget that this question can be interpreted in a way that allows clear practical answers, answers having to do with health and welfare. That these medical and technological answers provide no escape from the inevitable and normal conditions of organic life, that they can describe no alternative to isolation and death, is scarcely reason to despise them. It is petulant to insist that the only significant cure is a cure for being human. The questions and the answers that lie beyond health and welfare need not be complicated by mysterious and metaphysical considerations. What remains is a need to determine our affective relations to ourselves and to our world. What is left as a question and a hope for each of us is a problem of attitudes.

The question is hard enough even when stated in this uncomplicated way, but if one is determined to have conceptual confusion and is fond of dramatic effects, matters can be obscured again by introducing the idea of "decision." "Decision" is not necessarily a bad word in this context, but if it is to be used it must be with unusual care. It is not incorrect to say that answers to the question "How shall I live?" have the character of decisions, but the saying is ambiguous. Does it mean that people can consciously choose what their attitudes will be? Does it mean that they do? Does it mean that they ought to? Further, the simple statement will mislead us unless we read "decision" in a doubly *logical* sense. If we would talk of "first principles of conduct,"[15] we should understand that each such principle (1) has the *logical* character of a decision, seldom the psychological character of a decision; and (2) that its "firstness" is most often a matter of *logical,* not of temporal or psychological priority. These distinctions are often unobserved both by those who like and by those who dislike the thought that basic attitudes, first principles of conduct, or criteria of conduct are most intelligibly represented as decisions. Because these differences have moral importance as well as technical import, it will be worthwhile to try to make them clear.

i. Logic and psychology. To say that a first principle of conduct has the logical character of a decision is first of all to say that it does not have the character of a statement of fact, that it is *not* descriptive. Whatever its psychological character, whatever it feels like if ever we entertain it, if it were to be formally stated it should be given the logical form of a procedural or classificatory rule.

A procedural rule can be formalized as "If there is anything that has the characteristic f, let us consider it to fall under classification ϕ," or "Take any object that you will, if it is an a, then it is a Ψ," where this is taken as a principle of classificatory procedure. (It is by reference to a rule of this sort that we call a whale a mammal and a cockatrice a serpent.) Note that such a sentence makes *no* assertion of fact. It does not say whether there *are* any a's, but only that *if* there are, they should be regarded as Ψ's. Since no factual assertion is made, it makes no sense either to say that a rule is true or that it is false. To say "If there are any unicorns, they are quadrupeds" does not tell us that there are unicorns; it tells us a relation of classifications. Only in an extended sense can this sentence be called "true," since it can at best reflect a fact about our language, faithfully representing the way we use the words or classes named "unicorn" and "quadruped." Even so, when such a sentence is taken as a rule it loses its descriptive import, even vis-à-vis linguistic use, and expresses a decision about how the terms it names are to be used.

A descriptive or factual sentence is formalized as "There are some a's." It will be true if there are some a's—tigers or tables—

and false if there are not—unicorns or magic wands. Or it may say "There are some things that have characteristic ϕ and they also have characteristic Ψ." Such sentences will be true if there are objects of the sort described. To say that a first principle is a "decision" is to say that it is not this sort of factual assertion.

Later we shall have to see the relation of moral principles to matters of fact; here it is necessary only to make clear what can be meant by calling a principle a "decision." The most defensible meaning is not exciting and psychological, but technical and logical. To trade on this ambiguity, to slip from an accurate point about the logical character of principles to a doubtful speculation about their psychological nature is not to commit a harmless mistake. By talking as if the decisional nature of moral principles meant that the moral life were essentially a series of decisions in the most dramatic psychological sense, one misrepresents the character of human experience and misunderstands the role of those few acts of ours that *are* decisions in a dramatic, psychological sense.

ii. Logical and temporal priority. It may be objected that even if we have correctly discerned the form that a first principle should have if it were ever made formal and explicit, no one ever makes such an explicit formalization of principles; at least, no one does this before making particular moral choices. As a fact, this is often true, but as an objection it misses the point. Even if it were always true it would be no objection, for the sense in which a "first principle" as described is "first" is the sense of *logical priority.* Logical priority is independent of psychological facts and has nothing to do with temporal priority. In time, such a first principle is usually very late, or never. It is not a rule thought of and formulated before all practice, but one that in its greater abstraction and universality includes particular applications as special instances, one that is capable of serving as a general formula from which particular statements or acts can be derived. The classic illustration, although it does not perfectly fit the present case, has to do with Aristotle's formulation of the rules of the syllogism. Aristotle gave deductive inference a rationale, that is, a set of general principles sufficient to justify particular deductive inferences, but people argued deductively before Aristotle, and people now argue deductively who have never heard of Aristotle. Euclid formalized the principles of geometry long after surveying had become a practical art, and there was a practical science of ballistics before Galileo wrote.

The cognitive function of first principles is to systematize a body of knowledge or practice (generally an already existing, loosely organized set of particular practices), to display and codify its logical or practical relations, and to make inconsistency detectable and difficult. It is such logically first principles that have usually interested philosophers, and some philosophers have convincingly argued that principles of this sort are most accurately interpreted as decisions, in the logical sense of "decision." The reason for this interpretation is epistemological: there is always more than one way to systematize a set of particular propositions or practices, and while the choice among various systematizing formulae is in part guided by considerations of deductive and pragmatic convenience, this guidance is so far from absolute that first principles are better thought of as inventions or decisions than as discoveries.

To speak, then, of *first* principles of conduct is again not to make a psychological point about the development of morality in time; it is to make an analytic or linguistic or logical distinction. This is not to say that there are *no* cases in which decisions (in the psychological sense) are made prior to (in a temporal sense) particular moral actions. There are such cases, some of them are dramatic and important, and we shall have to return to the relation of principles to acts. The present point is that the distinctions between the logical and psychological senses of "decision" and "priority" are obfuscated by popular existentialism. When this obfuscation is taken at face value by opponents of existentialism, they may think to argue against the decisional character of first principles by saying that such principles seldom have the psychological character of decisions and are seldom prior in time to particular moral acts. (It may then be added that moral principles must therefore be descriptive of metaphysical entities, or natural laws, or social or psychological facts.) It is true that principles of conduct are not in general decided in the way we decide to have chocolate rather than vanilla. This objection to the decisional character of first principles is irrelevant to a proper understanding of the issue.

C. DECISION AND DISPOSITION

Philosophic confusion without moral consequences might deserve no more than academic indignation. The present case is not so innocent. Deliberate conscious decision in the psychological sense of "decision" *does* have a role to play in the moral life, and we can lose sight of its true importance by attending only to its more spectacular appearances. So far as popular existentialism pretends that one might wholly create his moral life at any moment (since moral "decisions" are made morning, noon, and night), it is not simply indulging its weakness for dramatics: it obscures the more basic operation of *habits* of choice, of underlying attitudes, of moral dispositions; obscures also, in its exaggerated concern for decisions per se, the fact that decisions differ in their consequentiality, and the need for criteria of relative importance among decisions.

It is true that we can, by deliberate choice and conscious practice, bend and alter the direction of our lives and it is important, but we are not as free of our past and present as some existentialists appear to believe. The creation of a moral life is as great and responsible a task—but not as singular, flamboyant, and desperate a performance—as they like to think. Conscious and deliberate decision, sometimes even dramatic decision, can play an important part, but if it acts it does so through some effect on the general and conservative structure of our affective lives—from which, of course, it comes.

The moral life cannot be understood in terms of decision alone. It should be obvious that an interplay of decision and given disposition lies close to the core of it. One may think that the apparently deliberate, otherwise inexplicable, ignorance of this truism reflects another aspect of the ambivalent relation of existentialism to Hegelianism. While they deny that Hegel's Dialectic limits or conditions man, the existentialists may continue to suppose that Hegel's is the only system of determinants which *could* limit man. In rejecting the determining System they may think themselves committed to the rejection of all causal influences, and thus to the assertion that man as a moral agent is unconditioned (save by a presently given situation, which in turn owes its externality to man's freedom).[16]

To take utter freedom as a presupposition of an authentically human life is an exaggerated reaction to an unfounded determinism. It is also morally dangerous to accept the false or meaningless belief that man is essentially free of his past as a necessary condition for the resolution of moral-affective problems. Later we shall see that "the unconditioned" is a self-defeating moral *goal.*

A man's character is more a matter of habits of action and choice than of the particular choices that express his habits. What would ordinarily be called "character" is a set of dispositions. It is evident to anyone who has started to smoke cigarettes, and more evident to those who have tried to give up smoking, that the formation of a habit is not a simple consequence of deliberate choice and that breaking a habit is far from accomplished by choice alone. We acquire habits by acting as if we had them. What we do, we become; but more often than not we drift into what we do. Nor is it necessary to be a Freudian to think it likely that many of our most important patterns of habit are established before we are old enough to practice deliberate choice. By the time we are old enough to choose, our choices are made against the active and influential background pattern of our affective lives. When we come to recognize the possibility of decision, of alternatives, whenever that may be, we are too far from innocence for any decision to be immaculately conceived.

None of this means that deliberate decision is unimportant. What it means is that no decision is without its roots in the past. The individual man, however great his solitude, at any given time sums up those experiences and those choices that have made him what he is. When he expresses himself in action or in thought, when at some moment of time he decides, the causal influence of what he has become is never wholly absent. It could only be to demonstrate the insouciance of metaphysical speculation in the face of well-known facts that one would hold the way we think and act ever to be wholly uninfluenced by what we and others have thought and done. It shows too romantic an assessment of novelty to hold that we *ought* to be uninfluenced by what we and others have thought and done. Decision is possible and important; that is why it is pernicious to misrepresent this possibility and this importance. Among the worst consequences of thinking that the moral life is either made with one decision or wholly made anew with each decision are that it leads the earnest but gullible to expect too many crises or to feel that only crises count or to think that all crises count equally.

From individual choices grow habits of choice, from the dispositions so established follow further choices, and further choices reinforce the habits. It is not dramatic choices but repeated choices that do most to determine the affective texture of one's life, since it is they that establish dispositions and that can, by deliberate effort, change dispositions. Alteration of the texture and even the structure of life can almost never be accomplished in one big moment. The texture of one's life is a matter of undramatic, day-to-day thoughts, feelings, emotions, moods, and choices. The mood in which one chooses his necktie or speaks to his children in the minutes before breakfast, the stray half-thoughts on the way to work, one's attitude toward the acquisition of the means of life, the things and moments that hold one's attention and concern—these are what give our days and the sum of our days their pervasive pattern. If life is not found satisfactory on this level, the chances are small that it will be found satisfactory at all. But the orientation toward crisis can make us overlook the times between in which the most part of our lives is lived, can let us drift through and ignore the usual human themes and moments in which the most centrally human fulfillments are found.

This effect of distraction is in itself bad enough, but there are further consequences that are worse. The rare, large, structural decisions arise from and represent a shift in established dispositions. The character we have made through a multitude of undramatic choices is that same person who makes our momentous decisions: dramatic decisions, if they are to have fruits beyond their own expense of spirit, must have some roots in time. Again, alteration through resolution is possible, but—to change metaphors—what we can reasonably hope to accomplish is a deflection of direction; habit is the inertia of the moral life. This is not an unfortunate inevitability; it is a beneficent, contingent fact, a fact without which human morality would be impossible. To deplore it makes all the sense it would make to ignore or condemn the law of gravity. If hopes and plans are to have a reasonable chance of accomplishment, the direction and force of our old ways must enter our calculations. The exhilarating illusion of beginning utterly anew—whether it is the relation between a people and its government which is to be newly established, or the relation between one woman and one man, or the relation of a man to his future—is, with tragic regularity, the prelude to a new calamity. We may never understand why all our programs come to nothing, why our lives drift irresolutely from crisis to abortive resolution, but the causes of inconsequentiality lie in a twofold ignorance: a failure to appreciate the instructive value of precedent and a failure to sense the causal debt of the future to the past.

These kinds of ignorance are not independent. If Spinoza's theory that causes are necessary cannot stand against Hume's demonstration that they are not, it is still true, even for Hume, that each of us is best understood as summing up in himself, at any point in time, his whole past. We shall fail to understand ourselves—our dispositions, decisions, actions—if we consider, in unreal isolation, only the moment before us and not those causes whose effects we are, which live in us, which have brought us just as we are to the moment as it is. To recognize this fully is, as we shall later see, to feel the burdens of isolation and responsibility in their truly human and bearable proportions. Failure to recognize it is human bondage. Even the few great and genuine crises that come are so intricately related to the past that the relation can nearly be called reciprocal: decisions are generally a simple or complex function of past patterns of choice, but it is also true that each further choice alters the pattern and gives ground for a fresh perspective on the past. Although we cannot change the past, the way we see it cannot help but change. Since we are complex and reflective creatures, what we are and do is not often a simple consequence of what we have been, but depends also on what we think and feel we have been.

Some terrible moments in life go beyond all hope of deliberate confrontation, but even these, and certainly crises that do not stun us so, can best be lived through to further life when a strongly established texture of affections lies behind them. Things can happen that cannot be comprehended, things that break us past recovery, but the best hope of comprehension is the existence of well-structured patterns of attention and habits of choice. When those few critical occasions come that call not simply for good sense, sensitivity, or endurance, but also for choice, our decisions will be made—whether we know it or not—in the light of our past. So far as the illusion or ideal of utter freedom from the past leads us to disregard that source of influence and light, it will lead us only into deserts and jungles, into the romantic and unlivable situations of popular existentialism.

6. *Patriotism*

Existentialism is an attempt to make philosophic melodrama out of human anxiety. Intellectually pretentious as it is, it has tended to excite a relatively small number of people. Greater numbers can be and have been reached by cruder attempts to meet or modify the felt isolation and littleness of modern man. For 150 years or more, such attempts have been secular and political, have tended to emphasize community to the exclusion of all else.

Nationalism-patriotism is an emotion, or a theory in the service of an emotion, which has ends other than the relief of the individual soul; given the variety of contexts in which it has flourished and become a force, it would be inadequate to explain it only in these moral terms. But we shall fail to understand the hold this religion has on its believers unless we see that its promise of community appeals to a widespread, uneasy need. That sense of individuality without precedents which can, to some fortunate few, seem the occasion for a new creation will seem to the many who never sought it an excuse for anarchy or indolence, or a burden too awful to be borne. Patriotism can offer itself as discipline for the disorganized, as a tonic for the demoralized, and as an intoxicating loss of self to all the frightened and frustrated little men. To merge one's own insignificance with a hundred thousand others, to rise together into a supremely significant synthesis—that is the looked-for liberation of the patriotic man.

But patriotism is effective only as a very strong solution. It is not easy to feel at one with all the members of one's nation even in times of stress, and it may be impossible at any other time.[17] In the past men may have felt at home within some small and well-known group, some *polis* in which personal and political life merged in the single ideal of citizenship, in which neighbor was known as friend and fellow-soldier, but such groups scarcely exist today. Now crisis is the requirement of patriotic community. The sense of nation as a saving grace can be sustained only at high tension. Each can lose his aloneness in the nation only when patriotism is a passion. It is in fascism that the religion of the nation becomes at once ceremonious and evangelical. The Dionysian salvation it offers its devotees is loss of the weak and unworthy self in the omnipotent and supremely valuable state. The better self hidden in the humble and uplifted follower is revealed in the will of the leader. The sullen isolation of the self is seen as an illusion, and gives way to a massive vision of unity of race, of blood, of hope.[18]

It is necessary to the effectiveness of fascism that intellect be abandoned for something less divisive. Intellect must be hounded into exile, penned up, or killed in favor of the supreme value of feeling together. Mind, which sees and makes distinctions, must be stifled in the loss of all distinction, in the drunk, unanimous roar of blind and saving passion. All barriers down, the mass can feel in the loss of individuality a common immediacy, or an intense surge of infinite and nameless emotion felt not as that of each, but as the mysterious union of all. In the intensely sentimental, romantic, and animal atmosphere of the party rally the feeling of community can be achieved.

It is discreditable to admit, but it is dangerous to deny, the crude and atavistic appeal of such an atmosphere. Although its production may be achieved by a cynical and perverted manipulation of the manly values of courage and comradeship, those values remain in themselves perfectly genuine. To say that the marching, the banners, the spectacle, the show of power and the counterfeit of glory *ought* to leave all unmoved—this may be the saying of a rarely wise and gentle man, but it is just as likely to reflect the reaction of a prig. If the emotions touched and stirred were utterly unreal or without value, the appeal felt by honest men, if only to be rejected, would be in the first place impossible.

But the cost is too high and the consequences terrible. Fascism saves almost in the sense that death does. Its victory over self is achieved at the sacrifice, not simply of mind, but of humanity. It is bad enough to wish to be one with the beasts in the field, but that further depth of romanticism that takes as its model the beast in the jungle saves at the cost of all worth saving. We, in our day, know too well the results of the abandonment of humanity. This evasion of self has ended only in berserker rage, sodden bestiality, and total destruction. Its condition is the extermination of mind; its instrument is the inversion of love; its real goal is the annihilation of self; and its sole and perfect creation is ruin.

7. *Communism*

For every philosopher who understands that he can say all that need be said without reference to Platonic universals, for every lay intellectual who knows the mistakes of Moses and can specify the fallacies in St. Thomas's proofs of God, there are ten thousand men who have simply lost interest, and millions who never had it. To explain fully the loss of authority of theories and consolations long thought to be sufficient would require an entire theory of cultural change, a theory in which philosophy would figure only as one agent among many. More accessible attempts to account for the eclipse of accepted myths are likely to be planks in a party platform, straight-hewn, simple, and crude. The Christian explains the haplessness of his religion by saying that men have lost faith in God, that social and personal disorientation can be set right only by return to forsaken ways. It is true that men have lost faith, but this is to name a fact, not to explain it. The economic-political conservative also laments a loss of faith: faith in a free and self-regulating market and in rugged individualism. It is true that such talk is special pleading;

it is also true that the world keeps changing, economically, politically, and socially. The conservative who explains such change by reference to loss of faith in Adam Smith is, like his Christian counterpart, confusing causes with effects. If he intends to suggest that the political and social concomitants of modern technology and mass democracy can be undone and molded again in the patterns of nineteenth century capitalism, he is being naïve or, more likely, disingenuous. G. K. Chesterton said that it was easy to turn back the clock: with one's right index finger one pushed the hands counterclockwise. Unless directed at witless determinism, this is a witless joke.

Useful and reasonably accurate sketches of the economic and social backgrounds of our personal problems are popular and available. One virtue of empirical, impressionistic, and paperbacked sociology (such as that of Mills, Riesman, and Whyte) is that it keeps before us a recognizable set of pictures of our social situation. On the other hand, we have to rely on imagination to discover what would be said of our situation by a Marxist who, instead of arguing a priori from his texts, looked to the actual conditions to be explained. The Marxists find it easier to explain the conditions that Marx predicted than to account for the conditions that have in fact come about.

The world of the Western bourgeoisie may be dying, but if so its death is indistinguishable from metamorphosis. Of the American scene, at least, one could say with equal accuracy either that the middle classes have disappeared or that they are on the point of absorbing the other classes. The lords of the bourgeois creation, the power elite, may be more sinister than any class that Marx envisioned, but they are less conspicuous, operate with more subtle efficiency, and are far more adept at public relations than Marx could have foreseen. No one in the more highly industrialized parts of the world seems to be thinking of rebelling against them just now. The masses are eager neither to rise against them nor to rise when they enter the room. The powers that be are so pleased with the former that they are willing to forego the latter. To the people, the notion of rising does not mean an attempt to destroy their economic superiors, but the effort to join or at least to imitate them.

In this there are gains and losses on both sides. One result is that people have more *things* than people have ever had, and while this is nothing bad and may conduce to content, it has followed that those harsh and informing virtues that can attend social struggle have suffered the same decline as have more humane and constructive values. Marx himself struck close to home with his dictum that the cash nexus destroys every other nexus in a capitalistic society, but to account for the vapid and lonely individualism of Western man by reference to class war is to explain something that has happened by reference to something that has not.

There are any number of people to whom evidence does not matter, and it is not original to remark the analogies between evangelical communism and militant religion. Marxist indignation at this analogy depends on identification of religion with supernaturalism, and this identification is largely just, reflecting what religion has always been. As an objection to the analogy it can be set aside when we see that materialistic metaphysics is as extra-empirical as the doctrine of transubstantiation, and if we consider principally the emotional results of its acceptance. It is as it is accepted by its true believers that we can pertinently consider the newest of the world's great faiths.

Communism comes to save, comes to the lost individual as a saving grace, and takes its saving mission no less seriously than have other faiths with different visions of salvation. Its vision is grounded in a metaphysics largely implicit in the writings of Marx and Engels, elaborated and altered by Lenin, and since developed or at least ramified with ingenuity and finesse. The Marxist makes play with the word "'scientific," but when he says "scientific" he means "materialistic," and materialism is no more and no less than a metaphysical vision. Science as we know it in the Western world is metaphysically neutral: in that lies its flexible strength and its fruitfulness for understanding and control; in that lies its ideological weakness. It is unlikely that a genuinely scientific spirit could ever serve to animate a fervid and popular religion. Only the grand and transempirical, only the stirring and unconfirmable certainties of metaphysical belief can provide the ground and motive of general enthusiasm. Marx's intentions in this respect are no more relevant to the development and present condition of communism than are those of Aristotle to the present state of Catholic theology.

It is as a source of metaphysical confidence that dialectical materialism—Hegel's Dialectic translated into material terms—sustains the morale of its believers. It furnishes belief in a common ground, the ground of material interactions on which all men stand. It holds that we are all appearances of one reality, manifestations of one universal ground. That ground, matter in its dynamic, dialectical structure, is the essence of us all. Failure to recognize this as the ultimately real gives rise to the illusion of individuality. To take the existent individual as fully real is simple-minded, a piece of class prejudice, or absurd. To hold the individual to be the final locus of value is a bourgeois superstition. On the deepest levels of reality, beyond possibility of mere observation, there exists not merely human community, but essential unity. More superficially and lifted to the level of appearance, there is the solidarity of the destined conquering class. The solidarity of the proletariat manifests the creation of this class by a particular and culminating movement of the dialectic of material forces. These forces, economically expressed, produce a people effective only in the mass, a class that must triumph only as a class. All matter conspires to produce community: the antecedents of the struggle, the conditions of the victory, and the world that must emerge from the suffering.

The appeal of militant communism is not to the physically hungry alone. For the spiritually homeless it provides its emotional identifications: with the comrades of the cell, with the international proletariat, with the future, with the dialectical march of reality itself. But equally given is the demand for essential obedience, for unconditional surrender of the self. The achievement of social salvation is, in any case, inevitable. If final victory is inevitable, its inevitable conditions include the re-patterning of personality, the elimination of useless idiosyncrasy, and the abdication of individual will in action. In this, the Marxist must say, nothing of value is lost. It is not as individual that man is real and valuable, but as the product and agent of irresistible and more than personal forces. Revolution and salvation alike demand a perfect conformity. But who would not conform to the truth? How could the believer see in this service less than perfect freedom? Salvation in terms of this vision demands what it promises: the disappearance of a trivial and burdensome individuality. For this it substitutes belief in a ground of metaphysical unity, a sentiment of class solidarity, and the exhilaration of being on the side whose rightness is wholly proved by its inevitable victory.

The result is automatism. The giving of oneself to be an instrument is an abdication that can produce a somnambulistic peace, and there can be a kind of metallic beauty even in human tools. The exact, narrow, and finally mindless certitude of an instrument can come as a blessing to the man who must fulfill himself in action, but who is afraid to accept responsibility for its instigation. The commitment of such a man to an organization that orders and absolves his action can be absolute, and so, according to one fashionable definition, religious. Such allegiances may lie beyond argument, may be among the fixed points around which moral disagreements circle. If, as his deepest and most central need, a willful man requires an alien rule for his will, if fear of lonely responsibility lies close to the springs of his action, he may fall below the possibility of a fully human life. He can always argue that the moral gain was not worth the mortal candle. Faced with his refusal of humanity there will be little we can say. We may point out possibilities of life that his tough cowardice forfeits and some of the hard-bought beauties that creators but never tools can know, and be met by the hidden fear of freedom and the smugness of willfully thoughtless certitude. When arguments, persuasion, and exhortation fail to move him toward the achievement of humanity, we may have to conclude that we are in the presence of a known and sometimes dangerous species of man. We might then do well to check the strength of our own position.

C. PANIC FORWARD

Ours is not the first time in which traditional or accepted "solutions" to Protagorean problems have lost their hold on the affections of men, and we ought not readily accept the view that Kierkegaard invented anxiety. What is peculiar about our situation is our exacerbated self-consciousness, our clearer awareness of our situation and the consequent sense, not merely that some one traditional solution must be abandoned in favor of another, but that no answer of the old kind could do. We feel entitled to think that we have not failed the answers, but that the answers have failed us; we begin to wonder whether we have been asking the right kind of question. It is hard to say whether such numbers of literate people have felt this way before; large numbers seem to feel this way now, and this quantity itself qualifies our problem. We can learn the most valuable lessons from our past but, romantic conservatism to the contrary, ours is the only time in which we can live, and ours is a time in which the fabulous cement of society has chipped or weathered away. The effective and illusory supports of social life and personal character have been intelligently condemned, leaving suspended uneasily in the air a world whose organization is a vulgar accident and felt to be such, and individuals distinguished by nothing but the types of their covetousness and fear and the aimless variety of their lack of purpose. There is no society that earns our full respect, and most of the attempts to deny or modify our sense of meaninglessness resemble nothing so much as that operation on the brain that, to cure madness, destroys its higher centers.

Understanding one's situation is not enough to resolve it. A man can retreat to any of the obfuscations already mentioned, or he can panic forward into attempts to intensify aloneness; extreme reactions come more easily than appropriate responses. Intelligence is not enough, willing as it is to follow every fear and to fawn on any passion. Our situation and our hopes will be clear only to those with steadiness enough to see them plainly, courage enough to do without mystification, and sense enough to disengage the most useful lessons of our past. After epistemological and ethical analysis and before therapy comes the recognition of what Santayana calls our "normal madness," then the acceptance of responsibility, and then the moral question of how we are to live. It is a question of moral philosophy whether, in our situation, we are entitled to hope for honest solutions; whether in all good sense we can hope to find some possibility of life, not in denying our felt isolation, but in consciously accepting these feelings as setting the initial conditions of the problem to be solved. The danger that lies closest to this acceptance is taking the initial conditions as the final solution.

1. *The Desert Islander*

One might hope to find advantages in the intensification of isolation, and so one can for a time, but the cost is very high and the sense in which isolation is desired turns out to be a sense in which it cannot be maintained. This last phrase could be misleading: in its problematic sense, isolation is not so much deliberate as inevitable; the characteristic poignancy of this feeling is partly caused by the apprehension that it is inevitable. It is rather that this awareness cannot protect the prisoner against the invasion of pain. We might like to think that since each man is an island, he should be able to live on his property undisturbed, but it seldom works out well. Those advantages of isolation we might hope to enjoy—fruitful warmth, rich tranquillity, happy peace—we find to be no sure consequence of island existence, and those aspects of island existence we might think to avoid we find to be inevitable.

What is involved here is less a paradox than an inequity. It is not fair, we may feel, that there should be suffering where there is no communion. If we are to be alone, we think, we ought to remain untouched. What we find is that the world breaks in on us; we more than half invite it. We find that the world will not leave us alone, that we cannot leave the world alone, but that so far as we succeed in separation, we lose what we had run away to save. That when the world breaks in on us we may find our way out to the world is a theme to be developed later; here we can consider isolation and invasion and take for text Joseph Conrad's *Victory,* a novel students read in Freshman English, when its moral is inaudible to them and has come too late for their professors.

It is not unduly didactic to derive moral lessons from this novel.[19] The story of Axel Heyst, the detached observer of human concerns, in retreat on his desert island, is an explicitly moral tale. What is less clear is exactly what the moral is. The possibilities are multiple and overlapping. Axel Heyst is a man who meets isolation more than halfway, who accepts and exploits it and asks only to have the advantages one might reasonably think to go with it. The moral of the story is that Epicureanism fails, practically and morally.[20] This statement is agreeably straightforward and misleadingly simple. Does Epicureanism fail Heyst, or could it be that Heyst is not a good enough Epicurean? Heyst sometimes leaves his island—·is the moral that he must? Heyst's island is invaded—is the moral that invasion is inevitable? Or is it that the attempt to exploit the advantages of isolation is so demanding that to buy a chance of success in it one must pay with most of his humanity, must become either something more or something less than human? There are at least these possibilities: that the practical difficulties in the way of detachment are insurmountable, that man is a social animal, that even under ideal conditions one remains open to pain, or that the degree to which one succeeds in detachment from things and people brings with it a proportionate inability to act or feel.

Is the point that, *practically* speaking, you cannot detach yourself? Beneath the possible moral point that something about your humanity tends to pull you from your island, there is the sordid and visceral fact that you have to eat to live, and that it is difficult to be materially self-sufficient. The practical is no doubt less important than the moral point, but the practical difficulties of literal or physical detachment from society are still in themselves prohibitive. It is an old insight that the division of labor is a primitive justification of society, and a refined division of labor a necessity for the highest civilization. Plato and Aristotle head the list of those who would see in *The Swiss Family Robinson* no more than a charming story for children and insist that to live in literal isolation is to live in some degree like a savage, obsessed with the single thought of daily bread. It can be said again and again that the only island that would really content us is a dream, an impossible dream that even as dream has gone stale. It can be said again and again because it is a dream we are never quite rid of.

"You live in a thatch hut with the daughter of the king, a slim young maiden in whose eyes is an ancient wisdom. Her breasts are golden speckled pears, her belly a melon, and her odor is like nothing so much as a jungle fern. In the evening, on the blue lagoon, under the silvery moon, to your love you croon in the soft sylabeluw and vocabeluw of her langorour tongorour. Your body is golden brown like hers, and tourists have need of the indignant finger of the missionary to point you out. They envy you your breech clout and carefree laugh and little brown bride and fingers instead of forks. But you don't return their envy, and when a beautiful society girl comes to your hut in the night, seeking to learn the secret of your happiness, you

*send her back to her yacht that hangs on the horizon like a
nervous racehorse. And so you dream away the days, fishing,
hunting, dancing, swimming, kissing, and picking flowers to
twine in your hair. . . ."*

"Well, my friend, what do you think of the South Seas?"

*Miss Lonelyhearts tried to stop him by making believe that he
was asleep. But Shrike was not fooled.*

*"Again silence," he said, "and again you are right. The South
Seas are played out and there's little use in imitating Gau-
guin."*[21]

Heyst's island is set up for self-sufficiency; his outward and
visible defeat is practical, but this seems to be a consequence
of incursion by appropriate representatives of the outside world
—and the girl, Lena, whom Heyst in pity brings to his island,
must be counted as the first invader. Heyst cannot cope with
invasion. The girl comes too late, the desperate men too soon,
and the result is an almost Elizabethan slaughter. Reserve the
fact that Heyst's practical failure is the consequence of moral
failure: coldly considered, meanly considered, Lena could no
more save Heyst's life than he could save hers. Let "save" be
taken literally or spiritually, she could not save him. We are
all but told that the girl, through love, has been victorious
over the greatest inevitability. She has stolen one invader's
dreadful knife, has pulled his sting of death. Through her
love for Heyst, and through the invader's lust for her, she has
won a sort of victory. But hers is a moral victory; it is only
moral, and it is only hers. Her practical victory comes to nothing, as it has to, being pitifully incomplete. To say that the
victory was hers alone is not to say that Heyst had no part in
its causes. He was her inspiration, her final cause, even if he
moved her in the austere way that Aristotle's God moves the
world. What we must mean is that, morally speaking, she saves
only herself. Her triumph is for his sake, but it is not his
victory. His essential loneliness is touched too late.

Heyst fails, but his practical failure is a consequence of a moral defeat. He sums up the immediate cause of his unsuccess in a terrible and accurate piece of self-knowledge: "After all, why should he trouble about these people's actions, why this stupid concern for the preliminaries since, when the issue was joined, it would find him disarmed and shrinking from the ugliness and degradation of it?" Exactly so—but why?

It is too simple to say that detachment fails. This might mean that one cannot remain detached, that the attempt to remain morally uncommitted or disengaged cannot be maintained, either because one must go out to the world or because the world will always break in on every island. It might also mean that detachment was to a degree possible, but led to unwanted consequences. These points may be good or bad, but they are distinguishable. They are possible themes for different trage-dies, but the particular tragedy of Heyst exhibits a combination of them. First Heyst loses his detachment; then he loses every-thing else. We may be too quick to blame the damning rem-nant of Epicureanism for ensuring his defeat, to say that he could not be committed enough, that he was given too little time to recover from his father's philosophy of detachment. But a consistent Epicurean (say Braz Cubas in *Epitaph of a Small Winner*) could well argue that it was the invader Heyst in-vited, the girl Lena, who destroyed Heyst, that all else was a consequence of this weakness.

Give the advocate of detachment his argument. What is the weakness Heyst might better have controlled? Heyst accepted, embraced, his aloneness and thought to be safe in his detach-ment. Perhaps he thought aloneness the same as detachment, so that having the former one always had the protection of the latter. He discovered that these are not the same. What he lost was not his aloneness, but his invulnerability: he opened him-self to the invasion of pain. The reason for his loss is clear. The elder Heyst had left a gap in his son's defenses, had failed to warn him against a terrible and subtle passion. It was

not love that exposed Heyst. Against this vulgar outgoing his
father, disillusioned past sensitivity, had inoculated him with
Lucretian antitoxin: "Of all the strategems of life the most cruel
is the consolation of love—the most subtle, too; for desire is
the bed of dreams."[22] But Heyst was too coolly clear-headed, too
self-contained for this until half-broken by a much more subtle
force. This invader, less easily guarded against, was disastrously
underestimated by Heyst's father:

[Heyst] had listened. Then, after a silence, he asked—for he was
really young then:

"Is there no guidance?"

His father was in an unexpectedly soft mood on that night
when the moon swam in a cloudless sky over the begrimed
shadows of the town.

"You still believe in something then?" he said in a clear voice
which had been growing feeble of late. "You believe in flesh
and blood perhaps? A full and equable contempt would soon
do away with that too. But since you have not attained to it,
I advise you to cultivate that form of contempt which is called
pity. It is perhaps the least difficult—always remembering that
you, too, if you are anything, are as pitiful as the rest, yet never
expecting any pity for yourself."[23]

And yet it is exactly pity that breaks Heyst, that pity which
Spinoza condemns as a terrible, powerful passion, more destructive than love. "He could not defend himself from compassion."[24] It is after he is broken by pity, but only after that, that
it can be said, "All his defenses were broken now. Life had him
fairly by the throat."[25] The same thing had happened once
before when Heyst came to the help of a person who called for
his help; of his compassion toward Morrison Heyst says, "I had
in a moment of inadvertence created for myself a tie. How to
define it precisely I don't know. One gets attached in a way to
people one has done something for. But is that friendship? I

am not sure it was; I only know that he who forms a tie is lost, the germ of corruption has entered his soul."[26]

In this story, at least, it is compassion that leads to action, and action to involvement. Conrad makes Heyst say ". . . woe to the man whose heart has not learned while young to hope, to love—and to put his trust in life!"[27] In fact there is no living alternative. If we are to feel at all we will find in fear and hate the other side of hope and trust and love. To panic forward into detachment provides a viable solution no more than does the flight to assimilation by the social machine. Men take their society with them, and most will not refrain from reaching out toward what they have forsworn. To leave is easier than to stay away, for it takes either dullness or strength to live alone, and strength alone confronting only itself turns too easily to hallucination or to savagery. But even supposing that rare strength—if it is ever the strong who run away—detachment brings no certainty of freedom from invasion. So long as any feeling remains to us, it is possible to be hurt; so far as we are human, we are vulnerable. In the furthest reaches of self-willed isolation we may find that it is only ourselves we mourn for, but we will find cause to mourn. Even if we fight off the pity and pain of involvement with other creatures, we are inextricably involved with ourselves, and hope, hate, pity, fear, and death break in no less surely, and often more meanly, to the self that has held its commitments to itself.

Still, cannot the Epicurean say that Heyst should have resisted the attack of compassion, that he was not detached enough, that if he could not be perfectly passionless, he should at least have come closer to this happy state? Heyst is an imperfect Epicurean, an incomplete Hellenist, and it is not impossible to draw the moral that it was the first invader he should have resisted, and that had he done so he would have had a better hope for living on in deeper isolation. To see this is to leave clear a further question: what is the price of detachment constantly guarded? Suppose Heyst had closed himself against Morrison and the girl—what then?

Most morally relevant qualities of character are brought to their relative perfection through practice. Passionlessness is the condition of acts and refusals that lead to the extinction of passion. The cost and the reward of desert island life is the refusal of affective involvement, the escape from disturbing attachments; this should be made clear. The advantage sought in detachment is invulnerability, and it would be foolish and sentimental to say that no advantage accrues to non-commitment, to pitilessness, to lovelessness. But absolute invulnerability is humanly impossible, and relative safety comes at a high price. Not only is invasion all but inevitable, but the more one improves his defenses, the less there is to defend.

It is not the business of this chapter to argue the point fully, but it would be well to see the alternatives and to avoid a possible misunderstanding. Invulnerability is the Epicurean ideal. Because man is mortal and subject to pain and to inadvertent attachments, invulnerability is an impossible ideal. If one especially so gifted could be completely passionless, could have no commitment beyond cool and disillusioned observation, his life would be completely lacking in affective depth, wholly free of deep intensity. Most of us can succeed in this only to a degree; but to whatever degree we approach this ideal we are protected from intensity. Since intensity is one essential aspect of the good life, the desert island life will be less good as it is more perfect.

The classical or humanistic ideal of balance and integration cannot be bettered, but it reduces and caricatures this ideal to suppose it to be accomplished by the elimination of strong feeling: that is to balance the scale by removing all the weights. What requires integration is emotion, and without emotion there is nothing worth the effort of integration. We say this now to forestall a false impression, for before showing the essential role of intensity in a life found good, we must say some hard things about its use as the *sole* criterion of goodness.

2. *The Anarchist*

Few people are prepared to become hermits; it must be assumed that most of us will live in some kind of society. But this is not a time in which one can, without terrible concessions, take his intellectual, cultural, or moral standards from the gross and visible society around him. Perhaps there have been great societies in which this could be done, perhaps there are imaginable societies in which it could be done, but it is not possible in our time and place.

If it is difficult literally to leave society, it is not easy for a man to live in a society whose practices and aspirations are substantially different from his own. It is not impossible. One reaction to taking the difficulty as an impossibility is the Hellenism of Axel Heyst. Another is the way of organized rebellion, in the hope of molding whatever survives destruction into something closer to the heart's desire. Today, and perhaps always, the attempt violently to overthrow an entire social order entails the acceptance of some other and equally specific social order. The acceptance of new allegiance required by total revolution can mean no more than the exchange of one bondage for another more extreme, and we have already seen that the cost of this will be too high for many of us. This is probably to say that we value autonomy, but it is not perfectly clear that the initial acceptance of the new system cannot be autonomous.

Most of those who are estranged from their society in feeling and values want neither literally to leave it nor to accept the loss of autonomy required to overthrow it. These are the people to whom it is hopeful to speak. But there is a subgroup of this minority about whom it is necessary to speak: those who, in their attempt at solution or escape, accept their given society as a sufficient antithesis. These can be called "the moral anarchists." Despite a coincidence on many points, and even their co-incidence in the same person, anarchism can be distinguished from romanticism. From its rich range of meanings we shall take "romanticism" as a label for the belief that intense, immediate experience liberates one from himself, puts one in touch with something transcending the self, and is the only good-making quality of a life found good. Anarchism is rather the attempt to achieve pure freedom of spirit by pure negation. Its tragic-comic trouble is that personal rebellion defined by negation alone tends to be limited precisely by local custom; it is an antithesis that takes its whole meaning from the particular thesis it opposes. It looks for the liberation of the self, and provincially interprets freedom as negation of the one social order it happens to know. It thinks to find an entire program in saying "No!" to the conventions it feels at first-hand. Posing as an attempt at pure liberation, an attempt to overcome insignificance by rejecting all that limits the self, it remains perpetually dependent on its local social forms, since it understands freedom to consist just in defiance of those forms. One finds few anarchists on desert islands.

The failure of the anarchist to escape into limitless freedom or even to achieve a modest autonomy is tritely marked by the way he clings to some like-minded group and depends for his self-esteem on their approval. Attempts to live outside the conventions always produce their own conventions, and the patterns of parasitical rebellion are as monotonous as their parent societies. If what it is to be outside is determined wholly by the would-be outsider's conception of the inside, then in his catechism to be outside the outside is the unforgivable sin. Perhaps from inside the outside it is different, but from outside the outside—a position the ignorant rebel cannot distinguish from the inside he has rejected—nothing could appear more minutely and unimaginatively regulated than the life of the militant outsider. From Murger to Kerouac, each generation of anarchists has shown only marginal differences from the type, and we find convincing evidence of plagiarism in their lives even more than in their work. The harmlessness of these people is recognized by all but the dullest of those whom they set out to shock. The amusement their poses provide for the philistines might justify the slight social expense of their maintenance if their cheap substitute for freedom did not capture or confuse some people who might otherwise achieve a more fruitful liberation.

Behind the easily observable facts, beneath the all-or-nothing turn of mind, lie ignorance, confusion, and an incoherent myth. It is bad enough to have one self-defeating ambition, but the moral anarchist has two: the attempt to achieve freedom of spirit through negation of his given society, and the attempt to achieve self-fulfillment by denying all that limits and conditions the self. The first limits him to being an antithesis of his society, and success in the second would mean not the realization of self, but its disappearance. Pure freedom, unconditioned freedom, is not only mythical, it is self-contradictory. We are not pure spirits and we cannot even conceive what such a situation would be. The self *is* a product or function of some set of conditions. "Spirit," if it means anything at all, is something that has a local habitation and a name. The attempt to define or to realize the self by denying all conditions is initially incoherent. This confusion may help account for the lapse of would-be free spirits into patterns as unnatural as those they have tried to transcend.

An argument against confused and petty rebellion is not an argument in favor of a petty and oppressive *status quo*. Even if it is impossible to be unconditioned, it is not impossible or even unreasonable to throw off this or that particular condition. The usefulness of trying to discard or transcend a particular social, moral, or aesthetic pattern of society will depend on the person, the principle, and the society. But the attempt or aspiration to have *no* principles, to reject those of one's familiar place without replacing them by others, ends in self-defeat, triviality, or crime.[28] The appropriate mean between mindless acceptance and ignorant rejection is not easy to find or to maintain. The moral anarchist, in the bravado of panic, throws himself toward an impossible extreme of negation. His is the *Jacquerie* of ignorance.

When the program of rebellion fails to go beyond negation, the result is never less ludicrous or ugly than its cause. (To stand Mrs. Grundy on her head merely displays another unlovely exposure.) The anarchist has nothing to say but "No!" and this is so far from a solution to affective meaninglessness, so far from a door to escape from isolation, that it usually leads to self-frustration and consuming bitterness. There are times when one must say "No!" but these are specific denials on particular principles, forerunners or defenses of positive values; the virtue of the negation lies in the affirmation for which it clears the ground.

The fallacy takes many forms, and in different ways we will have to insist on the platitude that neither life nor art can be based on negation alone. The anarchist's illusion that they can be rests on a false opposition between freedom and form. Disliking or fearing the forms of his given society, which may indeed be ugly and repressive, he concludes that his loneliness can be overcome and his freedom achieved by defying or outraging the only forms he knows. Since no other patterns of life seem possible to him, he thinks to find himself in utter freedom. He finds frustration, for the idea that there ought to be no limits, no order, is self-defeating. It is not only self-contradictory as an ideal, it is self-frustrating in practice. Choices must be made, that relative emphasis of experience that gives life its shape cannot but be practiced, and the only question open to us is the degree of autonomy, sensitivity, and consciousness with which we choose. Freedom is significant insofar as it is freedom to create an order of life found good by the person who chooses. If we merely contradict the conventions of our society, our ideal life will be wholly dictated by what we affect to despise. Then our heteronomy or dependence will be complete. If we choose nothing beyond rejection of all conditions of human and social life, our ideal is not distinguishable from an aspiration toward nothing at all. Of course we can so choose. We can in ignorance choose nothing deliberately, or we can make the unchoice of refusing to think of such things, of deciding to wait on the event of spontaneous inspiration—which is to leave our lives to apparent accident and to unrecognized drift.

III

THE ROMANTIC ATTITUDE

Burke:* [Reynolds] was a great generalizer . . . But this disposition to abstractions, to generalizing and classification, is the great glory of the human mind. . . .

Blake: To Generalize is to be an Idiot. To Particularize is the Alone Distinction of Merit. General Knowledges are those Knowledges that Idiots possess.

Reynolds: Raffaelle, it is true, had not the advantage of studying in an Academy; but all Rome and the works of Michael Angelo in particular, were to him an Academy. On the sight of the Capella Sistina he immediately from a dry, Gothick, and even insipid manner, which attends to the minute, accidental discriminations of particular and individual objects, assumed that grand style of painting which improves partial representation by the general and invariable ideas of nature.

* These selections from Reynold's *Discourses* are accompanied by William Blake's annotations (in italics). The first comment is by Edmund Burke, quoted in the preliminary account of Reynolds, which appeared in the edition Blake used.

Blake: Minute Discrimination is Not Accidental. All Sublimity is founded on Minute Discrimination. I do not believe that Rafael taught Mich. Angelo, or that Mich. Angelo taught Rafael, any more than I believe that the Rose teaches the Lilly how to grow, or the Apple tree teaches the Pear tree how to bear Fruit. I do not believe the tales of Anecdote writers when they militate against Individual Character.

Reynolds: When the artist is once enabled to express himself . . . he must then endeavour to collect subjects for expression; to amass a stock of ideas . . . to learn all that has been known and done before . . .

Blake: After having been a Fool, a Student is to amass a Stock of Ideas, &, knowing himself to be a Fool, he is to assume the Right to put other Men's Ideas into his Foolery.

Reynolds: A Student unacquainted with the attempts of former adventurers, is always apt to over-rate his own abilities; to mistake the most trifling excursions for discoveries of moment, and every coast new to him, for a new-found country.

Blake: Contemptible Mocks!

Reynolds: The productions of such minds are seldom distinguished by an air of originality; they are anticipated in their happiest efforts; and if they are found to differ in anything from their predecessors, it is only in irregular sallies and trifling conceits.

Blake: Thus Reynolds Depreciates the Efforts of Inventive Genius. Trifling Conceits are better than Colouring without any meaning at all.

Reynolds: Following these rules, and using these precautions, when you have clearly and distinctly learned in what good colouring consists, you cannot do better than have recourse to nature herself, who is always at hand and in comparison of whose true splendour the best coloured pictures are but faint and feeble.

Blake: Nonsense! Every Eye Sees differently. As the Eye, Such the Object.

Reynolds: Instead of copying the touches of those great masters, copy only their conceptions . . . Labour to invent on their general principles and way of thinking.

Blake: General Principles Again! Unless You Consult Particulars You Cannot even Know or See Mich. Anglo. or Rafael or any Thing Else.

Reynolds: But as mere enthusiasm will carry you but a little way . . .

Blake: Mere Enthusiasm is the All in All! Bacon's Philosophy has Ruin'd England. Bacon is only Epicurus over again.

Reynolds: Though a student by such praise may have his attention roused . . . *He examines* his own mind, and perceives there nothing of that divine inspiration, with which, he is told, so many others have been favoured.

Blake: The Man who on Examining his own Mind finds nothing of Inspiration ought not to dare to be an Artist; he is a Fool & a Cunning Knave suited to the Purposes of Evil Demons. . . .

Reynolds: But on this, as upon many other occasions, we ought to distinguish how much is to be given to enthusiasm, and how much to reason—taking care . . . not to lose in terms of vague admiration, that solidity and truth of principle, upon which alone we can reason, and may be enabled to practise.

Blake: It is Evident that Reynolds Wish'd none but Fools to be in the Arts & in order to this, he calls all others Vague Enthusiasts or Madmen. What has Reasoning to do with the Art of Painting?

Reynolds: . . . and the whole beauty of the art consists, in my opinion, in being able to get above all singular forms, local customs, particularities, and details of every kind.

Blake: A Folly! Singular & Particular Detail is the Foundation of the Sublime.

Reynolds: Thus it is from a reiterated experience and a close comparison of the objects in nature, that an artist becomes possessed of the idea of that central form . . . from which every deviation is deformity.

Blake: One Central Form composed of all other Forms being Granted, it does not therefore follow that all other Forms are Deformity. All Forms are Perfect in the Poet's Mind, but these are not Abstracted nor Compounded from Nature, but are from Imagination.

Reynolds: There is a rule, obtained out of general nature, to contradict which is to fall into deformity.

Blake: What is General Nature? is there Such a Thing? what is General Knowledge? is there such a Thing? Strictly Speaking All Knowledge is Particular.

Reynolds: It is true, indeed, that these figures are each perfect in their kind, though of different characters and proportions; but still none of them is the representation of an individual, but of a class.

Blake: Every Class is Individual.

Reynolds: . . . the painter . . . must divest himself of all prejudices in favour of his age or country; he must disregard all local and temporary ornaments, and look only on those general habits, which are every where and always the same. . . .

Blake: Generalizing in Every thing, the Man would soon be a Fool, but a Cunning Fool.

Reynolds: The general idea constitutes real excellence. All smaller things, however perfect in their way, are to be sacrificed without mercy to the greater.

Blake: Sacrifice the Parts, What becomes of the Whole?

Reynolds: If you mean to preserve the most perfect beauty in its most perfect state, you cannot express the passions . . .

Blake: What Nonsense! Passion & Expression is Beauty Itself. The Face that is Incapable of Passion & Expression is deformity Itself. Let it be Painted & Patch'd & Praised & Advertised for Ever, it will only be admired by Fools.[1]

All the issues are here. Painting is the ground of the exchange, but the shots carry far beyond the studio: Reynolds and Blake represent attitudes toward life itself. It is the romantic attitude of which we must speak, and speak with the deference deserved by a great half-truth. Romanticism, in the sense in which we shall discuss it, is an affective response to what is recognized, although seldom clearly, as an affective problem. (Where there is an appended "philosophy," its vagueness, fancifulness, and dispensability are enough to show its *post hoc* or ancillary character.) In this respect, at least, it is honest and hopeful, but its very closeness to an adequate answer makes it less a solution than a temptation. Romanticism has hit on an essential part of the truth about what can make a human life good, but it has taken its part for the whole, and in this its danger lies. Blake is right in seeing passion and expression—aspects of particular and immediate experience—at the heart of beauty, but he is wrong in taking these to be Beauty Itself. It is precisely passion and expression that require and repay an attempt at order, at a rule obtained out of general nature, to contradict which is to fall into deformity.

If Blake is not the great exemplar of the romantic attitude, it is because he was too little known, because his own peculiar vision lent a kind of fantastic discipline to his work, and perhaps because he was too honest. While no one man can be assigned responsibility for a tidal movement in art, manners, and morals, much less for the attitudes on which it rested or which it expressed, Rousseau does come close to this distinction. If Rousseau is not the entire devil that Irving Babbitt takes him to be, he must still stand as the subsequently sanctified and detested prophet of romanticism, as the liberator of many dark continents within, as the spiritual ancestor of all the sensitive young men from the provinces, and as the author of considerable mischief.

Nothing could be plainer than the extra-artistic bearing of Rousseau's doctrine and his example. His was a major influence in spreading the fertile idea that the inhibited life is not worth living. Think of Rousseau in personal rebellion rejecting the standards of a world he never made; of Rousseau retreating from forms of civility he was unable to imitate, flying off to a utopia of pastoral flummery; of Rousseau hugging his sensitivity and disposing of his children; of Rousseau listening to his own heart and cultivating his ineffable personality.[2] All these themes —rebellion, rejection of responsibility, dreams, intuition, inspiration, personality—are still with us, with results not inevitably evil or inane. What needs to be pointed out now is that the last four refer to something inevitably individual, subjective, and immediate. The romantic attitude is not only characterized by an emphasis on what is idiosyncratic and by a theoretical contempt for discipline: it opposes itself to what is clear and universal, and contends against the very concept of discipline. It finds its *summum bonum* in the undefined and peculiar, the untrammeled and intense, above all in immediate experience.

A. IMMEDIACY

"Immediacy" or "the immediate" refers to the direct apprehension of first-personal experience, to the intuitive awareness of one's own occurrent sensations and states of mind, and to the felt qualities given in experience. Considered in itself, the immediate is non-referential: it is the given content of consciousness, or consciousness itself, *not* some object beyond experience to which experience is supposed to refer. "The given" and "the immediate" have this same meaning regardless of whether we take our experience as indicating the presence of something beyond us, or as having primarily personal reference. We generally take the experience of shapes or colors to show the existence of shaped or colored objects, and the experience of happiness or boredom to be aspects only of the experiencing self. There are some exceptions to this generalization: spots before the eyes, happy scenes.

It is not possible to furnish verbal examples of the immediate, and for a basic reason: all "knowledge" of the immediately given is "knowledge by acquaintance." To give you knowledge by acquaintance of the color called "purple," it would be necessary to put a purple patch just here. Literally, nothing other than a sample of the color would do. The name "purple" is not a description and cannot convey the quality that you would immediately sense in the presence of the color itself.

"Knowledge by acquaintance" is, strictly, not yet knowledge; it is *only* acquaintance, intuition, immediate apprehension, particular awareness not yet organized by patterns of thought; immediate awareness is but the raw material of knowledge. Knowledge is confirmable or arguable, true or probable; experience just happens. Knowledge, stated in sentences or in formulae, stands at some conceptual distance from immediate experience, from which it departs to return for confirmation, but knowledge is always more abstract and communicable than its terminal points. Without the immediate intuition of the given in experience, there would be no ground for knowledge, but without the abstract and systematic organization of concepts and terms, we would never get off the ground; the world would remain for us a "buzzing, blooming, confusion." There may be some minimal order in the inchoate buzz and bloom of immediate apprehension, but when we speak of "knowledge" we are speaking of the conceptual interpretation of the given.

The difference is clearest in simple cases of perceptual immediacy, which involve nothing emotional.

The distinction between [the] element of interpretation and the given is emphasized by the fact that the latter is what remains unaltered, no matter what our interests, no matter how we think or conceive. I can apprehend this thing as pen, or rubber, or cylinder, but I cannot, by taking thought, discover it as paper or soft or cubical. While we can thus isolate the element of the given by these criteria of its unalterability and its character as sensuous feel or quality, we cannot describe any particular given as such, because in describing it, in whatever fashion, we qualify it by bringing it under some category or other, select from it, emphasize aspects of it, and relate it in particular and avoidable ways. If there be states of pure aesthesis, in violent emotion or in the presence of great art, which are unqualified by thought, even these can be conveyed—and perhaps even retained in memory—only when they have been rendered articulate by thought. So that in a sense the given is ineffable, always. It is that which remains untouched and unaltered, however it is construed by thought.[3]

David Hume, too, pointed out that the mystics have no corner on ineffability. That immediate experience subsequently declared to have signified the presence of God is no more and no less ineffable than the immediate apprehension taken to be the taste of a pineapple. One can name the taste of pineapple but the taste cannot literally be put into words. One can say "the smell of old books," but this is only a label; it will mean nothing to illiterate noses. Labels can be useful in classification despite disparity in what they call to mind. The teetotaling clerk in the liquor store does not disappoint his customers by confusing the scotch with the bourbon. A person who hears a labeling word and who has had the kind of experience he supposes the word to name can call to mind what he supposes to be an appropriate recollection. Whether he succeeds, whether his presently entertained immediate experience truly reproduces another experience now past or whether it is like the experience of another person who uses the same word, is an unanswerable question. Sameness or difference of first-personal experience is impossible to confirm. The attempt to communicate it causes something less like communication than like contagion. This is true of what might be called "external ineffability," that is, the incommunicable apprehended quality of a certain shade of red, a certain tone, taste, or smell. It is even more true of "internal ineffability," our immediate awareness of our own feelings, moods, emotions, passions. It is the despair of lyric poets that "alas!" is so uninformative. It enrages the lover that the best he can say is "I love you!"

It is not without cause that we often feel it to be just here that we must look to find what is most truly real and most deeply valued. There are times when it seems to be just these givens of sense and feeling—intense, unclassified, wordless, always escaping through our verbal nets—that are most truly *ours,* the quick and dying center of ourselves. (Schopenhauer and Bergson have each raised a whole metaphysics on this seeming.) No word or concept or abstraction could feel so close, no description so intense, no understanding so valuable. And we may twist in despair that this, just this which is so piercingly real, so finally important, so valuable, is most incommunicable.

There is an enormous consolation: the impossibility of communicating the immediate is the inseparable other side of an advantage, for in the surge and flow of immediate experience there may seem for the time to be neither need nor place for discursive thought, for the effort of abstraction thought requires. Indeed, when the intuition of experience is sufficiently intense, the sense of inspiration overwhelms us, and thought seems a properly banished impertinence; along with abstraction we seem to lose ourselves, and ourselves seem well lost. Utter absorption appears magically to dissolve the barriers between subject and object, melting the abandoned self and the overcome otherness of the other into one luminous and noetic whole —so it is said. One could say either that the ego was extended to infinity, or that all its limits or boundaries were destroyed; both reports have been issued. It is the way of the romantic, in his one-pointed devotion to intense, immediate experience, to meet the egocentric predicament by burning through the limits of the self, by losing all sense of separateness in a final consummation that leaves nothing to be desired. If cooler heads find the "knowledge" that is claimed to come from such experience unintelligible, even they should allow that in immediate experience men often or always find the most intense and lyrical moments of their lives. Intensity and lyricism are the symptoms and the fruit of intuition.

The less pretentious but still inestimable gift of immediacy is this: immediate experience is capable of perfect finality. If we distinguish things found good into "intrinsic goods" and "extrinsic or instrumental goods," perceptual and affective immediacy are ideal examples (perhaps the only examples) of intrinsic value. The intuition of one's own states of consciousness can do without any further justification or excuse for being. At the moment when experience itself is all-absorbing, in states of pure aesthesis, there is no need for reference beyond the immediate. When, later, we would express that which has been experienced as finally valuable, when we would communicate our sense of escape from the limits of singularity, when we would justify what seemed to call for no justification, we find to our surprise that all words fail. We may tell ourselves that communication is irrelevant to the experience we have had; it may be, but its failure here seems precisely to throw us back into the self we thought we had transcended. The experience that in the having *was* self-justifying and final seems then to have been transient and partial, to require a completion perhaps to be found in some wider prospect of time, self, and society.

1. *"Could I make tongue say more than tongue can utter!"*

For the romantic in his political role the attempt to overcome aloneness, to achieve genuine community of being, is likely to end in totalitarianism. "Adolph Hitler, we believe in thee! Without thee we would be alone! Thou hast given us the great experience of our youth! Thou hast made of us a people!" For the apolitical romantic the same attempt will end in love. Romantic love is the purest strain and perfect consequence of this attitude; predictably enough, we shall have much to say about it. For the moment we shall focus not on communion, but on communication, remembering that this distinction may seldom be felt as such. It may be the attempt to transmit from isolation, to communicate with perfect faithfulness what has been felt as most intensely real that peculiarly fascinates the romantic artist, and by extension all of us who have intensities to value, to re-create and to share.

The communication of scientific information is surrounded by no such bittersweet complexity. The states of mind or contents of consciousness of those engaged in cognitive communication are all but irrelevant to the successful transfer of information.

Idiosyncrasy of intuition need not make any difference, except in the aesthetic quality of the experience of one as compared with that of another. Let us take it for granted (it seems fairly sensible) that the sense-data of one are seldom precisely those of the other when we address ourselves to the same object. That, by itself, will in no way impede our common knowledge or the conveying of ideas. Why? Because we shall still agree that there are three feet to the yard; that yellow is lighter than blue; and that middle C means a vibration of 256 per second. In other words, if we define any one of the unit-ideas or concepts which enter into the expression of our thought, we shall define it in the same or equivalent fashion, and we shall apply the same substantives and adjectives to the same objects. So far as we fail in these two things, our knowledge will be really different and the attempt to convey our thought will break down. These, then, are the only practical and applicable criteria of common knowledge; that we should share common definitions of the terms we use, and that we should apply these terms identically to what is presented.[4]

Unfortunately it is exactly the immediate itself, the idiosyncratic intuition, the sense-data and their aesthetic or affective qualities, that seem to be most *ourselves,* and that we would comfort our solitude by sharing and justify by public celebration. He who would express the immediate seldom wants merely to sing to himself; he wants to communicate, to convey his unique sense of the particular and given. The romantic especially wants to utter, and thus to comprehend or capture, the unutterable: the taste of failure, or of winter apples, the coming of April, the colors of autumn, the sense of time, the growth of love, the death of feeling, the sense of mortality, the terrible struggle to speak what cannot be said. *"Ach, was ich weiss, kann jeder wissen —mein Herz habe ich allein."*

2. *Lyricism*

It is no more than half-true to say that the maker of lyrics is concerned only with expression and not at all with communication. It *is* half-true that the pure extreme of lyric expression is a sigh, a shudder, a shriek, or a squeal, and one inspired to squeal scarcely cares whether anyone hears him or not. A squeal has not yet reached or has short-circuited art, but that art closest to the squeal is lyric art. A sigh is neither an art form nor can it be true or false, but it can be used to propagate emotion, and even to suggest to its hearer a true or false hypothesis. It can do this because even the least-formed noise can accomplish a counterfeit of communication. It can *evoke*. Perhaps the purest poet of the immediate, the purest lyricist, simply sings to himself, but few poets are this pure, and those who may be are only doubtfully poets. Even if it were possible to use sounds that were at once linguistic but suggested no familiar expectations, no relation to experience, no public classifications, few would be content to babble their response to immediate experience wordlessly. Such persons may exist, but we never hear of them. Those we know of are the frauds who publish books in which we are told that only lyric experience and expression can make for good and who seem (though in principle confined to animal noises) to recommend as an ideal the sheer accumulation of immediate experience—tastes, smells, sounds, spasms, speed . . .

Of course we can be affected by this. A powerful, rhythmical, repetitive, insinuating, or savage expression of the immediate can evoke the most profound response. Because celebration of the immediate inspires, touches, evokes what is immediate, animal, and passionate in us the celebrant seems to speak to us in a language we had forgotten, to have found the words we had sought but could not utter. The emotional impact can be overwhelming. If it strikes at the right time it can leave a mark on one's whole life, both on its open expression and on its secret style. But why is the right time adolescence? And why is the single-souled celebration of the immediate finally dissatisfying? Always satisfying in moments, at certain times, or in certain moods, and some few passages at almost any time. But when it is the whole, it palls; as a style it is outgrown. We should ask why.

There are bad reasons and good reasons, unhappy causes and sensible second thoughts. Among the causes are getting old and getting tired, growing weary with any strenuous pace. Worse than this is loss of responsiveness of body or of spirit. Those who best deserve the name "philistine" were born old and unresponsive. Theirs is a kind of innate dryness or sourness of heart that would deny all value to expression of immediate sense and feeling and even to the experience that underlies the expression. Those who suffer this affliction have nothing to outgrow; having weak roots, they scarcely grow at all. We can for the moment leave such stalks out of account.

There are better reasons for dissatisfaction with pure lyricism as an aesthetic ideal and with the lyric emphasis on immediacy in life. One of the sad causes has a happier corollary. If one stays alive as he grows older, he may come to recognize more complex beauties, may come to realize that there are themes more communicable and objects of attention more enduringly rewarding than the kaleidoscopic stream of immediate experience. This is what may happen, not what must. The common standard of evaluation probably remains quantitative. Most of us would ask, if we asked at all, "How great an emotional impact? Does it make me cry? Or jump? How high?" The most complex response of the many is to run or to clutch, to sulk, to weep, to wallow, to stare, or to squeal. It is not easy to remain open to the impact of experience and be neither cowed nor dazzled, trying instead in full consciousness to comprehend. A certain steadiness, discrimination, and discipline are necessary for this. One must find points to stand on or to steer by; a man can neither navigate nor understand the river in which he is drowning.

Strange time, forever lost, forever flowing like the river! Lost time, lost people, and lost love—forever lost! There's nothing you can hold there in the river! There's nothing you can keep there in the river! It takes your love, it takes your life, it takes the great ships going out to sea, and it takes time, dark, delicate

*time, the little ticking moments of strange time that count us
into death. Now in the dark I hear the passing of dark time,
and all the sad and secret flowing of my life. All of my thoughts
are flowing like the river, all of my life is passing like the river,
I dream and talk and feel just like the river, as it flows by me,
by me, by me, to the sea.*[5]

Immediacy and dreams, transience and loss: many of us as
adolescents find in expressions of the romantic attitude a miraculous anticipation of what we feel or think we ought to feel about
life. When one is very young, sheer emotion, if sufficiently poignant, seems the aim of art and the end of life; when almost
every experience is new, almost any experience is exciting. But
experience need not be exhausted by these simplicities of novelty
and transience, love and death, time and the river. In its various
complex and recurring patterns we can begin to see and in
understanding almost hold the shape of human life, and of our
own. It is true that love, like the particular rose, grows old and
is forever dying, but there is more than consolation in the seed.
It is true that each man burns like one candle in the dark, but
it is also true that from one candle a million others can be
lighted. No one can keep his immediate experience, and no one
can bequeath exactly what he has felt, but to say that what
passes is lost is not to say all is lost.

To begin to sense this is to grow in wisdom. To our good
fortune, few of us are born wise: the emotional heights and
depths we touch in adolescence give soundings for the rest of
our affective lives. To avoid the open crossing of this country—
to slip through in armor or disguise, to fly over, or tunnel under,
or work around—is to remain ignorant of the most romantic
ground we have to cover. To stay in it is to have a desperately
false vision of life as a whole.

Like knowledge, wisdom begins with the recognition of signs
and a sense of analogy: first the recognition of connection and
recurrence, then the apprehension of continuity through change.
The adolescent has not had time to discover the existence or to

learn the value of continuity. Unacquainted with the attempts of former adventurers, he is apt to overrate his own uniqueness, "to mistake the most trifling excursions for discoveries of moment, and every coast new to him, for a new-found country." (Blake: "Contemptible Mocks!") Dazzled by the discovery of himself, unable when each particular is important to recognize the universal themes through which he lives, his only plan of life is to experience everything, his only art to express everything he feels.

If the ancestor of *Look Homeward, Angel* is Rousseau's *Confessions,* the same could be said on a higher level of *Portrait of the Artist as a Young Man*—but the end of the line is *On the Road* or *City of Night.* The literary-moral line for all the sensitive young men has to do not simply with subject matter, but with technique. The romantic egoist can have no more characteristic vehicle than the prose-poem, the stream of borrowed consciousness, or the extended lyric squeal. The idea of the artist as craftsman, responsible to standards of excellence in his craft, is lost in the picture of artist as licensed exhibitionist. Calculation of effect may go into such performance, and the display may be warped or guided by some wholly private standard. The value of a piece of pure expression or pure reportage may be great in some rare cases, but this will depend entirely on our interest in the passing and particular experiences recorded. The expression of the immediate has established its place as case history, as pathology, or as pornography: all of us would at times peek through keyholes. What we see will at best be work in progress, the experiential raw material of which a finished work might be made.

When immediacy itself becomes less novel, most of its lovers sink without trace into lethargy or quiet desperation. Some few begin to discriminate; the demand for arrangement and order, for something to satisfy understanding as well as mood can be sensed. It is nearly a necessity of growth to have been lost and almost drowned in unchosen and unrefined experience, but along with the premonition of tiresomeness can arise a more than compensating sense of discipline, of transparent architecture, of patterns that do not supersede the immediate, but give it form. It is not only the artist who must learn that it takes cutting and editing, elision, renunciation, to make a self-contained and significant work. The romantic attitude, the single emphasis on the immediately given, is not simply an evasion of this recognition; it would deny its truth. "Perhaps the rest of mankind, but not me!" So time and again the dream that happiness and self-realization are to be found in mere accumulation of immediate experience, accumulation with neither form nor order but in greater and still greater intensity, leads to triviality, to inanity and dissipation, to fatigue and boredom broken by shocks, like explosions in a sewer. Reasonableness, humanity, and order are abandoned in the retreat to sensitivity, and life and art go to the dogs. The result is not self-realization and it is not happiness.

3. *Sincerity*

Of all the virtues, sincerity is the most easily overrated. In common evaluation it does not matter that a man is a fool, as long as he is a sincere fool. Our estimates of personal quality are nowhere more haplessly sentimental than here, and this softness is perhaps the most dilute and pervasive contemporary effect of the romantic bent toward the natural.

It is worth noting what the advocates of sincerity, naturalness, and realism have been reacting against; it is reasonable to believe that only faulty conceptions could lead to so many miscarriages.[6] Austerity, when overdone, leads to enthusiasm no less forced, no less unnatural. Samuel Johnson was speaking of poetry and wit when he commented on Abraham Cowley, but as always his words had a moral bearing.

If by a more noble and a more adequate conception, that be considered as wit which is at once natural and new, that which, though not obvious, is, upon its first production acknowledged

*to be just; if it be that which he that never found it wonders
how he missed, to wit of this kind the metaphysical poets have
seldom risen. Their thoughts are often new, but seldom natural;
they are not obvious, but neither are they just; and the reader,
far from wondering that he missed them, wonders more frequently by what perverseness of industry they were ever found.*[7]

The *less* adequate and noble conceptions of "wit" that Dr.
Johnson rejects are those of the metaphysical poets, but they are
also those of Pope, whom Johnson here takes to represent an
extreme against which eighteenth and nineteenth-century romantics conceived themselves to stand. Despite its elegance and
brilliance, perhaps as a partial corollary of its elegance and
brilliance, neoclassic formalism seemed to many to reflect nothing more than shallowness of spirit, to epitomize the opposite
of the cult of sincerity. The word that comes most naturally
to mind is "artificial." As in art, so in manners the significantly
Aristotelian notion of "good form" had tended to degenerate
into a set of mechanical rules. What it was to be a gentleman
had been reduced to a matter of external signs not necessarily
symptomatic of any inner grace. It was against *this* situation,
which even Dr. Johnson could condemn, that there occurred that
phase of romantic rebellion whose consequences, themselves
much degenerated, remain with us yet. It was against a momentary extreme of neoclassic artificiality, which even Sir
Joshua Reynolds was far from endorsing, that the romantics
reacted in the name of original genius and sincerity. The reaction was essentially negative, despite the positive ring of its
key terms. To be "original" was to be free from neoclassic rules
of decorum. To be "natural" was to be unspoiled by the social
forms of a court, a nobility, or an upper bourgeoisie. To be
"sincere" was to act and speak in response to the prompting of
a heart untutored by the conditions of civilized life.

The first phase of the romantic search for naturalness has
always been anarchistic. Although sincerity is supposedly valued
as a precondition of uninhibited and lyric experience and ex-

pression, the question "What is sincere and natural?" tends to be answered in terms of reaction against local social forms. The romantic attitude condemns the standards of its time and place as artificial, and "natural" is then defined as opposite to "artificial." The relatively clear social situations which once made this negative semblance of definition plausible scarcely exist today. Is "to be natural" the same as to be absolutely unrestrained? We shall think so if we are able to imagine only extremes: a mindless conformity to some imposed or mechanical code and barbarism. The courtiers of Louis XV had the same effect on Rousseau that the organization man may have on us. We go rocketing to dreams of noble savagery. Even Rousseau knew that this was only a dream, but Rousseau liked it that way. We should know better. The self-conscious posturings of the "beat" are uglier and less interesting than the poses of Rousseau, not only because pseudo-motorcyclists are less lovely than Dresden shepherdesses, but because the inheritors of romanticism are putting a negative sign before something in part produced by their spiritual ancestor: a sincerely sack-suited, vulgarly sentimental society that owes much of its character to the romantic movement. Perhaps there was distinction to be gained by negating standards that were distinct, that were hard and clear even if brittle and shallow. It is hard to see how anyone could think that hard standards or clear criteria of distinction are forces of repression in our time.

The *avant garde* has failed to notice that the front has been reversed, so that now it leads the enemy's advance. In a culture characterized by an almost invertebrate absence of firmness, by emotionalism limited only by its own viscosity, the modern romantic still argues that life and art are at their height when experiencing and expressing what is natural, that originality of experience and expression ought not to be restricted by artificial rules. There may once have been justice in the romantic reaction against neoclassicism, but that this antithesis no longer fits the literary and moral situation leads today's would-be ro-

mantic into a false position. If the romantic *attitude* retains its
negative "freedom," romantic *art* has become a common denominator of popular culture. "Romantic" as applied to art does not
name an absence of artifice, it names the commonest kind of
artifice. The distinction is far less noticeable in artistic practice
than it is in aesthetic theory, but if there is a doctrinaire emphasis on universals in neoclassic theory, there is an equal
emphasis in the opposite direction in romantic theory. If there
were a choice between "classicism" and "romanticism," it would
be a choice between conventions.

Rebelling again, the enthusiast of sincerity may bring realism
forward as a model, as the sign of a way between conventional
extremes, a way utterly natural and free of contrivance. If he
is not just a theorist he will find that realism too is possible
only as the product of another kind of discipline, another set of
standards of selection. The advocate of perfect sincerity who
looks toward realism as an aesthetic paradigm will find what
satisfies him only in photographs of disaster and court reports;
he will scarcely find it in a newspaper story. There is considerable moral significance in the reason for this: if the ambitious
realist tried to notice and record everything that happened in
any little time, he would find he had set himself a task too
monstrous and too trivial for words.

The reason much of our experience does not capture our attention is that it is not worth our attention; attention is already
a minimal exercise of discrimination. Without this much discrimination life would be impossible. The creation of that order
which we call a work of art is accomplished by the still more
deliberate exercise of selection and emphasis. The artist who
would do no more than convey the effect of "what really happens" does not have a problem of sincerity, but one of discrimination; not of inclusion, but of exclusion; and exclusion pre-
supposes principles of choice. If it were easy to express without
artifice the sense of commonplace experience, there might be a
surplus of Zolas in the slums, or a new Marquand in every easy

chair in the Somerset Club. To take perfect sincerity as an affective paradigm, and to understand by "sincerity" the absence of discrimination, is to have an ideal indistinguishable from chaos.

B. ORDER

This is not to deny the trivial truth that any arrangement of things is some kind of order. Throw a handful of marbles into the air and the points at which they come to rest will form a pattern. Throw a bottle of ink at the wall and it will splash into a pattern. All of our lives have this much order, this kind of order; most have little more. But in any attempt at communication, however humble, however subartistic, there must be something more; there must be selection and ordered emphasis. If, in the Platonic phrase, we look away to works of art, we see an outline or pattern that directs and fixes our attention on certain of its aspects, which then take on special significance in the light of the whole. All experience comes in some sequence, but in the unconsidered stream it is almost impossible to sense what is significant. The gift and burden of the artist is to find in the babble and flow of time some possibilities of affective order—order that is *felt* as order and not as ordinary motion. By discrimination, selection, and emphasis there can grow under one's attention an order that *feels* intelligible and whole, which we sense as a significant and satisfying pattern. In a successful work of art this has been done for us; it is the basis of the wholeness we find there.

1. *Naturalness*

The romantic attitude cannot comprehend the limitations of genuine choice, fails to understand the number or nature of the alternatives truly open to the artist or to the would-be free and moral man. Our viable choices are always choices among principles, among conventions, among limitations. If the attempt at pure negative freedom tends to a new conformism, parasitical and dull, the exclusive and unprincipled emphasis on immediate experience leads to chaos. If the latter is touted as natural, original, and sincere, that must be because the touts have not seen that to be natural qua man is not the same as to be natural qua animal. Other animals may be unable to act other than spontaneously, and the life of uncomplicated animals may be purely lyrical. There is no reason to think that man is not an animal, but neither is there reason to think that man is a simple animal. We live a good part of our lives in a presently projected future and a constantly recreated past. At any moment we may sum up in new patterns what has gone before, each moment giving a new perspective on our vision of what has been; at any moment, though confined to that moment, we look into an imagined future, finding terrors to avoid or themes to be lived through. There is neither need nor reason to make metaphysics of this, nor to complicate what we can see for ourselves into religious or neohumanistic mystery. Man is a complex, self-conscious, reflective creature, and these natural facts are sufficient to show the inadequacy of holding the life of immediacy and impulse to be a fully human life.

Immediate experience is at the core of all the facts of life, cognitive and affective; it is always pernicious to pretend that man can or ought to live by thought alone. To emphasize the need for order is not to overlook the fact that it is precisely experience that calls for and gives fullness of content to form. On this point Plato is more easily misunderstood than is Aristotle. Perhaps Plato did not intend to advocate asceticism, but the unhealthy results of Western asceticism can in part be laid to his charge. That asceticism represents an unnatural extreme no longer needs argument. What is hard to see is how anyone could think that the opposite extreme is in need of defenders.

Here the analogy between experience and art draws close.

Asceticism, the refusal or fear of experience, like classicism, cuts out too much, thins down the vital texture of life in the name of some invariant, abstract, and transcendental structure. The refusal to refer beyond experience as it happens to come, the fear of any attempt to create a structure for the given, is the romantic attitude, and the program of romantic art. Neither of these extremes is appropriately humane, and neither is humanly natural. Here Aristotle is morally and aesthetically on perfectly human ground. For Aristotle what is natural is what is normal, that is, what is universal. Goodness and beauty alike are to found in arranging particulars so that their patterns approach the perfection of appropriate universal types. For conscious and rational creatures there exists the possibility of deliberate imitation of exemplars of their kind, of particulars so ordered that in them a specific universal seems incarnate.[8]

2. *Art and Experience*

If a work of art were created wholly without discipline and without selection, it would be a freak of nature. It is a truism that the novelist, poet, painter, musician, must impose some pattern on sounds and meanings, colors and tones. In what does the artist exceed other men but in this mastery? Many of us are sensitive, imaginative, fresh-eyed, or neurotic, with consequences no more artistic than pain, daydreams, awareness, and misery. All of us are condemned to profound events and a few of us may be aware of them, but fewer still are artists. The artist is not simply a man who has had more experience or who has felt it more profoundly and expressed it most sincerely. It is rather that the artist sees in all experience the possibilities of order, that he brings to events the perception of possible forms. So far as the artist's experience is qualitatively different from ours, it is in his constant thought that "Here is raw material!" One difference between great artists and good artists may lie in the intensity of their passions or the universality of their concerns, but the major difference between artists and other people lies in the perception and execution of possibilities of aesthetic order. However striking and intense experience may be, without order there is no art. "There is experience, but so slack and discursive that it is not *an* experience."[9]

It would be a mistake to suggest an absolute difference between artists and other people. All of us have in some degree the ability to sense possibilities of order. This is not merely a matter of the way we attend to experience as it comes, the relative emotional weight we allow to aspects of the given. This *is* of moment, since we contribute selective attention and attitude to the present experience. We take the given into the patterns of our moral economy, and the affective significance of our experience will depend in part on how we take it. But of equal import is the extent to which we live in our past and in our future.

In a trivial sense we are at each moment confined to that given moment, but we carry our past with us and can at any moment summon a vision of it; in imagination we can project some picture of our future. The past does not change and the future is what it will be; we are and will be what we have become, and sanity and hope of happiness require that we give our deepest deference to truth and fact. But it is also a fact that our past as we know it is a reconstruction out of historical data, our expected future a reading of present signs in the light of memory. Respect for the data is paramount, and a disregard for the actual past is one way to disaster, but the light and shadow in which we see that past, the weight and affective prominence events take on in their summing-up is not wholly a function of the past events themselves. Such summing-up and projection can be the work of any time, and sometimes comes without an invitation. The structures that our lives are then felt to have will be a function of what has been, but also a function of the texture of attention, of criteria of relative importance, of discrimination, of selection, and of emphasis.

If we were to adopt Dewey's terminology we could say that the hope of finding life good lay in the possibility of making the experience of life, so far as possible the whole of it, *an* experience. The aesthetes have it that the best moments of life are moments of response to works of art. We should rather say that the life found best is that which in its wholeness approaches the affective character we can find in works of art—the relation of matter to form, of intensity to order, of expression to discipline that characterizes, say, *The Musical Offering* of Bach. Because we shall return to this analogy, we must insist on what should be obvious: that the accomplishment of the artist is based neither on depth alone nor on skill alone; that the art which survives the judgment of historical and personal time, which continues to inform our lives, comes neither from the madhouse nor from the schools. Discipline without the warmth of life is pedantic and inhuman, but life without discipline is a waste of time.

The need to find a balance between the demands of order and the desire for free expression is not just a problem for artists; it is the aesthetic version of the wider moral-affective problem of order and freedom, principles and passions, discipline and spontaneity. If we take our ideals of life from our ideas of art—a thing more often done than thought or said —and suppose the artist to be marked by no more than intensity of experience, by passionate or sincere expression of the given, we shall find ourselves running a round of experience that soon grows exhausting and stale. We shall find, inevitably and perhaps too late, that human happiness requires something more distinctively human than this, something more reasonably informed. "It is discipline that renders men rational and capable of happiness, by suppressing without hatred what needs to be suppressed to attain a beautiful naturalness."[10]

The human being who merely suffers his experience, or merely expresses it, is not only less than an artist, he is less than fully human. The exclusive concentration on immediate experience, the rejection of form, the expression of flux—the romantic attitude—are not only anti-aesthetic, they are anti-human. Artists do something with their experience: they organize their vision and inform ours; they are the great disciplinarians of vision and emotion. Like a realized work of art, a life found good will not be passionless. In both cases immediate apprehension is brought to its most intense expression, but in both cases passion is expressed through intelligible forms. The appearance and the sense of form, of limit, of intelligibility, is achieved by selection and by emphasis: what we feel as form is the pattern we give to the given. To fail in this exercise of discrimination, to attend accidentally and in the absence of principles or models, is to risk the loss of all sense of order, or to feel nothing more than the animal sequence of birth, copulation and death, birth, copulation and death, the hope of life and beauty lost in distraction and inattention. To the achievement of a sense of order, the language of immediacy and the life of immediacy are necessary but not sufficient.

IV

THE USES OF SUFFERING

Surely I haven't suffered, simply that I, my crimes and my sufferings, may manure the soil of the future harmony for somebody else. I want to see with my own eyes the hind lie down with the lion and the victim rise up and embrace his murderer. I want to be there when every one suddenly understands what it has all been for. All the religions of the world are built on this longing, and I am a believer. But then there are the children, and what am I to do about them? That's a question I can't answer. For the hundredth time I repeat, there are numbers of questions, but I've only taken the children, because in their case what I mean is so unanswerably clear. Listen! If all must pay for the eternal harmony, what have children to do with it, tell me, please? It's beyond all comprehension why they should suffer, and why they should pay for the harmony. Why should they, too, furnish material to enrich the soil for the harmony of the future? I understand solidarity in sin among men. I understand solidarity in retribution, too; but there can be no such solidarity with children. And if it is really true that they must share responsibility for all their fathers' crimes, such a truth is not of this world and is beyond my comprehension. Some jester will say, perhaps, that the child would have grown up and have sinned, but you see he didn't grow up, he was torn to pieces by the dogs, at eight years old. Oh, Alyosha, I am not blaspheming! I understand, of course, what an upheaval of the universe it will be, when everything in heaven and earth blends in one hymn of praise and everything that lives and has lived cries aloud: 'Thou are just, O Lord, for Thy ways are revealed.' When the mother embraces the fiend who threw her child to the dogs, and all three cry aloud with tears, 'Thou are just, O Lord!' then, of course, the crown of knowledge will be reached and all will be reached and all will be made clear. But what pulls me up is that I can't accept that harmony. And while I am on earth, I make haste to take my own measures. You see, Alyosha, perhaps it really may happen that if I live to that moment, or rise again to see it, I, too, perhaps, may cry aloud with the rest, looking at the mother embracing her child's torturer. 'Thou art just, O Lord!' but I don't want to cry out aloud then. While there is still time, I hasten to protect myself and so I renounce the higher harmony altogether. It's not worth the tears of that one tortured child who beat itself on the breast with its little fist and prayed in its stinking outhouse, with its unexpiated tears to 'dear, kind God'! It's not worth it, because those tears are unatoned for. They must be atoned for, or there can be no harmony. But how? How are you going to atone for them? Is it possible? By their being avenged? But what do I care for avenging them? What do I care for a hell for oppressors? What good can hell do, since those children have already been tortured? And what becomes of harmony, if there is hell? I want to forgive. I want to embrace. I don't want more suffering. And if the sufferings of children go to swell the sum of suffering which was necessary to pay for truth, then I protest that the truth is not worth such a price. I don't want the mother to embrace the oppressor who threw her son to the dogs! She dare not forgive him! Let her forgive him for herself, if she will, let her forgive the torturer for the immeasurable suffering of her mother's heart. But the sufferings of her tortured child she has no right to forgive; she dare not forgive the torturer, even if the child were to forgive him! And if that is so, if they dare not forgive, what becomes of harmony? Is there in the whole world a being who would have the right to forgive and could forgive? I don't want harmony. From love of humanity I don't want it. I would rather be left with the unavenged suffering. I would rather remain with the unavenged suffering and unsatisfied indignation, even if I were wrong. Besides, too high a price is asked for harmony; it's beyond our means to pay so much to enter on it. And so I hasten to give back my entrance ticket, and if I am an honest man I am bound to give it back as soon as possible. And that I am doing. It's not God that I don't accept, Alyosha, only I most respectfully return him the ticket.[1]

FYODOR DOSTOYEVSKY, *The Brothers Karamazov*

To talk sensibly about suffering is as difficult as to talk reasonably about love. The extremes of mysticism and philistinism, sentimentalism and cynicism are easier to strike than is a proper understanding of the place these experiences can be given in a life found good. Romantics fall into profundities that are as often unintelligible as illuminating, and rationalists specialize in sensible platitudes; the former always seem too drunk, the latter too sober. The romantic plummets from fire to ice and flies again to fire; the advocate of reason always seems lukewarm.[2]

Mindful of these difficulties, but discounting the opinion of those who think that a man has neither experienced nor understood anything intense unless he speaks of it at the hysterical top of his voice (as if a book on hemophilia could only be printed in blood), we must approach the problems of suffering and pain with a diffidence that verges on pedantry. It is never easy and is almost always thankless to try to talk in a useful way about those aspects of emotional life that feel to us most central: whether of self-esteem or suffering, of love, of loyalty, of death. Any attempt to be clear about these matters will depend on distinctions and discriminations that must be more carefully articulated, more lucid and schematic than their subject; that minimum degree of intelligibility essential to understanding will always seem pedantic to the purely passionate, the impatient, and the uninformed. It is rare for a man to have important things to say about a crisis he has not lived through, but the man who tries to speak of such things in defiance or disregard of the minimum requirements of communication will contribute no understanding of his problem, only another instance of it. If on the other hand he observes the least degree of clarity or form, some fervent soul will inevitably cry that this dispassionateness bars him from discussion of the problem.

Someone must try to speak reasonably of love and pain in their immediacy. Somehow these givens must be taken into our lives. We would not avoid love and we cannot avoid suffering; if these are to be more than accidents, unmeaning disturbances, they must somehow be incorporated into the structure of life, given a place that lets their significance stand clear. The problem is more difficult with pain, but even of pain we can ask whether it can be taken up into a life in any way that will allow us honestly to see it as other than sheer negativity, pure and useless loss. It cannot honestly be said that there is any intrinsic good in suffering; suffering is intrinsically bad. But a question of which we can make sense is this: how can that immediacy found bad in itself be comprehended in a life found good as a whole?

There is a further question, although the attempt to answer it is more presumptuous still: can suffering be given a *use?*

A. THE UTILITY OF A TEXT

It is difficult at once to experience the depths and to illuminate them. Where the difficulties are greatest it is useful to lean on a text or to borrow a theme, to make comments in the margin, to appropriate material distant enough and public enough to permit both pertinence and intelligibility. This is said partly to account for the long, circling trip we must make away from Aristotelian views, and partly to apologize for giving a great novel a use extrinsic to its immanent purpose, for using it as a text to show the tragic inutility of one attempt to put suffering in its place. This being done we can turn to a theme less profane and more fruitful. The texts will be drawn from Dostoyevsky, primarily *The Brothers Karamazov;* the theme is that of redemption.

Suffering is the emotion or experience that seems to give the novels of Dostoyevsky their essential motif. It is true that the stories often end with talk of love, but it is also true that in Dostoyevsky the answers are never as clear as the questions, and that hate and rage, pain, suffering, and despair have been overwhelmingly in evidence before the concluding, but never quite conclusive, chapters. It would not do to claim to have discovered what Dystoyevsky says about suffering: with what character in which novel should we unambiguously identify their common author? It will be better to claim only to use his work in a way he might not approve in order to understand not Dostoyevsky, but ourselves; to talk about the use to which we can bend our destructive passions—hate, rage, the desire to destroy—and the good that may be wrung from pain. Although suffering, deformity, and death are by no means Dostoyevsky's private preserve, their presence in his work is seldom merely for the sake of the *frisson*. What he has truly felt, we feel. No one can guide us more faithfully into the depths; there are better guides when it comes to getting out.

B. AMBIVALENCE

"Romanticism is sickness. Classicism is health." This is Olympian enough, but like all such pronouncements it requires exegesis, and in the amplification its sharpness is lost. We can take Goethe's dictum as a warning against love of darkness for its own dark sake, but we can take it little further. Sickness and health, darkness and light, seldom come unmixed. Even that which all would like to think of as pure light, and that which all condemn as dark and bitter, even love and hate are not accurately thought of as opposite passions or best understood as polar extremes of feeling. Love and hate, when pushed to some extreme of intensity, seem almost to merge, or at least to lose clear marks of difference, but so do hope and despair, pleasure and pain, intense satisfaction and suffering.

Others have made this observation before. It is only an observation: it is not to say that things ought to be so, or to celebrate the ambiguity of passion. It is Dostoyevsky and the romantics who have most fully observed the ambivalence of intensity, but from observation they have tended to go to praise. Leaving aside the latter, their recognition of this central fact of affective life deserves respect. What they have realized—which is not to say "explained," but "recognized," "displayed," "made real"—is that those capable of the most intense love are those also capable of the most intense hate; that these two classes probably have the majority of their members in common. There may be some people who can know only one extreme and not the other, but these pure strains are rare.

It may be that most of us, for better and for worse, fall into neither class. We are capable of neither the greatest love nor the profoundest hate. For us there are the milder crises which the extremes display as larger than our lives, but perhaps the more easily visible for that. And even for us there are times when the easy road opens into chasms before our feet, when a crack in the teacup opens a lane to the land of the dead. If we ever do experience intensities, we will learn that love can slip into hatred, that there are deep aversions indistinguishable from desire. And this is to consider only the paradigms, the affections in which we might hope to find the most distinct extremes. Few of our deepest intensities escape ambivalence.

Despite the commendably good-natured, positive preference that emphasizes only hope and love and bliss, the ambivalence of intensity suggests that where manifestations of these heartwarming, constructive things occur quite free of all less pleasant affections, there we have little to fear and less to hope; where hope, love, and happiness are intense, we shall never find them in perfect separateness from despair and hate and pain. It may be possible for some people to keep from themselves all but safely happy, constructive thoughts; we shall see before this chapter is done that their lives leave much to be desired. The rest of us, to understand ourselves, must try to understand at least hate and pain; at least these we should prepare to have with us in some degree. In fact, it may be salutary to insist on one possible value of hate: there are lives we will never understand unless we admit that a large, clear, consistent, and controlled hatred can give unity, force and, in an affective sense, "meaning" to a life. Most kinds of hate cannot do this; neither can most kinds of love. More often than not hate is petty, mean, and trivial; then, like any demoralizing force, hate is contemptible and ugly. But hate can have its beauty, can give a stark significance, even an awful nobility, to some lives. Only a sentimental, moralizing, and politically ignorant psychology could deny this; if it does it will be found to have little knowledge of love.

It is equally mistaken to think that the intensities we want can be had unmixed with those we would avoid, and to think that hate and suffering can never be turned to good. In life and literature of any depth what we do and do not want are not only tangled together, but each is always surprising us by coming out of the other. A poem or a novel can display this more clearly than life itself, but like life it must stop with showing; a poem or a novel seldom provides its own exegesis; that is not its business. We can count on Dostoyevsky to show us much, but for exegesis we have to count on ourselves. Moral clarification cannot be accomplished by plain description and will fail if it is not less ambiguous than the facts. Its object is not to re-create the facts but to show their significance. Yet, the clarity it hopes to create is more than intellectual, it is also affective and moral.

The books are balanced. The credit of clarification has been established and the debt to ambivalence charged against it. We can make the distinctions we must and talk for the rest of this chapter about the uses we can hope to force from pain.

C. METAPHYSICAL PHILISTINISM

There is a species of hatred which might be called a love of integrity, negatively determined: it is the hatred of hypocrisy. The paying out of counterfeit pieties, the concealment of moral poverty behind a façade of general benevolence, is a species of fraud so mean that it deserves to be hated. "How beautiful is noble sentiment: like gossamer gauze, beautiful and cheap; which will stand no wear and tear! Beautiful, cheap gossamer gauze, thou film shadow of a raw material of Virtue, which art *not* woven, nor likely to be, into Duty; thou art better than nothing, and also worse!" Carlyle is almost too kind. Rage may be the only appropriate reaction to this duplicity, especially when we find it in ourselves.

It would not be easy to defend personal hypocrisy, although cases deserving of pity could be found. But there is a less personal, theoretical manifestation of the same doubleness that is at least as disintegrating in its effects and that enjoys great intellectual respectability. It was this public monument that enraged Ivan Karamazov to the point of madness, but the moral situation of Ivan Karamazov is far from clear. He belongs to the intelligentsia, and Dostoyevsky had no love for that class. He is in no obvious sense the hero of *The Brothers Karamazov.* His anger and suffering have not been useful in any obvious way. At the end of the story he is sick, mad, dying. And yet in Ivan is acted out a problem that is for some few an intellectual puzzle, for many a sacred mystery, for others an excuse for moral fraud, and for some an intense personal agony. This is the so-called "Problem of Evil," an expression of hypocrisy on the grandest possible scale.

1. *The Problem of Evil*

The "Problem of Evil" revolves endlessly around the question, *"How can there be* pain and badness in a world created by a wholly good and benevolent God?" Starting from but never leaving the notion that the world has been made to a benevolent plan, the speculator wonders how there can be pain and suffering on every side. The man who accepts this problem as real, and who in addition feels in himself the reality of human suffering, is less likely to take it as an excuse for dialectics than to endure it as a deeply personal crisis.

"I am trying to explain as quickly as possible my essential nature, that is what manner of man I am, what I believe in, and for what I hope, that's it, isn't it? And therefore I tell you that I accept God simply . . . and am glad to, and what's more I accept His wisdom, His purpose—which are utterly beyond our ken; I believe in the underlying order and the meaning of life; I believe in the eternal harmony in which they say we shall one

day be blended. I believe in the Word to which the universe is striving, and Which Itself was 'with God,' and Which Itself is God and so on, and so on, to infinity. There are all sorts of phrases for it. I seem to be on the right path, don't I? Yet would you believe it, in the final result I don't accept this world of God's, and although I know it exists, I don't accept it at all. It's not that I don't accept God, you must understand, it's the world created by Him I don't and cannot accept. Let me make it plain. I believe like a child that suffering will be healed and made up for, that all the humiliating absurdity of human contradictions will vanish like a pitiful mirage, like the despicable fabrication of the impotent and infinitely small Euclidian mind of man, that in the world's finale, at the moment of eternal harmony, something so precious will come to pass that it will suffice for all hearts, for the comforting of all resentments, for the atonement of all the crimes of humanity, of all the blood they've shed; that it will make it not only possible to forgive but to justify all that has happened with men—but though all that may come to pass, I don't accept it. I won't accept it."[3]

How can a concrete, personal sense of the world as it truly is be reconciled with the conviction that the world as it is is sustained by the goodness of God? It cannot be; if any feelings can be incompatible, these feelings are. The attempt to hold to both, to appreciate fully the force of both in one's own affective life, must be given up or leads to madness. "I meant to speak of the suffering of mankind generally," Ivan says, "but we had better confine ourselves to the suffering of children. That reduces the scope of my argument to about a tenth of what it would be." To reconcile the suffering of the children with the ultimate goodness of the world . . .

"This poor child of five was subjected to every possible torture by those cultivated parents. They beat her, thrashed her, kicked her for no reason till her body was one bruise. Then, they went to greater refinements of cruelty—shut her up all night in the cold and frost in a privy, and because she didn't ask to be taken up at night, they smeared her face and filled her mouth with

excrement, and it was her mother, her mother did this. And that mother could sleep, hearing the poor child's groans! Can you understand why a little creature, who can't even understand what's done to her, should beat her little aching heart with her tiny fist in the dark and the cold, and weep her meek unresentful tears to dear, kind God to protect her? Do you understand that, friend and brother, you pious and humble novice? Do you understand why this infamy must be and is permitted? Without it, I am told, man could not have existed on earth, for he could not have known good and evil. Why should he know that diabolical good and evil when it costs so much? Why, the whole world of knowledge is not worth that child's prayer to 'dear, kind God!' I say nothing of the sufferings of grown-up people, they have eaten the apple, damn them, and the devil take them all! But these little ones!"[4]

The world as Ivan Karamazov sees and feels it—and if we feel less than he, we have seen more—is characterized just as much by hatred as by love, by cruelty as by kindness, by wickedness as by good. Our world is the stage for the destruction of innocence, the betrayal of trustingness, the failure of love. Perhaps we must say that Ivan goes beyond reason if he hates the world itself for this suffering—that is the pathetic fallacy in reverse—but how shall we exempt from hatred those who taught him that this terrible world is right and good? It is they who deserve his hatred, not the world. He does not see this; had he seen it he might have been able to live. If we are sensitive we shall suffer for the world; that is part of the price of full awareness of the world, and necessary to that end. But Ivan's suffering is not just a consequence of openness to pain; the crux of it is in the intolerable contradiction between the goodness of God's plan and the suffering of the world. *That* is what makes the pain unendurable, what pushes his pain past reason and necessity. Of that the world is not guilty.

Those guilty of his unnecessary pain are the philosophic hypocrites who would urge the higher optimism, who tell us that they can morally justify the world. Those who tell us that this is a world in which suffering is unreal, or in which everything happens for the best in the very long run or according to some great design that we must accept on faith, ask us to disavow our deepest moral feelings, to approve what is hideous, and to accept what is not humanly acceptable. Never doubting the reality or goodness of the cosmic plan—for after all the people who talk this way have an important place in it—the metaphysical philistines conclude that it must be the suffering which is not quite finally real.

It is the terrible smugness of those who would justify things as they are by calling them good that Ivan ought to hate. Instead, he is destroyed by its presence in himself.

2. *The Wrong Problem*

The "Problem of Evil" is wholly created by those theories that claim to solve it. Since it rests on a view of things that is fantastic, to dispel the fantasy is to dispel the "problem," and to be left with questions that admit of sensible answers.

The existence of pain and suffering in the world is perfectly and terribly *natural;* it is not humanly *good,* and no theorizing can make it so. In a physical engine of the complexity of our world there is bound to be friction and what is, from a human point of view, dysfunction. From the human point of view we can say that it ought to be different, meaning that we might be happier if it were, but the inhuman world has no point of view, and it is pathetic to think that it ought attend to ours. Where there is no deliberate purpose or plan there can be no dysfunction, but only surprises for those who must bet their lives on regularity. There is nothing foolish in calling a leaf of Cuban tobacco "good," and a cancer "bad"; such intelligent judgments reflect the relation of these things to our interests. The foolishness lies in thinking that they have an interest in furthering or frustrating ours.

Unlike things, humans have intentions, act for ends, and are subject to moral praise and blame. Here there are genuine problems enough, but for consideration of real problems the "Problem of Evil" substitutes the manipulation of emotion-laden words. "How can it be that man should do evil?" Some will say that man's essential goodness has been destroyed by civilization, or urbanization, or capitalism, or socialism, or television. Others—hardheaded realists, these—blame it all on Adam and Eve, remind us that our ancestors were told to stay away from that tree, agree that they should have, and conclude (with a peculiar relish) that of that first disobedience the fruit is essential corruption. Those who debate on human perfectability and original sin have their whole business with words, and if this employment is not quite innocent, obscuring or replacing as it does the recognition of genuine moral problems, confusing or distracting as it does the few moral men who get lost in its verbal mazes, at least it is comfortably endless.

If man is essentially anything, he is essentially mixed. Between the assertion that man is essentially good but in part corrupted by institutions and the assertion that man is essentially bad but in part redeemed by grace, there is no contradiction. There is no ground for choosing between them as descriptions of our situation, since every extra-verbal prediction that follows from the one follows equally from the other. Men are, from our human point of view, good and bad, or good-and-bad, but "essential goodness" and "essential depravity" are figures of rhetoric, not hypotheses about our good-and-badness. They are cries of hope or disappointment, not alternative explanations of human conduct.[5]

There is in man much goodness and kindness of heart, much charity, much viciousness, depravity, and lust for pain. For so wonderfully complicated a nature there can be none but complicated natural explanations, and it will always be easier for the many to rest in a simple myth. Yet man's natural good-and-badness is exactly what thought unclouded by metaphysical fancies would predict of creatures so intricately formed; it is what sensible, untheoretical men in practice expect of beings as cruel and kind and various as they are. Nothing more unnatural has ever been imagined than a human nature essentially good or totally depraved.

When a sensitive and honest man mistakes his version of what a morally good world would be for a vision of the benevolent plan that in fact orders the world, when he takes his picture of a fair consummation as an insight into the *telos* toward which the world in fact must tend, the terrible inconsistencies he will find between his vision and the natural world may break his heart. It is this possibility that can turn intellectual farce into personal tragedy, unnecessary tragedy, since beneath the genuine crisis in feeling lies a spurious paradox. The paradox disappears when we abandon the groundless belief that the actual world is essentially good, or that it operates according to principles set by some morally interested party. Give up this fantasy and the paradoxes go with it. Suffering and evil do not then disappear, but the "Problem of Evil" does. The problem about suffering that then remains is not the tragically useless pseudo-question, "How can this be?" The question that remains is hopeful and can be answered. It is "What can we do?"

D. THE AFFECTIVE PROBLEM

It is necessary to make and to justify one major exclusion from our argument. The obvious and true first answer to the question of what to do about suffering scarcely needs argument: suffering should be alleviated; pain should be lessened. There is a level of action on which the practical problems of sickness, poverty, and prevention of war have priority over the questions we shall consider. Most of us have enough moral common sense to agree that the relief of suffering is a desirable end. Arguments that would touch those outside this consensus could fill another book—which would not be read by those it tried to touch. The question of means to this end involves technology and politics as well as morals, and consideration of it would lead away from the ground we shall cover here. The questions with which we are concerned are more limited in scope; our problems are those that begin by considering the quality of individual life. If social problems have practical priority over this, that is because so many social evils are so glaring that they unambiguously cry for remedy, and because no great moral refinement or complication is needed to see that the cry must be answered. When it comes to feeding the hungry or tending the sick, what is needed is not philosophy, but compassion, or at least good will. For those with these qualities, arguments are seldom necessary; for those without them, arguments are seldom sufficient.

When social issues are more complex, theoretical and practical priorities may be reversed. Then it begins to make sense to say that a man must have some viable idea of what the individual good life might be if he is to take a viable stand on wider problems. If social policy and social action do not have their final bearing on the lives of individuals, they have no bearing at all. In this sense to consider the experience of life is to consider the beginning and end of policy. Within this focus there are problems equally and immediately practical, but presenting difficulties of a different order. Here we must cope with lack of distance, with questions too close to permit clear formulation, with answers that have always appeared in a mist, looking larger than life. We must ask what we can do with the pain that will come to all of us whatever we do, whether we can make use of the intensities we would avoid, the hurts and losses that are among the inevitabilities of natural life. We will avoid the pain we can avoid, and lessen that which we cannot. But what can we do with the suffering that remains, beyond the reach of alleviation?

1. *Discipline*

It is rightly considered perverse or frivolous to discuss whether pain in itself is good, or whether suffering is intrinsically valuable. Pain is our very paradigm of what is to be avoided, and the immediate experience of suffering is the most obvious example of negative value. If we hear of a man who asks that his veins be cut so that he can bleed, we are likely to conclude that the man is mad. Suppose, however, we were to learn that the doctors agree that bleeding is the proper cure for every ill. Then, if this person were suffering a dropsy, we should with equal sense conclude to his sanity. Pain is universally rejected as a reasonable end. What we can ask is whether it is ever a reasonable means.

a. THE COST OF ACCOMPLISHMENT

Consider pain first not as a means in itself, but as a consequence or by-product of some means. Then pain can be thought of less in terms of the distinction "valuable-disvaluable" (in which terms it is clearly disvaluable) than as an all but inevitable condition of accomplishment, an almost necessary concomitant of those achievements we tend most to admire. In some other world very different from this one, everything worthwhile might be accomplished without pain. If we were immortal or infinite beings we might hope to do everything and to be everything. In the only world and time we have to live in, effort is the cost of accomplishment, and renunciation the oldest lesson of wisdom.

Although this is a platitude, it is often misunderstood. The attempt to inflate the truism into something more impressive may be a chief cause of misreading its simple lesson. There is nothing intrinsically valuable about renunciation, and nothing but impotence in renunciation that will not stop short of Nirvana. This extreme may have its nihilistic thoroughness or its oriental charm. It may even be appropriate when the slightest hope is not—but only then. So long as our situation is not altogether hopeless, or rather so long as we do not give up hope, we will find the creation of self of greater worth than its annihilation. It is also more interesting. To this creation renunciation and the pain of renunciation are only means. There is less than the whole truth in the saying that we value things in proportion to the pain they have cost us. This is too simple, since it would seem to make suffering a sufficient condition for the presence of value, and we know that triviality also has the pain appropriate to its condition. The lesson is rather that suffering and renunciation are usual and predictable, conditions, if not quite necessary conditions of accomplishment.

It is not only *doing* something rather than nothing, but *being* something rather than nothing that is accomplished in pain. Many are willing to believe in the pain of the artist who looks away to an ideal, who judges, accepts, and rejects his inspirations in its light, and who knows better than anyone else how far short he has fallen. It should be even clearer that any attempt to inform our lives, to give them a satisfying rhythm or order, will require the sacrifice of what is attractive but incompatible with the form we have chosen; every choice is in some degree exclusive. There is sadness too in learning to live within one's intellectual and emotional means, in learning that there are aspects of the self beyond one's power to change. These things and more will come to us unless we remain children, and some will come to us even so. Such pain is the price of accomplishment: doing and being have this as the cost. We need not pretend to like these conditions, or lie to ourselves by calling intrinsically good what we do not find so; yet the conditions themselves we must accept.

But this is so plain that no one could fail to see it. There must be further questions to be asked.

b. CRIME AND PUNISHMENT

Sometimes the question "Is suffering valuable?" signals an attempt to understand the place of pain not obviously incidental to the accomplishment of an end. Leaving aside the possibility that the question is asked by a sadist or a masochist, what it may intend is this: "Is pain *itself*, not as the concomitant of some necessary means, but pain itself ever a means to an end? If it is, then to what end?"

The first suggestion for an answer to both questions can be sought in the various meanings of the English word which derives from the Latin *disciplina*. All six meanings in *Webster's Collegiate Dictionary* apply:

1. *Obs. Teaching; instruction.* 2. *That which is taught to pupils.* 3. *Training which corrects, molds, strengthens or perfects.* 4. *Punishment; chastisement.* 5. *Control gained by enforcing obedience or order, as in a school or army; hence, orderly conduct. . . .* 6. *Rule or system of rules affecting conduct or action; esp. Eccl., practical rules as distinguished from dogmatic formulation.*

For further suggestion we can turn to Werner Jaeger's *Paideia.* "Aristocracy in all ages and all nations is marked by *discipline*, the deliberate formation of human character through wise direction and constant advice."[6] Yes—but there are also the rod, the birch, and the back of a hairbrush; there are scorn, shame, and penance. These are the uses of pain itself as a means. Discipline in this direct sense is paradigmatic of a class of cases in which we can see the *use* of suffering, the use of what cannot be avoided.

We bring much of our suffering on ourselves as a result of our excesses and deficiencies. It is not administered by a transcendent disciplinarian, but follows as the natural consequence of our own actions. And yet the Greeks, who sensed in nature the operation of Nemesis, and the Jewish prophets, who saw in the life of their people the hand of an angry God, cast into an appropriate rhetorical form the recognition that suffering can be given a moral use. Some of us are still incapable of distinguishing the mythical or poetic formulation—the figure of purposive, deliberate, divine discipline imposed by a super-natural disciplinarian—from the moral insight it qualifies. If we take the rhetoric for the essence, we fall into confusions analogous to the "Problem of Evil." The operation of Divine justice, as nearly as we can make it out, is too irregular, erratic, whimsical, and arbitrary to be understood on any compre-hensible human model of justice. The conduct of this court is an ancient scandal; for every time that the punishment fits the crime, there are ninety-nine times when it does not. The prophets are right to call our attention to the hundredth time, but they go too far when they ask us to respect or even to love a judge whose average is no better. Only the hundredth time shows a moral lesson.

What can we learn from the suffering we ourselves earn? First, we can learn not to do it again, and learn it the only way that makes the lesson stick.[7] There are exceptions to the rule—very cool or serene natures, or very dull and phlegmatic people who do not need the rod and can see no good to be got by suffering—but most of us learn our moral lessons only by making mistakes. Wise direction and constant advice are not to be despised; they help. But every philosopher, every friend, every lover, and every parent must suffer again in knowing that the benefit of his past mistakes is only in the smallest part transferable. If we thought our children could learn from our errors to avoid the same mistakes, we would willingly endure ten times the pain originally earned by our fault; we suffer no less than this in knowing that our children must learn for them-selves. Words fail us here just as they do when we try to com-municate happier intensities.

Because the force of the lesson is affective each of us must learn from his own mistakes. We need not be without help, and those who have learned can help to teach, but where the cost of learning limitations is set at suffering, no man can adequately learn another's lessons. Agamemnon sent a great soldier, a great schemer, and an eloquent teacher to persuade Achilles to take the field. They did not succeed, and the Greeks understood the lesson paid for by Patroclus' death and Achilles' pain. Strength and reason, eloquence and wisdom when they touch the heart have some effect. Art can go deeper than thought. But the force of discipline lies in the immediate experience of pain, depends on intensity, and is lost in verbal communication.

In the double sense of "chasten" we find the last use we can give to the pain we bring on ourselves. "To chasten" means not only "to correct or discipline by punishment," but also "to render pure in character or style, to refine." If we take our suffering as chastisement, it does not merely curb or lop off a particular intemperate shoot; it can force strength back into the whole fabric of our lives. Most of us are barbaric and wild in the beginning; we need to try our strength by trying its limits. We find the strength that lies in limits by throwing our strength away; our strength is informed, is used, and grows. It is by suffering the consequences of unrestraint that we learn the value of restraint. It is through dissipation that we discover the point of concentration, in the waste of disorder that we find the need for form. Those who have felt themselves close to madness, those who have suffered despair, know best the uses of balance, value it most, and may be the ones who can use it best. Where matter is most full of possibility, where there is great natural strength and great hope for form, there is great need for that purification which comes of feeling the whip and tasting the bit.

All of us need refinement of soul, but where it is most valuable

—in those most passionate and most powerful, most extravagant in invention and strong in thought—there it is hardest to achieve. If most of us come from the run of a mine far below this hyperbolic height, about us too is a deal of dross, much lead mixed with our little gold, and we too need the refiner's fire and the fuller's soap, even as the sons of Levi. Of course these are metaphors, violent metaphors, not to be excused by saying that what is good enough for Malachi (3:2) is good enough for us. The difficult thing is to get past the figures to the affective patterns they represent. It is easier to see symptoms, even accurately to prescribe a discipline, than it is to understand the emotional basis that permits us to give a penitential use to suffering. This ground will be complex and natural, but uses and effects can be described in some ignorance of it. It will be possible for each of us to find a practice between the extremes advised by those who tell us never to think of past mistakes and those who tell us to think of nothing else, a degree of attention to our errors that is distanced without detachment, painful but not malignant. By thinking of our errors and the suffering they have earned, and equally by knowing when we have thought enough, we can achieve a penance that is also absolution.

No sacrament is more humane than Penance. From contrition, confession, satisfaction, and absolution one can return not merely equal to the man he was before transgression, not merely with an error canceled out: one can be made stronger at the mend. This is the use we can give to the suffering we earn: we can consciously recall the occasion of error, judge our mistake, take its consequences as just punishment, and deserve self-absolution. We can feel—not just say, but feel—that as humans we are imperfect, but not for that reason depraved. We can learn to accept the consequences of choice and that conduct is amendable. We can learn the tact of forgiveness by forgiving ourselves, whom we have most to forgive and always forgive too little or too much. We cannot accomplish this without attending to our past, but the exact quality and degree of fruitful attention cannot be prescribed. The Church measures out penances as it does indulgences, and both must be earned with attention and effort. If its precise bookkeeping is fantastic, there is a solid emotional foundation beneath the fanciful superstructure. There is both justice and foresight in the insistence that our ways are corrigible. There is truth in the recognition that remorse is at best an opportunity for reformation, and that without absolution remorse can lead to despair. Moral sanity requires the realization that all mistakes are not equally important. We must try to make this kind of estimate if we are to act freely and then to live at ease with ourselves.

If we are to achieve a form of life in which we can feel a reasonable satisfaction, each of us must learn to judge his actions with justice and with mercy. We will never know how to strike a perfect balance, but we can practice, knowing that nothing about us will ever be perfect. From our practice may come the tact that is celebrated in the sacrament of Penance. Standing behind its ceremonial form are natural facts of central moral importance: if we intelligently attend to our particular choices and their consequences, we can discover the relative importance of the various commitments in our moral economy; we can also learn the degrees of contrition that tend to the restoration of reasonable hope for improvement of life.

2. *Unearned Suffering*

The glass of metaphor is never clear; if it were, metaphor would be description. Where it is affective matter we must attend, metaphor may be as close to description as we can get. The figurativeness and imprecision may be regrettable, but they will not be dangerous so long as we do not take our metaphors for literal truths. This case calls for such caution.

Through metaphor we must try to see the use of unearned suffering, of pain we have not incurred through our fault, but which comes to us without reason, from causes that can be given no sensible relation to our choices.

To speak first of the suffering of others, we have already seen one response to it: the rage of compassion. This is honest, even admirable, for it reflects a moral sense that will not accept as worshipful and good what common humanity cannot find so. Although it is brave and honest, passionate pity is often naïve and uninformed; then it tends to run to indiscriminate extremes and to exhaust itself in fruitless hatred of the world. Pity that constitutes itself as indignation toward the cosmos commits the pathetic fallacy in reverse.

There is a better insight—although bending too much to the less just extreme—into that suffering which the world lays on the innocent. Of human beauty, Baudelaire says in his *Journal,* "I do not pretend that Joy cannot associate with Beauty, but I will maintain that Joy is one of her most vulgar adornments, while Melancholy may be called her illustrious spouse—so much so that I can scarcely conceive (is my brain become a witch's mirror?) a type of Beauty which has nothing to do with Sorrow."[8] But his brain was a witch's mirror, and this makes sorrow too universal and efficacious a condition of good. What has sorrow to do with a beautiful child? And yet the very fact that children are one obvious exception to this doubtful romantic rule does suggest a kind of beauty which children in their innocence cannot have.

This suggestion, even when we allow for its source, does force to mind a disturbing question. We *do* tend to attach a peculiar value to the person who has suffered. We must ask what that value is, and why we feel it. If the simplest answer is true, it is disconcertingly true: perhaps we do find an intrinsic good in pain. It may be that we take its stigma as a mark of distinction, that there is some primitive depth of our being that accepts the

victim with awe. This has nothing to do with pity; pity is sometimes an impertinence. "Terror" is too strong, "respect" too
weak; "awe" is the best available word.

The causes of our response are hidden from us; the ground
of the use of pain remains obscure. What must be made clear
is that gratuitous suffering can be justified only by giving it
a use; only if it can be forced to good account can it be considered other than purely bad. This is to reject the view that
there is any intrinsic good in pain; to think there is is to confuse
a means with an end. Whatever this use may be it is possible
only to the sufferer himself. If its possibility is suggested by the
suffering of others, even if one in part re-creates their experience to his use, this does nothing to justify *their* pain. "Why
should he know that diabolical good and evil when it costs so
much? Why, the whole world of knowledge is not worth that
child's prayer to 'dear, kind God!' " No one can afford the
price of the children's pain; it is not ours to pay. But the
price has been paid for us, against our will, and from what
we can assimilate we can hope to learn—until the cost goes
beyond our comprehension. There are magnitudes which stop
the thought of use: there is no way to assimilate Auschwitz.

It may be a rational fear of going too deep that has kept
some discussion of suffering too shallow. It is sensible but
inadequate to suppose that pain has its whole use in making
felicity more valuable (presumably by its usual absence) or in
showing us the difference between good and evil. Pain can be
given these uses, but the heart of the matter is deeper than
this, and less intellectual. We must listen when the pagans
tell us that through suffering we acquire strength and single-
ness of soul, that these qualities are not only tested, but are
often formed, in adversity. It is true that steadfastness and
endurance are virtues, that courage is a great virtue, and that
the goodness of these qualities is not merely in their utility
in a world like ours; those informed by these virtues find them
good in themselves, as we find them good to see. It is true that

triumph over adversity or compulsion is inspiriting, that the human spirit can stand forth most clearly in defeat and seem to gain its greatest dignity when all else is lost. These are the lessons of tragedy, and are not to be undervalued because they are partial.

The ancient world finally found this too thin, and so must we. The notions of victory in defeat, of the triumph of spirit, or reaffirmation of cosmic order, have never made a wholly satisfactory theory of tragedy. Even if they did they would seldom furnish lessons for life. Used as such they tend to degenerate into moral melodrama, a category into which falls "the tragic sense of life." The danger here is not just preciousness, refined melodrama, but the foreclosure of other insights and other uses. Unless the word is stretched past all clear meaning, we cannot call most human suffering tragic.

When suffering seemed to earn for its subject not admiration for the spirit that triumphs through tragedy, or scorn for the weakness that falls under pain, but rather the awe that is due to sanctity—then pagan morality was at its end. The sense of life of the Greeks or Romans cannot be made our own. Rightly or wrongly we have lived too long with the feeling that there is something beyond their insights to be gained through suffering. If the clear language of cognition cannot convey what we feel we have learned, if the noble rhetoric of virtue cannot express the sense we think we have gained, so much the worse for them. We must try to speak as clearly as we can, with as little mystification as we can, but our talk must be about traveling into the dark, about touching depths. Our language must be that of metaphor.

a. THE METAPHOR OF REDEMPTION

When those of us who have had a slight acquaintance with pain speak to those who have suffered deeply, we can have the sense that they have been somewhere we have never been, that they "know" something we have yet to learn. They have no words to tell us; they did not choose to go and we do not choose to follow, yet we are in awe at their journey. It is not that they have explored a possibility of life that few can realize. On the contrary, it is that the possibility made real in their suffering has its ground in the furthest depths of our common nature. Nowhere are we so much at one as in the experience of pain. The masks we hold before it for the world to see will differ, but in the experience itself we are stripped of difference almost to community. If, sunk in this intensity, a man can hold to his humanity—can know that he is a man and that he suffers—then he can comprehend his suffering, and so in feeling comprehend our universal condition. We speak only of possibilities, it does not always happen this way, but we know that among those who have suffered there can be the strongest of wordless bonds, the deepest affective communion. Where this exists, it rests on their mutual sense that they have touched the ground of mortality common to us all. For this sense Christianity has found a perfect symbol. In nothing does the Christian God— perfect God and perfect man—show His humanity more than in His openness to pain; in His vulnerability we are one with Him, and He with us. It is in Christ that men's deepest attitudes toward suffering find their best *persona*, One who suffers for us, Who goes there in our place, to hell and to heaven, to hell before heaven, showing the course and measuring the extremes of human possibility, earning our salvation.

At the center of this story is the sense that redemption can be gained through suffering, and it is the metaphor of redemptive suffering that we must try to understand. The first thing to understand is that whatever benefit is here, it cannot be earned by proxy. This is not so far from Christianity as it sounds. The Christian believes in the supernatural benefit to him of Christ's one perfect sacrifice, once offered, but he also believes that he too must suffer on the cross. Considering only this latter insight and leaving supernatural mysteries aside, all come down to the same questions. How is it that suffering can be a deliverance? From what can we be saved by that suffering we do not deserve? What can we use our suffering to gain? If we cannot justify the suffering of others—even Christ's except as a paradigm—from what use can we force a meaning for our own?

The natural sense of redemption can be found in the supernatural figure; that is what gives the figure its life. The metaphor has at least two affective meanings, probably not distinct in operation: (b) through our unearned suffering we can come to have a sense of expiation; (c) in the immediacy of suffering we can feel walls of separation break, feel that the pain which destroys our defenses relieves our isolation, opens our way to communion.

b. ANXIETY AND EXPIATION

Guilt is only possible where there is complexity, and vague guilt belongs to the luxury trade in suffering. Those who have what seems to them too much good luck may be afraid of Nemesis, and those whose outer circumstances have been more singular or more fortunate than have those of their neighbors, if only because they have survived and their neighbors have not, may be most susceptible to anxiety. The guilt of the man who kills his brother will, if he feels it, be hard and clear; the suffering of their mother will have a terribly specific cause; in neither case could we speak of "anxiety." The soldier facing a bayonet charge and the farmer whose crops have failed feel, with respect to their concrete situations, neither vaguely anxious nor vaguely guilty; they are clearly and reasonably afraid.

Why generalized guilt and anxiety are chronic and endemic in certain groups is a psychological question that may someday be answered. Meanwhile it is plain that great numbers of more or less innocent people feel more or less guilty, feel that they are to blame, feel that there is something for which they must atone—but the ground of their anxious guilt they do not know. Such people might do penance if they could, but how? And for what sins? "The remembrance of them is grievous unto us; the burden of them is intolerable." But we cannot remember what we have done. We would confess, do penance, amend our lives; we would seek absolution—but there is nothing to confess except mortality, and for that original sin there is only one absolution.

When concrete suffering comes to such people, when the world gives them specific cause for deep and personal pain, they can, if they will, find in their pain a sense of expiation. Those guilty without due cause can accept their suffering as if they deserved it, accept it as a penance, and in this way feel they have earned at least a partial absolution. If there is nothing very rational in this, there is also nothing mysterious. A conscientious child who has done a thing he has been told and feels is wrong may not feel right until he has confessed and accepted his punishment. Merely feeling guilty is not sufficient. Expiation and absolution require more objective and dramatic suffering. Conscientious adults are not very different. The need for a general confession takes us all at one time or another, though the times are more often inopportune than not. Or we feel driven to confess to a person we have wronged, to expose ourselves to his punishment. Our motives are seldom as noble as we make them out to be. We give credit to our honesty, but what we want is relief.

If vague feelings of anxiety and guilt are a common affective affliction, the need for punishment may be universal. Although it may seem that we value the suffering itself, the truth may be that we value it as a penance, as a condition of the sense of absolution. (Not only the Crucifixion, but three days in hell had to come before Easter. Even if in our childlike hearts we still believe in sympathetic magic, we cannot believe that this once has done for all. To have been shown the way is not to have traveled it.) There are severe limitations to this search for absolution: obviously suffering does not always have this effect;

there are probably better ways to assuage anxiety and guilt; the sense of absolution may come of itself, without preparation or thought. Nothing said here should be construed as a recommendation of suffering! There is no mystique of pain here. Pain is exactly what ought to be avoided, but it is not possible to escape it wholly; after saying pain ought to be avoided, the only sensible recommendation that remains is that we try to make good use of the pain we cannot avoid.

This is not clear in the models to which we should look. These are ancient and customary, beautiful and mysterious, but then it is not as naked schemata that they have their affective bearing. If it were a novel sense of humanity that Penance embodied and redemption symbolized, neither the sacrament nor the symbol could serve as stable or effective moral patterns. Behind them lie their history and their associations, the central place they have held in our common cultural past, all the emotional significance with which piety has surrounded them. All this working together with their directly human import makes them appropriate models. They are that at least; they are nothing more. The facts behind these figures are pragmatic, affective, and natural. Their true significance lies in showing us this: if we need and if we will, we can with conscious attention shape our attitudes toward our pain; we can inform the patterns into which we take suffering and loss; we can learn in time to accept our unearned suffering as chastisement for our unknown sins, as an installment on the cost of their redemption.

This is not rational. The ways of non-thought behind this use are childish or primitive, but that is in part the way we are. Such facts tend to give irrationalists unwarranted reassurance and cause rationalists undue chagrin. Both species of extremists think human nature is or should be simpler than it is. If this use of suffering rests on subrational causes, it does not follow that the use itself is irrational. Indeed, if the foundation of the moral life lies in our affections, it does not follow that only the ground exists, or even that the structures raised from it are less rational than rationalists believe. But the lovers of reason become unreasonable when they insist on attributing all efficacy and virtue to what they love, showing in this the exaggeration usual to infatuation. It is at once intemperate and jejune to say that we are or ought to be purely rational clean through. We can demand as much rationality as it is reasonable to demand, and, in recommending sensible means to the end of a life found good, adapt Burke's most famous dictum to our use: moral discipline "ought to be adjusted not to human reasonings but to human nature; of which reason is but a part, and by no means the greatest part."

c. VULNERABILITY AND HUMANITY

Through most of the dull and extraordinary events that mark our lives, but not deeply, we live in uneasy isolation. We are pulled between pride in our difference from all the others, in our separateness, and fear that difference is a kind of crime. We set to work to mend our defenses, fearing equally invasion and escape; but then we come to think that we are our walls, that life has spent itself in fortification, that nothing exists behind the façade. For all our care, because of all our care, the structure is empty.

Add to that metaphor this: the most proud and mistrustful have built without a door. Self-committed to solitary confinement, or being themselves no more than a system of defenses against life, fearing even the illusion of openness, they stand imperviously as the last extreme of human isolation. They have achieved invulnerability. If they discover that their defense has nothing to guard, theirs is the most desperate situation. They have kept out all that might cause them pain, but this is the same as to keep out all that could bring them life. So in their hollowness nothing grows but coldness, pale as a weed in a cave, the very sense of emptiness itself. Then at last they may try to call for warmth and hear in answer only an echo,

> *. . . quiet and meaningless*
> *As wind in dry grass*
> *Or rat's feet over broken glass*
> *In our dry cellar.*[9]

From this last little room no one escapes by his own efforts. There is no hope except that the walls be broken, but all strength has gone to the building of walls; inside there is only dust and darkness. Help, if it comes at all, can only come unasked for, accidentally, from outside.

If there is a difference between building a keep and finding a desert island, it is that the former is more warlike. Set as it is among men, it is more likely to have been thought of first as a base for offensive operations, to have been useful as a safe, strong place to strike from, becoming then with time and age primarily defensive, necessary then as a place to hide, a prison, and a grave. The stronger the walls, the harder they are to break; that is obvious. If a man has given all his life to his defenses, when he wishes that they might crack to let in warmth and light, it must be the breaking of himself he hopes for; that is less obvious. It is hard to lose the only life one has just for a chance to gain a life long feared. Some, insofar as they have a choice, draw further in and spend the last of whatever strength they have in defense that can be successful. They cannot be greatly blamed for this: they have seen that it is themselves that must be broken, and that for this no force is sufficient but pain.

This is the last and most desperate use of suffering, no more to be invited than war or martyrdom. More often than not our differences from each other are more valuable than our resemblances, and we cannot live without defenses. If we could consider our common humanity somehow in itself, beneath or behind the forms it grows to and the forms we give it, we might find it big with life and warmth, but within the broadest limits of humanity still an almost amorphous potential, a matter with all distinction still to be achieved. We might find what Schopenhauer and perhaps Bergson claim is there to be found: emotion without objects, attention without focus, mind without structure.[10] Without this ground there would be no life, but our actual lives are the patterns this matter grows to, our achievements are the forms we give it.

Pattern and form are the contour of life; they can no more exist apart than can any form without matter, but the man-become-wall comes as close as a human being can. Aristotle's language serves here even in its faults. It is on the point of God that Aristotle is caught at his most incongruously Platonic, and the hollow man has a likeness to Aristotle's God: unnatural, matterless form, perfectly self-centered and self-contained, capable only of self-reflective thought, circling eternally, coldly, on itself. This God is neither natural nor humane, and Aristotle's argument that we ought to take it as our ultimate moral model —since God and man have the same metaphysical essence, God being the purest actualization of intellect and rationality man's essential nature—is the least natural part of his system.[11] What is natural is to find that this extreme is humanly untenable, so much so that those who approach it most nearly may be the most desperate to break out, may be willing to welcome any shock that will break the circle and send them back toward the human mean.

While the hollow man stands at an extreme, dangerous if less critical cases are common. (A humanitarian front is the best cover for an absence of humanity.) These produce milder but similar symptoms: uneasy detachment; vacillation between pride and fear of difference, between need and fear of human commitment; and finally a growing, guilty coldness. Words are not an adequate cure for this; they may well make the matter worse. Popular canting on the insignificance of human difference, easy claims that nothing human is alien, have as their danger the possibility that the noble words will become a wall, will hide both the differences and the likenesses that count, and keep those who stay hidden behind the words from any genuine human warmth, any sense of affective communion. The patterns into which life falls are a kind of universal, but an intellectual recognition of human likeness may be without moral effect.

What we need is not merely knowledge, but wisdom, and there is a difficult saying, often abused, that wisdom comes only through suffering. The suggestion of noesis gives this old saw a dangerous edge, but "wisdom" need not be taken to mean a peculiar kind of cognition. It is better used as an honorific name for affective tact, for informed emotions. (This is not to claim that a perfectly clear line can be drawn between cognition and affection.) Under the name of wisdom in this sense we can list what we need to learn to become answers to this problem. First, we need the sense that there is nothing wrong with difference, that otherness, separateness, form, are not due cause for guilt. But then with the same sense we must feel that we are and must be both different and the same, both unique and fully human, ineluctably ourselves and rooted in common matter. We need catharsis of the fear that sometimes spoils our difference; catharsis also of fear of intensity, a fear not always without cause, but exaggerated by recoil or pushed to terror by mistaken belief that intensity is incompatible with form. Intellectual acceptance of these wise maxims cannot have the moral effect that suffering can. It is in our vulnerability that we feel our common mortality, in suffering that we sense our common humanity, and equally in suffering that each can earn the guiltless sense of his own uniqueness.

To know that this can happen is not to know how it happens, nor will it be other than a confusion—a sinister confusion since it might seem to ground a case for the goodness of suffering itself —to assimilate wisdom to knowledge. Our knowledge of the circumstances that have caused our suffering is in part properly called knowledge, but the only "knowledge" we get through pain itself is "knowledge by acquaintance," that is, immediate apprehension. What we get can *feel* like knowledge, can give us a sense of noesis in the absence of cognition; from this comes the quarter-truth that suffering brings knowledge. If knowledge were what suffering brought, it should be possible to state the knowledge that it brings, but requests for such statements are always met with metaphorical, mythical, or expressive answers. This is because the sense we get is affective and amounts to a shift in attitudinal and emotional patterns, a change brought about by the intrusion of an unlooked-for intensity. Any intensity has its effects on one's emotional set, but where the patterns of affective life have at once hardened and emptied—and this happens in some degree to all of us—the only invasion likely to break through old forms is the experience of pain. It is indeed ourselves that break, but we can break to be filled and to re-form. It is true that destruction sometimes goes beyond possibility of restoration; it always does at last, but of all the times we think are last the last comes only once, and every time before that time the pain that destroys our defenses can bring with it the sense of common matter. The possibility of fresh form is inherent exactly there. We have only touched the surface if we feel it is sympathy we learn, and it is something better than pity. We seem to ourselves to touch that life in us most like the ground of every other life. This touch transforms us: we become the answer.

This is the natural mystery of redemption from egocentricity. It would be senseless to say that this redemption ought to be other than partial. It cannot be, for it is a change worked in the life of each who earns it; there is no other place for it to happen. It is not our particularity or separateness that is lost; our sense of self is intensified. What is destroyed is the exaggerated sense of separation. It is not that our form is shattered to allow our matter to merge in some blissful, amorphous, metaphysical sea: the relation of jug to water is too naïve an analogy, panpsychism is a myth, and The Sea of Being exists only as a name on fantastic maps. The sense of communion that can be achieved is the sense of each who has it, who feels himself at once himself and all. It exists as a pattern of feeling created when the invasion of suffering is comprehended, when the intensity found least good in itself is accepted into patterns that have been and its force used to restore and reshape our lives.

Beyond the sense of communion and the possibility of fresh form, there is one further restoration pain can make us: through it we can return to innocence. Some of the vague but pervasive disquietude we feel, the uneasiness amounting to guilt, may be based on nothing more culpable than the fact that each of us is himself; or, better, based on the apprehension that all of us do not amount to one indifferent whole. At some irrational depth may live the fear that we ought not to be many, but one—one undifferentiated, darkly luminiferous ocean of immediate feeling, The Sea of Being again. The prenatal ground of this fantasy gives it no less strength, rather the contrary. That it is beneath the reach of reason means that it can be altered only by force.

At least to a little degree the force of pain can be bent to this use, although its operation is neither direct, efficient, nor simple. It would seem that the way we attend the experience we undergo, the place we can try deliberately to give our affections, can sometimes drive the patterns we build around them into the unknown irrational depths, where changes follow. Our affections are shaped by habit, and changes in habit are brought about by acting as if they had already been made. It would be too much to hope that useful or reasonable patterns of response could in this way be made perfectly to inform our emotions, but it hopes too little to give up hope that all our ways are past breaking and mending. If it is true that difference or otherness can be a source of guilt, this feeling rises from depths that may lie not only out of sight but beyond the reach of deliberate change; to say this is to be honest about the odds, to make it clear that a regimen suggested is not a cure guaranteed. After this qualification it remains true that our unearned suffering can be accepted as a penance for individuality and forced to pay the ransom of its guilt.

The same intensity that can open the way to communion, that

can break us and leave us whole, can also earn us the sense of innocence. It seems a sacrifice acceptable to our aboriginal gods whose childish judgment is absolute in the darkness where they govern. They—we—cannot understand absolution without payment; or, since "understanding" at this depth is a sense of affective adjustment, it would be better simply to say that we cannot feel ourselves to be forgiven except at a price. There is no virtue in calling extortion a favor, no need to pretend to like to pay, and only confusion, hypocrisy, or perverseness in the claim that the pain we offer is in itself found good. The good to be had is not intrinsic, but only instrumental: it lies in use. Perhaps all the uses of suffering can be seen as means of redemption; here it is a ransom we can give for the chastened sense of particularity, for the innocent appreciation of our separateness. Having earned the sense of absolution we can go on—now guiltlessly—to create the sense of form.

3. *The Affective Answer*

Only the use of suffering, not suffering itself, can in reason be justified. Each of us can use his own pain, but no one else's pain can be justified by our use. Whatever its uses, pain can never be recommended or prescribed, not even in the sense that amputation and shock treatment are. It would be terrible for this to be misunderstood. We must not suppose that suffering ought to be looked for or deliberately induced, even as a cure. We have already pushed to the limits of good sense in trying to see a reasonable use for a kind of experience it is reasonable to avoid.

But if pain and loss are not certain, they are as nearly certain as anything human can be. Times will come when our only choice will be between simply suffering our pain or trying to use it. Much suffering is past use, but where there is a chance for suffering to be other than passive and useless, it is unreasonable to decline the chance. Given the near inevitability of pain, any attempt to win back some good from it will leave us no poorer than we were before. The conditions of the venture are that we have already lost. Let the odds against gain be as great as you will, we must take the chance of gain if we take any chance at all. This should be added: when life itself is in question, it is always too soon to decide that no chances remain.

It is in suffering that one's own life comes most in question; only one's own life can be the answer. Beyond the attempt to alleviate human misery there is no "Problem of Evil" except that which has an affective and personal resolution: the answer to suffering is a form of feeling. The answer is an affective pattern that feels like an answer—it is an answer because it feels like an answer—immanent in the life of each who achieves it. Each resolution is thus (as Santayana describes the feelings of lovers) original but not novel. The deeper resolutions depend on the possibility of feeling a direct awareness of common matter, on an apprehension we accept as a sense of communion. Our sense of this ground and the ground itself are affective. Our sense cannot literally be put into words, and that sense and its ground resist literal description. The recourse to metaphor and analogy would represent defeat for theoretical description, but for practical purposes figurative language can force to attention possibilities of action and use. The most appropriate figures are those of discipline and redemption.

No wonder affective consequences of such complexity have been held miraculous; we have been in the presence of one of nature's best imitations of miracle. The causes of these events are obscure, but natural and human. They lie in the breaking and re-formation of patterns of feeling, dark figures that cannot be touched or moved except by a force that reaches to their depth. No wonder it seems a miracle when from this darkness there comes to consciousness a sense of transformation, communion, or forgiveness, even a sense of having taken up the whole burden of humanity and earned it absolution. To fail to try to make this possibility real is not to escape suffering; it is to be shattered or to suffer uselessly. To try to shape suffering to this realization, to accept for these uses great loss, great pain, all grief—this is to become as perfectly human, and perhaps as God-like, as it is appropriate for a human to become.

V

ESTIMATES OF MATTER AND FORM

The Devil speaks:
Has the sun better fire than the kitchen? And sane and sound
greatness! Whenever I hear of such, I laugh! Do you believe in
anything like an ingenium *that has nothing to do with hell?*
Non datur! The artist is the brother of the criminal and the
madman. Do you ween that any important work was ever
wrought except its maker learned to understand the way of the
criminal and madman? Morbid and healthy! Without the morbid
would life all its whole life never have survived. Genuine and
false! Are we land-loping knaves? Do we draw the good things
out of the nose of nothing? Where nothing is, there the Devil too
has lost his right and no pallid Venus produces anything worth
while! We make naught new—that is other people's matter. We
only release, only set free. We let the lameness and self-conscious-
ness, the chaste scruples and doubts go to the Devil. We physic
away fatigue merely by a little charm-hyperaemia, the great and
the small, of the person and of the time. That is it, you do not
think of the passage of time, you do not think historically, when

*you complain that such and such a one could have it wholly,
joys and pains endlessly, without the hour-glass being set for
him, the reckoning finally made. What he in his classical decades
could have without us, certainly, that, nowadaies, we alone have
to offer. And we offer better, we offer only the right and true—
that is no longer the classical, my friend, what we give to experience, it is the archaic, the primeval, that which long since has
not been tried. Who knows today, who even knew in classical
times, what inspiration is, what genuine, old, primeval enthusiasm, insicklied critique, unparalysed by thought or by the
mortal domination of reason—who knows the divine raptus? I
believe, indeed, the devil passes for a man of destructive criticism?
Slander and again slander, my friend! Gog's sacrament! If there
is any-thing he cannot abide, if there's one thing in the whole
world he cannot stomach, it is destructive criticism. What he
wants and gives is triumph over it, is shining, sparkling, vain-
glorious unreflectiveness.[1]*

THOMAS MANN, *Doctor Faustus*

Whether we like it or not, the only material each of us has to
work with in the making of his life is the person he finds himself *now*. We cannot start to live unless we start from where we
are, and that starting place is given: each of us on every morning
finds himself as a given structure of character, temperament,
emotions, and tastes. Whether the main lines have been laid
down at three years old, or by the age of reason, or the day
before yesterday, matters only in degree. Life today and tomor-
row will be a balance, sought or stumbled into, between circumstance and personality as we find them and the goals toward
which we tend. There are two conditions under which we may
fail to start at all. We may think so highly of ourselves as we are
that we feel no need to change, or think so little that any attempt
at change is felt as forlorn in advance. Our evaluation of ourselves

as given can be too easy or too hard; since what we are makes a difference to what we can be, a proper appreciation of the given self is essential to the sensible conduct of life.

A. THE SELF AS GIVEN

The importance of given gross differences seems too obvious to deny. One is born in America, or China, or Germany, or Sicily—and this makes a difference. One can grow up in city, town, or country, aware of the turn and circle of nature only as a nuisance or as life itself—and this makes a difference. One is born a male or a female; one may grow very tall or stay very tiny; one is born more or less intelligent, more or less stupid; one is the only child, or the first child, or the second or third or last or lost child; one is born of rich parents, or poor parents, or parents at neither extreme; one grows up in an atmosphere religious, or areligious, or irreligious; one is Catholic, Protestant, Jew, or unbeliever. There is a difference, for instance, between a Protestant and a Jewish intellectual, and between a rural and an urban intellectual. These differences can still be seen after the Protestant has lost his faith and the new Thoreau has left Walden for Washington Square.

None of these things is sufficient to send a man spinning down the iron rails of Spinozistic determinism. Determinism is not an information-giving or scientific hypothesis; at most it is a heuristic device, and at least a human attitude. What can be said is that these factors give grounds for reliable predictions. We are born, live, and act in a personal, social, and historical milieu, and that context is not wholly one's own creation. Our vision of the past and future is indeed a reconstruction, a constantly renewed reinterpretation, but the past that has really been continues to work in our lives, even bears on our present vision, and ignorance of its present force is one form of human bondage. Our reconstruction must do justice to the historical data, must be tied to the truth of events as far as we can tell it even when the affective significance of the events emerges long after the time of their original occurrence.

The notion that the real past is present in memory need be no more than a harmless confusion, but the claim that the past can be ignored in favor of our present vision of it, that we are practically free of all we have been, is a dangerous fantasy. This is not simply a question of honesty: the ignorant or sophistical idea that the past has no lien on the present is one way to an unhappy future. Those who are skeptical of second births must hope to find a less fantastic way of understanding the relation between the world and the self as given, and what we want to become. We need a language, a conceptual vocabulary, in which we can express a just understanding of these things, and then we need a standard of judgment that will allow us to accept ourselves, but accept ourselves as a somewhat plastic, more or less recalcitrant, material that we can hope to turn into better shape.

1. *Matter and Form*

Each man is, in the full particularity of his life, concrete, individual, and unique, and the life of each is much like the life of all. At any time a man is only and exactly what he is: his flesh and bones, his given emotions, beliefs, hopes, goals, and fears. Individuals existing at particular times and in particular places are the sole and concrete locus of humanity—but only the new or butterfly mind, completely captivated by the infinitely varied and particular surface of life, could deny that each human lives a life much like that of other humans and, in its most important occasions, like that of all human beings. This takes nothing away from the reality of the careers of particular men. The universal patterns of human life exist as Aristotelian "form" does, most clearly as abstractions, but each of us concretely lives through aspects of the pattern. Form is structure or arrangement, the organization that matter has or a pattern it could be given; form is the contour, the architecture of matter. Forms of life have no existence except as each of us lives them, but it would be hard to deny that lives repeat patterns of life.

In Aristotle's language we can say that a man's situation in any temporal cross section of it is a function of matter and form, of what is concretely particular to him with the patterns he shares with other things. But this distinction of matter and form is relative and comparative. Aristotle identifies matter with potentiality and form with actuality, and argues that what is form compared with some lower stage of development is matter compared with a higher one. The whole individual, matter *and* form, is matter to the form he might achieve. "Matter" and "form" are always applied in relation to each other: to claim that X (say an oak tree) is form to the matter of Y (an acorn), is to say that X is a further and more complex development of Y, that in X is actualized the best that lay potentially in Y. We say that the oak tree has greater form not only because it realizes the possibility inherent in the seed, but because to the familiar eye its pattern seems the most coherent order that the complexity of its elements admits. It is possible to use in a natural and descriptive sense the same examples that, when form is supposed to draw matter magically to its actuality, are taken to illustrate teleological explanation: the soil is matter, potentiality, to the vine as form; the grape is, potentially, wine. To the more highly ordered phases, all below is matter; to the lowest stages of development, the least informed, all else is form. We shall find nothing altogether without structure, but the closer a thing is to amorphousness, the more it is merely potential, having as yet little realized a specificity that can be seen as form. The same distinctions can be made in comparisons among species and in understanding the life and growth of individual things. If the soil is matter for all that is the vine, and the grape for the cup of wine, so also is the bud form to the shoot, but matter for the grape. The child is a potential man; the man as formed is matter to the man he may become. What a thing is at any time can only be told by telling what it was, what it is, and what it may be.[2]

In this manner of speaking we can say that one's given self and situation are matter, potential. This is true of one's abilities and hopes, of one's moods and affections, of the whole person who has grown to just this point. One grows toward specificity, but unlike the vine which has no choice of direction, unlike the acorn which cannot choose to be an elm, man can turn aside from the achievement of humanity, from growth toward those patterns of life which are most distinctively human. This is to say that man is a creature for whom choice is possible.

2. *A Manner of Speaking*

Here we must part company with the substance of Aristotle's thought. For him man's true goal was unambiguous and clear; it was set by the unique and metaphysically privileged form that all humans shared, their rationality. Progress toward rationality was natural growth, movement toward a universal form itself attractive as a magnet; all else was unnatural or perverse. The difficulties of defending or even of defining the assertion that man qua man has one true, positively valuable, and unambiguously determinable essence are insuperable, since no one can tell exactly what the assertion asserts or what would count as evidence for or against it. The Aristotelian doctrine that each species has one inherent and uniquely characterizing essence or form, and that knowledge consists in discovery of the essential nature of fixed species, has proved cognitively useless; worse, it has been used as an instrument of scientific and philosophic obscurantism. This, however, need not be the very last word. It is possible to ask whether anything useful can be saved here, after the metaphysics has been washed away.

It should not be surprising that the answer is yes. Whether

through the influence of Aristotelian ideas, or through the pervasive Aristotelianism of Western grammar and rhetoric, our ordinary ways of thinking, talking, and feeling find a congenial echo in much Aristotelian language. What can be saved is a manner of speaking, a conceptual vocabulary the appropriateness of which can best be shown by putting it to use. What we give up in getting free of Aristotelian metaphysics is the notion that one specific characteristic determines man's essential nature and thus sets him a demonstrably right direction for development. To give up talk in terms of antecedent essential natures need not be to lapse into wordless nominalism, nor into a general belief in the inutility of all general statements. We can feel as free to speak of human nature as any believer in essence—say of any Z that Z is a man and all of us will be able to make great numbers of predictions about Z that are likely to be true—but in our use of "human nature" it must remain a concept that is empirically and historically grounded, not rising to the status of a fixed metaphysical truth.

If man qua man does not have one predetermined actuality or goal on which all rational men must agree, it is still true that all men are much alike—have, as we say, much in common. It is not metaphysical insight but wise observation which can tell us that there are recurrent and (in a metaphysically neutral sense) universal human characteristics and human situations. Without the belief that each species has its fixed essence which can be apprehended by reason, our argument must have a character and conclusion that Aristotle might think disastrously modest. We shall have to say that the judgment "clearly patterned or chaotic," "more or less informed," depends to a degree on the temperament of the judge, on his sense of what is familiar, comprehensible, and just. Form does not lie in one simple sense in the mind of the beholder. There are two senses in which it is found much closer to his heart: (a) where our questions concern the life found good, it is "form" and "matter" in an affective sense and the relations between them, which argument must touch; and (b) we call "order" or "form" what *feels* like order or form.

a. THE BRASS AND THE SPHERE

To speak of the form of emotion is to a degree metaphorical. What has form and structure in the most obvious sense is a physical object; to speak of the form of a work of art is already a step toward metaphor. If we think or speak of informed emotion, emotion considered as matter, that must be to elicit a sense in which aspects of the affective life can be felt to have similarities to more literally structured things. But this sense is not distant or recondite. The problem of bringing it to mind is rather that it is too close and familiar. We do feel our experience to have its ebbs and flows, its peaks and valleys and plains. We speak of a day or a year as outstanding, or of an hour as marking a climax, meaning that the experience it brought seems to stand out from the rest, to rise from the level of passing life and command willing or unwilling special attention. The day of a man's wedding, his son's birth, his father's death, unless these moments are lost in an unconsidered crowd, can be felt to have peculiar force, and all that gathers around them seem as foothills to their height. The heights are the affective intensities, and it may not yet be metaphor to say that the surge and flow of feeling in the *Oedipus Rex,* or that we sense in hearing Beethoven's Opus 131, the *Quartet in C Sharp Minor,* are their affective organization or form. Even an ordinary day is felt to have a contour made by degrees of intensity, although the valleys may be shallow and the few hills low; wider perspectives of time may show patterns more distinct.

We cannot demand literal truth of this way of talking, nor claim that no more illuminating figure is possible; we can try to be consistent in our manner of speaking. We shall have to say that the form of our emotions is separable from them only in whatever sense the shape of a brass sphere is separable from that particular sphere. The form of life can be separated from the experience of life only abstractly or analytically; it can be spoken of separately and generally as the geometric formula for a sphere can be stated in mathematical symbols. If we call this abstraction a "principle of form," or its verbal statement a "statement of form," we must also say that the form itself is inherent: it is not another entity or thing apart from matter, but is the structure of the affections, the pattern made by the relative distribution of their force.

It is possible to recognize, mention, condemn, and recommend forms, but form itself exists as an actual or possible configuration of experience itself—of thought, will, evaluation, emotion, action. The statement of form is abstract and general, and exists in whatever way such statements do exist. It is applicable to each of those like things which have the characteristics it names. These characteristics are "universals," but they exist only as they characterize individuals. When a pattern described by such a statement is taken as a model, or when it is recommended as a form worth achieving, the statement may be taken to prescribe in general the aspects of life on which intensity is best spent, the objects or events to which it is best directed. But the form of life is not the statement; it is the contour made by the spending itself, by the disposition of affections and, below that, by the habits of evaluation and emphasis manifest in choices made and experiences lived.[3]

b. AFFECTIVE FORM

Just as the shape of a pearl is the pearl under one aspect, so the shape of a life is an inherent, formal aspect of it (though an aspect felt as peculiarly pervasive and comprehensive), and can be apprehended as such—but even explosions and rubbish heaps have some order. In moral and aesthetic contexts we

save the word "order" for what *feels* like order; what we
mean by "form" is not grasped by intellect alone. It is a tempting but useless speculation that Aristotle and his followers in
fact discerned essential structures or forms in the light of their
affective glamour; this is certainly not what they thought they
were doing. While we consider it a contingent fact that there is
much intellectual and emotional likeness among human beings,
and hence in their opinions about what patterns deserve to be
called "forms," Aristotle took the fact for a necessary truth about
the essence of humanity and its consequence for a cognitive judgment dependent on man's essential rationality. It is probably
unfortunate that moral topography is not so grounded in essence,
for if we cannot recur to essential forms to justify our evaluations, it remains true that our judgments of form are evaluative.
When our interest in form is moral rather than purely anthro-
pological or sociological, we will not ordinarily call a life
"ordered" or "informed" merely on the basis of finding in it
pervasive qualities and remarkable events—insensitivity, say, and
three divorces. "Form" and "order" used in normative contexts
are normative words; they apply to some works or days and not
to others, to some affective structures and not to others. It is not
the evaluative use of these terms that we must abandon, it is the
notion that their applicability can be determined on strictly
intellectual grounds. To insist that only such grounds can vali-
date choices, to refuse recognition to one's evaluations because
they do not come with strictly cognitive credentials, is never to
be able to choose or act at all.

This is not said to denigrate reason; one's decisions and evaluations should be as rational as they can be. Estimates of appropriate means, their ends being already given, can be thoroughly
scientific. But when we recognize that the estimate of order is
affective, that it is based on our sense that we would feel fulfillment in some pattern of experience if we lived it, we shall have
to allow that our use of "form" and "matter" and our judgments
of relative form are misrepresented when thought of as wholly

objective. This does not mean that the use of the distinction, the attribution of "form" (or "more ordered" or "less formed"), need be random and without inter-personal regularity; the very fact that we are much alike ensures against this. It does mean that judgment must be tentative, modest, and less than wholly universal. A degree of parochialism here is a mark of good sense. Aristotle was modest about arguments in ethics, especially when they descended to consider the concrete application of general principles, but it is in general that man is more open than he thought, less furnished with fixed, antecedent goals to gain or to disregard. We can argue and sometimes agree, we can make generalizations and live together, because the grounds of argument, principle, and choice lie not merely in reason but in the resembling modes and patterns of our affective life.

A morals which would demonstrate its conclusions must rest on a metaphysical system. Where affective likeness already exists the appearance of demonstration can re-enforce conviction; so far as this antecedent consensus fails metaphysical recourse is not likely to produce conviction. The loss of metaphysical belief has been seen by many as reason for despair, but to lose the hope of moral demonstration is perhaps to lose not a necessary illusion but something superfluous and distracting. If we can cut past metaphysical agreement and disagreement to the affective likenesses and conflicts on which it rests, we can hope to touch the true ground of moral life in more direct and effective ways.[4] The attendant liabilities are obvious: some affective similarity, though it may be minimal, must be taken as the ground for effective moral discourse; the only evidence that can fairly be offered for the existence of this ground, or in arguments built on it, must come from history and observation; any ultimate arguments offered must appeal to the emotions. Honesty here can work against effectiveness, and to say that an argument is at bottom persuasive may rob it of its power to persuade. Fortunately not many arguments are ultimate, and candor is most fatal among those who prefer to be fooled. It would have a fine rhetorical ring to say that no real or reasonable human being could reject our recommendations, but it would not be true. The truths we can return to and rest on are that humans are much alike, and that human likeness exists in varying degrees, being greatest in limited historical and social groups. This is a modest truth, and if it is necessary for moral generalization, it is also sufficient.

On such natural grounds we can still argue that some human possibilities repay actualization more fully than others. We can use Aristotle's language of "matter" and "form" with a part of the teleological weight it has carried, but the teleology will be proximate and descriptive, amounting to recognition that The Creature has a purpose, and his eyes are bright with it. Although only living things have the reflex of purpose, and artifacts the purpose they are given, and although these purposes may be explicable in non-purposive terms, it is still true that to understand creatures it is useful to know what they want. It is not false to say that men love form, but by refusing to take this fact as an explanation, by discarding the arguments which would demonstrate that some one *telos* is metaphysically justified, by allowing that all forms are equally real, we are left with nothing better than the facts: that the choice of ends is founded in affection and that arguments urging one form over another must have recourse to common experience, to probabilities, and to persuasion. There is no real line to be drawn between moralists who have such reasons and those who have better reasons. The only line is between those who know that such are their reasons, and those who do not know.

B. SELF-OPINION

"We know what we are, but know not what we may be." The tragedy in Ophelia's words is made more poignant by their irony—very few of us know what we are. Matter is given, but often not appreciated; form is to be achieved. At this moment each of us is exactly what he is, and less than he would be; it is sometimes hard to accept, but the former limits the latter. We could not possibly have sufficient reason to say that ourselves as given *determine* what we may be, but the proper estimation of the matter we have to work with is essential to the fortunes of our work.[5]

That we are limited is inevitable, and no reason for despair. Limits set the conditions of work, but do not determine its outcome; to say that we ought not uncritically accept ourselves does not mean that we ought to be despised. If a man does hate himself too fiercely to consider any possibility of cultivation, if no form of life meets his fancy and his only hope is for total and universal destruction, he may be that species of savage called "nihilist," and society will have to deal with him as it can. It enforces a proper diffidence to remember that there are many sorts of people who cannot be reached by any moral discourse, however that discourse may be grounded or conducted.

1. *Complacency*

It can be a dull or a calamitous mistake to have too high or too low a regard for oneself as given. The less interesting extreme is probably the more usual: a complacent, satisfied view of one's own sweet self, actual or potential; for the splendid fellow one is or would be if only circumstances were different and more favorable; or for one's inwardness, one's goodness or genius which seems always to be misunderstood by the hostile and insensitive outside world.

The trouble with having too high a regard for oneself as given is not just that one is probably mistaken. This, in itself, makes a man no worse than annoying, foolish, or pathetic. "Now the man is thought to be proud who thinks himself worthy of great things, being worthy of them; for he who does so beyond his deserts is a fool, but no virtuous man is foolish or silly. . . .

He who claims more than he has with no ulterior object is a contemptible sort of fellow (otherwise he would not have delighted in falsehood), but seems futile rather than bad. . . ."[6] The more serious consequence of exaggerated self-regard is not its silliness but the fact that it keeps the complacent from making better use of the materials they have. It would not do to slight the self-satisfaction a complacent man can have; with luck it may keep him happy his whole life through. What is lost is the hope for a better satisfaction, the more intense reward that comes with the sense of accomplished form. Since the complacent are unaware of or unattracted to the more perfect shapes they might achieve, the fact that they are likely to remain lumpish natural objects may call forth little pity. Past this there remains the possibility of waking up one morning to find oneself nothing at all.

2. Contempt

The extreme of complacency is more comfortable and tends for that reason to be even more sterile than the extreme of contempt. Too low a regard for one's given self may result in an inhibiting, paralyzing self-contempt, a Nietzschean disgust that sicklies over the rest of the world, but that is first of all felt for the self, for all the self is, or knows, or could become.

There are many middling talents short of genius—surely all that most of us could claim for ourselves—that might amount to more than a little in the world's eyes or in their own, except that they are smothered by an overwhelming realization that they are not first-rate. That genius could be thus frozen seems as likely. Great creative gifts, great possibility of life, can be accompanied by a powerful critical sense; sometimes the latter, regardless of its justice, can check or stop the former. The venom then distilled often seeps into the finest texture of the thwarted life, and all the world is seen as shot through with infection. There are also those who can tolerate everything except themselves, who can forgive all except what they have done, whose scorn, in concave reflection, is caught and focused, burning, on the self. All these are metaphors of death and sickness, and their appropriateness lies in the nearness of self-contempt to suicide; near also to disease, to cancer, overgrowing hope, feeding on despair.

Self-contempt and suicide come from the loss of hope for form. It is true that suicide can come from boredom, but "boredom" only names a state of spirit, it does not explain it. Boredom does not grow from lack of mental resource; if it did, intelligent and imaginative people would never be bored. The trouble is not that one is unable to think of ways to live or things to do; it is to think of a thousand reasons for living, and to find them all uninteresting, not worth the effort. To be bored is to be tired, tired to death. It should be known, but it can help very little to know, that the interest of interesting things is not an intrinsic quality of them, that nothing is interesting or worth doing or loving except as someone finds it so. When whatever inner light it is that shines on things and makes them bright burns low, delusion about the source of value in things may be a comfort, and we may say that the presence or absence of value has nothing to do with ourselves. The fault is not in the things, it is in ourselves; we are never bored unless we are sick of ourselves.

The affliction of self-contempt is impossible without ambition; it arises when ambition is combined with some misapprehension of matter and form. It is only a rough distinction, but the dangerously self-despising can be seen to fall into two classes: (a) those who overestimate the value of some particular form, and (b) those who understand the need but underestimate the value of all form. It is also roughly true to say that the first mistake is likely to be made by the too-critical second-rate, and the second by a few men of original genius.

a. FROM GRETCHEN TO HELEN

Imagine a musician who knew exactly the kind of music he wanted to write, whether like that of Haydn or of Schönberg, and knew also that nothing he could do could compare in value with the work of his models and masters. Or take an example closer to home. Imagine an ordinary man who knew exactly the pattern he wanted his life to have, whether like that of Alexander, Henry Ford, or Albert Schweitzer, and knew also that the cherished form was far beyond his reach. But this is less an example than a description. It is a paradigm of common misfortune, of a modern disease.

There are many people who, like one of the Borgias, wear on their signets "Caesar or nothing," but who decide that their only real possibility is nothing. The ideal form to which they look, and of which they despair, may be trivial and vulgar to other eyes; this fact will not ease their pain, and need not lessen our sympathy. These may be people who have achieved enough freedom to see that the life they have led represents but one alternative among possible ways of living, who see that there can be better ways, if not for themselves, then possibly for their children. That their notions of "better" may be narrow and naïve, that they have given up all hope for themselves, does not rob their dreams of the power to work changes in the world, changes which can make for good, but which in proportion to the narrowness of their inspiration can equally make for bad. Even here there may operate a dim appreciation of the possibility that life can be given a conscious and satisfying order, but the general possibility may be lost in the admiration for some particular and unattainable form. The most probable consequence of ignorant idolatry is hopeless bitterness, a dull and constant sense of unjust defeat, or the rage to destroy, especially to destroy all that stands close to the one form on which the heart is set.

The idolators of one form fail to see that their ideal, like their actual lives, is but one alternative, one possible form of life among others of no less value. By identifying perfection with their accidental ideal, by mistaking one particular order for order itself, they stake their essential self-respect on an accidental game, almost always some game in which most players are losers. It is "success" to which they look—success which, though a bitch, is still a goddess—and having a vision of her nature at once glamorous, exalted, and narrow, they try and fail or never try at all, saying that success is beyond the likes of them, and hating themselves and their world for a foregone conclusion. This is no less true of the would-be painter than of the would-be assistant to the office manager, just as true of the ghostly Judith, Shakespeare's sister, as it is of Willy Loman. What they mean by "success" will be vastly different and equally narrow, mutually incomprehensible, and in practice equally precarious.

To overestimate the value of one particular form, to identify "success" with its achievement alone, is to set oneself on a path that almost always ends in a sense of formlessness and failure. There are those who have tried and failed and are bitter, and those who are too wise and bitter to try, all living uneasily in low country, unable to take their eyes away from the one height they have seen. Only a few are wise enough to break free from ideal fixations, to estimate the relation of their given means to ideal ends, and to set themselves toward attainable heights that are worth attaining. What the entranced worshipers of one version of success fail to see is the very human ground on which they stand; they may be closer to an appropriate height than they know. For as well as "overestimation of an accidental form," the present formula for self-contempt could be called "underestimation of given matter." Its sadness does not only lie in the ugliness of unnecessary failure. Looking away to some distant, wished-for pattern of life, the bitter dreamer overlooks the possibilities of form that lie in the life he has. In identifying human satisfaction with some received and beatified form of life—at the country club or in a garret, on Madison Avenue or on Tenth

Street, seen in the newspapers or hidden in the woods—it is too likely that potentialities which truly inhere in every human life will be despised in advance. So neglected, so uncultivated, they fester and die, and we discover that we have spent ourselves to buy nothing within our means, and have to show for our extravagance one little plot of rank and sour ground.

Most of us know that we are neither Mozart nor Cole Porter, neither St. Francis nor Scarlett O'Hara, neither immortal nor in the *Daily News*. Our foolishness comes in thinking that since we are not Caesar, we must be nothing, or that nothing we can be is worth the effort. This is a deadly underestimation of the matter we are given, of the potential order in the humblest human life. Good sense may be enough to tell us that we ought to accept our limitations and be reconciled to our abilities, but the point that goes beyond this carries deeper: within the conditions set by our common humanity—in fact, as a function of those very limitations, and impossible without them—can be perfected the form of human life itself, can be felt a sense of wholeness and significance, of order and value. How this is to be accomplished remains in part to be said; here we have seen only that to ignore or to scorn this possibility leads to unnecessary pain, to peripheral defeat taken as essential failure. If it is one kind of moral mistake to live uncritically in our nature as we find it, the opposite extreme, the contempt that leads us to despise the cultivation of our gardens, is no less mistaken.

b. FROM HELEN TO PARALYSIS

There is a related but probably rarer problem, the problem of seeming to see through everything. " 'Why does almost everything seem to me its own parody? Why must I think that almost all, no, all the methods and conventions of art today *are good for parody only?*' "[7] Adrian Leverkühn "misdoubted form, calling it pretense and play,"[8] and so does the Devil:

Work, time, and pretense, they are one, and together they fall victim to critique. It no longer tolerates pretense and play, the fiction, the self-glorification of form, which censors the passions and human suffering, divides out the parts, translates into pictures. Only the nonfictional is still permissible, the unplayed, the undisguised and untransfigured expression of suffering in its actual moment. . . . The criticism of ornament, convention and the abstract generality are all the same one. . . . The claim to consider the general harmonically contained in the particular contradicts itself. It is all up with the once bindingly valid conventions, which guaranteed the freedom of play.[9]

If there are those who misdoubt form because they fail to see its value, and those who mistrust their ability to achieve some particular form, there may be a smaller number who are well aware of the virtues of order, but to whom all patterns seem obvious, played-out, and stale. (One might want to distinguish between those who really "see through" and those who only think they do, but their affective situation is the same. If what is to be said applies to the former, it will apply to the latter as well.) There may be men of original genius who understand so well the conventions that their time or their art has developed that they could do great things within these forms, and who for that reason think all such forms unworthy. The man who gets this far may be on his way to a breakthrough that will bring back new possibilities of life; he may also be on his way to the daemonic. His road will be darkest if he not only rejects the historical patterns of the person and the time, but seems to understand too easily all the possibilities of any new dispensation which could be devised.

The artist and the prophet of new forms of feeling may think in their beginnings to reject all form. They may try to put aside the received paradigms of their time and place, but if they have a true vocation they will learn that their calling is creative, and that the rejection of old forms entails the creation of new. If the creator's critical insight is sharp and his criteria too demanding, the new creations, like the old, will be mercilessly seen through, seen as senile in imagination before they are born in time. There is a truth here that is dangerous to grasp unless one also accepts its complement: of course it is true that nothing really matters. It is not only that there is nothing new under the sun or that what is fresh and innocent grows old and tired and corrupt; it is that to pure affectless intelligence all forms are equally forms, and equally vain. Men create patterns to give their lives direction and meaning, and these may seem no more than invented games with toys for prizes, dances we set ourselves to dance, mountains to climb, so that we can tell ourselves we have done something real. The sane magician never tricks himself, and in his pride of intellect may see only what seems to him the artifice and arbitrariness of any form that he or anyone could create. But what is not seen, or rather not felt, is that it is the heart's affections that make things holy. The patterns of feeling we find or create can give rise to a sense of purpose truly felt, to a genuine satisfaction. Pure critical intelligence creates the emptiness it feels, for seeing form as an empty or arbitrary trick, it cannot understand that the rewards of order are felt as perfectly real, or that there are some forms that suit the whole human so well that the more humane intelligence can call them "natural."

The too-critical creator may thus be caught in an affective paradox. Understanding the necessity for order, he may feel all order as artifice and feel that he sees through it to an emptiness beyond. Our question must concern the criteria by which he feels and judges. Against what standard shall our human devices be judged and declared artificial? The critic who says that nothing really matters, that nothing is really worth hoping for or loving, that one pattern of life is as good as another since all are arbitrary and none avails, must be made to tell us the model to which our sense of satisfied form is to be compared and condemned as unreal. Then the clue to his killing vision may appear. Knowing the penetration of his insight, contrasting his clarity with the foolish infatuation of other men, he is less likely to judge himself wanting by reference to what he in his proper person could accomplish or become, than by reference to what anyone could accomplish, what anyone could become. Taking himself at his highest value, he may despise mankind with a passion beyond that of other men because his judgment follows from criteria beyond theirs: he may be in love with the impossible.

Contempt for all possible form, when it is combined with an understanding of the need for form, is contempt for human potentiality itself. The man who sees himself as standing on some new frontier of humanity, and who sees the promised land as another desert, is despising humanity when he scorns himself. If he has pity, he will wear a mask to keep others from knowledge of his annihilating vision. If he speaks, he will speak in riddles. If he would still fulfill his calling, live at once according to his lights and honestly, his ambition will lead him to ways that are lonely, dark, and bitter—not least dark and bitter because the man who sees through the principles that have organized life and art still has these principles living in his conscience. His sensibility has been shaped by the forms he would now transcend, and transcendence cannot be distinguished from transgression.

The man who would give new laws suffers a bad conscience; his object is transformation, and he feels himself brother to the criminal and to the madman. He feels himself cut off from those he takes to be comfortably conservative, from the traditional, from the academic, from the bourgeois who lives and works within the bounds the new man would break through. He feels sick when he looks at the "normal," healthy, happily stupid men among whom he lives. From the shadows he looks with longing and contempt, sidelong at their blue eyes, then moves on, troubled and alone. Contempt and longing, for he is also they. So far as he is human they live in him, and it is his own humanity he loves and hates. Often the man so marked will despise the bourgeoisie in favor of peasant naïveté or coarse barbarian vitality. He can think that only the spontaneous is unspoiled, the *ur*-spontaneous and elemental, and that goodness and beauty must be found in the lowly.

Inevitably, when he finds himself in Auerbach's Saloon he does not like it very much, and inevitably he soon gets bored with Gretchen. This barbarism is too nostalgic, too sentimental, to be true. Most minds susceptible to this hankering are far too cultivated and subtle to find any approach to the real thing other than repellent or boring. The enchantment of the view requires distance: all traditions are stifling unless they are recondite, overripe, decadent, or dead. Any culture to escape condemnation must be far removed in time or space, or at least at that moment detached or cut off from the mainstream of common tradition. Once upon a time there was ancient Greece, medieval Europe, pre-colonial America; now there is the African or Australasian village, simple Mexico, dark Harlem. For everything else the deep and suffering genius feels a particidal hatred, a not-quite-confident contempt.

How much real uneasiness there is in this, and how much pose, is not a question that can be answered in general. What does seem necessary to the mixture is a strong if ambivalent conceit. The feelings of proud criminality, of *sehnsucht*, of sickness, of love and hate of one's unhealthiness, its privileges and its badges of alienation—these intensely ambivalent feelings flourish best in the climate of introspection, of supposed self-knowledge that never doubts the hateful superiority of its subject. The marks and scars of this self-scorning are taken by those who wear them to be the sign of genius itself. Thinking himself the only type of true genius, the sufferer may scorn all those who work within a tradition, even those who are the culmination and fulfillment of a tradition.[10] It is always easy to conclude that this or that pattern of expression—personal, artistic, social—is stale and exhausted, and not very extraordinary men may be tempted to conclude further that all propriety of form, all conventions, disciplines, techniques are worthless. But imagine the man who thinks that he has in himself not only the past and the present but also the future, who thinks that in him if in anyone lies the matter for so-far unrealized forms—and who cannot feel these forms to be other than contemptible devices.

Is this contempt for form or contempt for matter? The classification breaks down here; it is irrelevant. The man who has identified what can be done with what he can do can hate indifferently the possible and himself. Such proud contempt for the self and any forms it could devise is terribly close to our last form, close to *rigor mortis*. For many the road goes from Gretchen to Helen, and for some from Helen to paralysis. The latter few are those who combine in themselves the furthest extremes of self-consciousness, pride, and self-contempt.

C. THE DAEMONIC RAPTUS

The guilty genius is a man of bad conscience. He must break laws thought to be in need of breaking but felt to be most profound, felt so because they are a part of his deepest self. He would break through the old laws to create a new, but his standards are always set just the other side of the impossible, set at infinity; his judgment of the possible is absolute and damning. Held fast in the clarity of his vision, frozen in self-contempt, he may think that his only help can be found in the fires of hell. The recruits to the Devil's party are those who see in the Devil an ally against the established order of things in the world and in themselves. Those most desperate for relief are the paralyzed, the creators fixed into immobility by self-judgment. Immoderate self-consciousness is a polar extreme, and those who have abused self-knowledge so far cannot break free except by the invocation of a powerful and hateful force. It need not be syphilis of the brain, but it must be some sickness of the mind, some insanity that will serve as a liberation, something to kill the pain of criticism. What is needed is intoxication, the drowning rush of mania, delirium. A man will throw himself toward madness if he is desperate to destroy the awareness of limitation and the sense of criticism; this is the Devil who takes us away from our hateful, clear-seeing selves. The more we need the Devil the more we hate him and fear his visits and the more we hate ourselves for our need and our fear, but anything is better than the eye fixed on itself.

If it is obvious that this is the excess that leads to invocation of the daemonic, it may be less obvious that the scorn which leads to the Devil is in essence turned on the self. Its most visible and public expression is contempt for the world, for prevailing forms of morality, religion, or art, and this contempt may be sincerely and passionately felt. But first and last is hate of the self: conceit, ambition, and contempt; intellectual pride and self-consciousness; and a kind of proudly despairing seeing through in advance anything the self could become or accomplish. It appears to be the world that is condemned, and so it is, but the first to fall under the judgment, the first to fall and carry all else with him, is the judge. He cannot but condemn, for his judgment is made by reference to the impossible.

This is neurosis, almost by definition. To be neurotic is to be exhausted, unhappy, rigid, while madness can be an energetic, euphoric state. The madman has wings, or thinks he has; his warmth is the heat of fever, but he burns. To be in love with the impossible while keeping sanity enough to know that all such loves are hopeless from the start is never to begin; is, naturally, to accomplish nothing. If, frozen, a man remains ambitious not merely to pursue the Eternal Feminine but to live with the goddess herself, the daemonic may appear as his only hope. In madness he may think to overcome that criticism which shows the impossible in its proper light, but which to him makes any attempt at action, at creation, seem unworthy of the effort. So from ice he runs to fire, to elemental, passionate, self-forgetful activity.

The Devil, as Blake saw, is the great advocate of intuition; it is the Devil who clears the way for inspiration. The Devil blocks off some part of the brain, burns out the scornful, critical eye, and one sees through no more, at least not for the time being. Set free from intellect, from criticism, from paralysis, one seems to fly. And for the honest moralist here is the rub: sometimes one does fly.

In some particular cases the alternative of intoxication or paralysis may be genuine and exclusive. So far as calculation is then possible, each man must estimate probable losses and gains, the cost of madness and the likelihood that from it something worth the cost will come. The odds are poor for most of us. The voice of Daemonic temptation itself insists that "Where nothing is, there the Devil too has lost his right and no pallid Venus produces anything worth while! We make naught new—that is other people's matter. We only release, only set free." Our matter—and if what is set free is not worth the cost, the Devil has his usual best of the bargain.

But how much calculation can there be? And how shall the estimate be made? It would be false and dangerous to pretend to precision in the answer, or to an automatic application to particular cases. The particular judgment must be made by the particular man, and only the dogmatist would venture general prescriptions certainly applicable to concrete situations. To be honest here is to remember the empirical and affective grounds of moral judgment and to be tentative. We can say that the resort to madness is itself no proof of genius, and that even the genuine genius who needs this help is not the only kind of genius; in this, as usual, the Devil is a liar. We can say that the man who calls the fires of hell to his aid is likely the man who is frozen in self-contempt, that to be tempted to this desperate liberation is to be caught between a pride which probably exceeds its ground and a contempt which is in part a hatred of the possible. But how can we say that the bargain or bet is never worth making and should never be made? To know this we should have to know each man even better than he can know himself. It is always dangerous to trust the Devil, but there is no support for a general claim that the risk can in no case be justified. It is possible to describe the probable causes, costs, and odds, but if to a particular man there comes what seems a need and a chance to decide between ice and fire, the responsibility for the decision must be his alone.

d. THE USE AND ABUSE OF SELF-KNOWLEDGE

The last word is unexciting and plain. Self-knowledge is an instrumental good and, like many instruments, is dangerous when ill-used. There is little hope and much trouble for the man who fails to know himself, but in this peculiar reflection are inherent tendencies to distortion; those most sure of their grasp of themselves are most likely to have hold of a lie. All of us tend to think in extremes in thinking about ourselves, and often the more we introspect the more extreme our estimates become. It is easy to characterize the extremes: a lumpish contentment with all the accidents of the given self, and at the other extreme the Medusa of hateful pride, the paralytic conviction that in seeing through oneself one has seen through everything.

The problem of finding a hopeful mean between these can only be solved by each person who has the problem; its solution will vary with person and circumstance, with some best tending toward one extreme and others toward the other. The mean is never a mere mathematical average; we cannot be averaged that way. We are alike enough to recognize unhappy extremes when we see them, but we are not so much alike that we need fear all immoderations equally.

Insofar as we are alike, generally useful recommendations are possible. Because no object of knowledge and judgment is more singular than the self, the application of general recommendations must be left to each who would use them. It is a safe generalization that we are seldom so good or so bad as we think.

The plain and abstract statement is a platitude, and nothing is more important to the conduct of life than the proper use of it in one's practice of self-estimation. The problem for each of us is to strike an appropriate balance between acceptance and aspiration, between those aspects of our situation and ourselves which we must accept as setting the conditions of our work and those forms of life and feeling for which we can reasonably hope. Too great a disproportion between possibilities and hopes leads to defeat and to bitterness that might have been avoided by a juster estimate of given matter and attainable form. To think too little or too much of oneself, to place beyond reach or to value too little the lives and works one might achieve, are injustices that come more easily than does equitable self-judgment.

Since we will err, it is better to hope too much than too little; more good may be lost through diffidence than harm be done through pride. Allow for error, but also allow that the chances for a life found good and fruitful are bettered by a true and temperate knowledge of the self.

VI

THE BEARING OF TRADITION

And custom, for the spreading laurel tree.[1]
Where all's accustomed, ceremonious;
For arrogance and hatred are the wares
Peddled in the thoroughfares.
How but in custom and in ceremony
Are innocence and beauty born?
Ceremony's a name for the rich horn,
And custom, for the spreading laurel tree.[1]
WILLIAM BUTLER YEATS, *"A Prayer for My Daughter"*

What are the appropriately human forms? It is easier to understand the mistakes one can make in estimating the need and importance of order than it is to specify patterns that will be felt as meaningful. We cannot say with Aristotle, "The purpose of the present study is not, as it is in other inquiries, the attainment of theoretical knowledge: we are not conducting this inquiry to know what virtue is, but in order to become good, else there would be no advantage in studying it."[2] Although we may want to become good, we do not think we know in advance what virtue is. The essence of humanity seemed clear to Aristotle, and his recommendation of rationality was based on this assumed theoretical knowledge. Without such assurance on the score of essence, with a wider knowledge of human history than he had, our notions of good form can be neither so certainly based nor so specific. Even so, any attempt to specify patterns of the good life must justify their pertinence by some appeal to human nature and must show that the ways they recommend are likely to repay the devotion they cost. If our ideas of man are based on nothing more recondite than history, tradition, and experience, and our recommendations related to these in non-deductive ways, it is no less true than it ever was that a sensible moral theory must establish connection between human nature and the human good.

Such connection always exists, at least implicitly, not only in moral theories but in the moral life. Our notions of what we ought to do and be most often arise from secret paradigms of human nature. Whether we know it or not, most of our attempts at goodness and beauty are imitations. To deplore this is to lament an inevitability. It is more to the point to try to understand it and to put the understanding to good use. Not that there are new discoveries to be made here; there are only forgotten lessons to be recalled and common practices to be clarified. Plato and Aristotle have debated the question, and systems of education long successful in their object have recognized the affective import of moral models. To make this insight explicit and to apply it is only to justify and generalize what every parent knows. But the parent of all parents as moral philosophers is Aristotle, and we can best begin to see the uses of imitation by understanding the role he thought it played in life and art.

Plato and Aristotle both say that art is imitation, but they differ radically in their assignment of value to art. Their differences depend on metaphysical disagreement. For Plato there is a difference in reality between form and matter, universals and concrete things. With respect to the world of matter, the tangible world we see and feel about us, the senses, ourselves as given, Plato agrees with Protagoras. Matter means unintelligibility; feeling is the subversive agent of chaos. In this world, man *is* the measure—which proves to Plato that goodness and beauty must have some better home. In the world of sense you cannot step into the same river twice, which proves that earthly streams cannot be known; they can be felt, but it is exactly in our sentience that we are most individual and lost. There is no truth in the senses; they give only opinion. Knowledge must transcend the conditions of sense and rise to a wholly rational grasp of form, of independently subsisting universals: not the seen shape of this wheel, the feel of this coin, or the rim of that cup, but the essence which all of these share. The one timeless and immutable essence of Circularity is the object of knowledge. Circularity itself cannot be identified with any particular imitations of it. If Circularity could be found in any place, if it were just this wheel or just that coin, or a particular thought in someone's mind, it could not be that which the wheel, the coin, and the thought have in common, nor could we call the rim of the cup circular. Even in the context of geometry the moral bearing of this begins to be apparent. Circularity itself is perfect, while every seen and particular circle is only approximate, striving toward an unattainable perfection and inevitably falling short. Imperfect circles change their shape, are burdened with matter, and disappear. Their goodness, which lies beyond them, is not subject to accident and is always the same. We can know perfection because we have truer and better knowledge than sense can give us, but our knowledge is tragic, its object being a reality beyond sensible reach, beyond space and time, unrealizable in the world of changing material things. Our lower world is so incomplete, so desperately imperfect, that there must be another world— there *must* be. We look out of the world of sense and body as out of a prison, and our truest hope must be the hope to escape.

The One remains, the many change and pass; only the eternal can be truly known, and only the unattainable can content us. Our best course must be to detach ourselves from temporal things, free our reason, and try with the mind's eye alone to see forms in their purity. Plato never makes clear the relation of these supersensible forms to their wordly and possible imitations, but if this leaves the world of the possible beneath the reach of reason, we can only conclude that this is the world's misfortune. This world is weighted down with matter, shot through with chaos. It is not pure, not radiant. The light it has is stained or comprehended in darkness. The way to the only forms that could content us lies beyond the limits of mortality.

To make a positive aesthetics of this requires a deal of distortion. Art and imitation have a low and disreputable place in Plato's explicit theoretical scheme. In one of this artist's most famous phrases, art is an imitation of an imitation. Plato supposes that the artist takes as his task the exact and illusionistic reproduction of some particular thing, a particular which is itself an imperfect manifestation of a perfect archetype. The artist thus works at a third or even a fourth remove from reality, imitating from a particular point of view a particular thing that imitates a distant universal. The artist and the spectator-victim are pulled away from the real and learn to value illusion over truth. Poets are liars, and particulars are far less often ladders than they are snares. Operating on the lowest level of opinion and unreality, art appeals only to our emotional nature, stirs up the muddy depths of our affections, and distracts us from our better end, from the flight of unfettered reason to the good, the beautiful, and the true.

For Aristotle the matter is otherwise. Plato reserves the claim of full reality for abstract universals. For Aristotle particulars, "substances," are real. Substances are irrefragable conjunctions of universal and particular, of form and matter. Better, form and matter are aspects, separable only analytically, of substances. The materiality of things gives them their location in space and time; in its terms we distinguish this coin from that coin, this wheel from that wheel. As circular they are the same; as things that might be given distinct proper names they differ. On the other hand, two cups made of clay are alike in their matter ("matter" relative to the cup, but "form" relative to mud), which the coin and the cup are not. Two lumps of clay waiting their turn on the potter's wheel have like potentiality, but an ingot of silver and a tree trunk do not. While Plato saw change as virtual chaos, Aristotle tries to provide a framework in which change is intelligible: natural change is an ordered progression from matter to form, from potentiality to actuality. Actualization is the approach to an appropriate universal. A substance achieves its highest degree of reality, of naturalness, when it comes closest to manifesting the perfection of its type. An acorn is a potential oak; the ideal oak tree is its definition and goal. The essence of humanity is the formal and final cause of each human. Ideal form is not in another world, tragically removed from this. The appropriate ends of things are potential in their matter and stand as the natural limit in a course of natural growth.

The difference between form transcendent and form immanent lies behind the different lights in which Plato and Aristotle see imitation. For Aristotle, art imitates the universal, and the universal is embodied—imperfectly realized, partly manifest —in the particular; we must look to the particular to see the type. Art is not an attempt to reproduce a singular view of one concrete individual, but an effort to exemplify as perfectly as possible the universal which the particular has but dimly realized. "Art completes what nature cannot bring to a finish. The artist gives us knowledge of nature's unrealized ends."[3] It is because the proximate aim of art is to elicit the universal from the particular that Aristotle holds poetry to be more philosophic than history. The historian reports the half-intelligible course of things; the poet, not bound to report, can by his art make the form and import of things stand clear. His art is arrangement: he deploys particulars, shapes his material into a pattern more clearly rhythmic, complete, and arresting than are unnoticed forms of thoughtless life, and thus brings home to us the universal aspects of our common situation. The recurrent and typical in each ordinary life is obscured by distractions and by the very details through which it exists; the artist, by controlling our attention, leads us to the universal through the particular. The artist and the philosopher work in different ways to a similar end: each tries to disengage the themes of things from their particular occasions. While the philosopher presents these themes as a set of ordered abstractions, the artist embodies them in ideally ordered particulars. The arrangement and incarnation of universals, the re-creation of form, is what gives art its universal significance and its moral force.

. . . it is usually through artistic expression that the highest values acquire permanent significance and the force which moves mankind. Art has a limitless power of converting the human soul—a power which the Greeks called psychagogia. *For art alone possesses the two essentials of educational influence—universal significance and immediate appeal. By uniting these two methods of influencing the mind, it surpasses both philosophical thought and actual life. Life has immediate appeal, but the events of life lack universal significance: they have too many accidental accompaniments to create a truly deep and lasting impression on the soul. Philosophy and abstract thought do attain to universal significance: they deal with the essence of things; yet they affect none but the man who can use his own experience to inspire them with the vividness and intensity of personal life. Thus, poetry has the advantage over both the universal teachings of abstract reason and the accidental events of individual experience. It is more philosophical than life (if we may use Aristotle's famous epigram in a wider sense), but it is also, because of its concentrated spiritual actuality, more lifelike than philosophy.*[4]

To reject Aristotle's hypostatization of essences or natures is not to lose all hope of learning something useful from the system. There are common and recurrent patterns or themes in the human situation, and there are perennially recurrent types of character; each situation and each life is unique, yet none is without its correspondences. The order that seems to produce illumination, that does produce the sense of clarification and completeness (rather than a sense of distraction, pleasant or unpleasant), is one that exemplifies a humanly relevant universal. The creative imitation and the moral function of the artist combine in eliciting these patterns and making them at once concrete and clear, intense and luminous, more likely to feel to us informed than our cluttered and monotonous lives ever do.

A. IMITATION AND FORM

If there were pure and abstract forms of human goodness, and if these were directly accessible to reason, imitation in its most obvious senses would be unnecessary; theoretical knowledge of the good would be sufficient to lead the fully rational man to the practice of goodness. Since nothing supports these hopes, it is fortunate that moral virtue does not depend on a rational grasp of ideal forms by fully rational men. Human goodness exists insofar as it informs some humans. When Aristotle tells us that good is what the good man does, and recommends that we imitate the good man, he means that we can and should model ourselves on the man who realizes, as nearly as his matter will allow, an ideal form. The movement in which we take a particular as exemplary, take a real or legendary or typical life as a model for our own, creates for each who makes it an affective connection between fact and value, between the "is" and the "ought to be." The linguistic or logical break between factual and normative sentences is neither closed nor even patched by this; "ought" statements remain undeducible from descriptions. The last bridge between these is affective, although even the metaphor of bridging is not altogether apt. It is rather that our attitude invests some factual exemplar with the operative significance of a norm.

The ease with which we can conclude that Aristotle's recommendation is circular should lead us to suspect that we may thus miss his point. The apparently circular saying, "Good is what the good man does," marks a basic fact about our moral situation: to a large extent we become what we are through imitation. What we feel to be good, what we call "good," what we try to realize as our good, is what our idol is and does. Most of us, for longer than we could consciously know, pattern ourselves in imitation of some model. Our original choices are seldom deliberate. We fall into half-conscious commitment, and subsequent sophisticated definitions of "good" and "bad," "beautiful" and "ugly," are conditioned by the nature of our moral paradigm. What happens in the beginning is less like choice and more like a reciprocal relation of love and need. Later one finds that through habits formed in imitation of an ideal affective patterns have been established that shape the whole of life, that can be truly chosen only if consciously rechosen, and that can be changed in direction and form only by deliberate revision.

It is reassuring to be able to agree alike with Aristotle and with common sense that habit lies at the heart of the moral life. This is not to denigrate the factor of choice, but choice is generally a factor of habits of choice, and such habits are seldom chosen. One function of moral philosophy is to bring such habits to light, to show the individual what he has become, and to present him with the possibility of conscious and principled choice. The conscious moral life is always a balance or tension between ourselves as we have come to be and are—our given matter informed by habit—and our revisions and reconstructions of that ground, our attempts to find or to create order and form. But it is practice that makes perfect and imperfect: past choices have made our disposition; conscious choices must be exercised into habitual patterns of choice if they are significantly to shape our lives. There must be more to this than an ephemeral sense of harmony—a drug can produce that. It is rather that "real harmony, by which eventual conflicts and mutual destruction are obviated, must be partially established in the realm of matter before the feeling or the love of harmony can be a guide for rational ethics."[5]

The ground of such feeling is affective and habitual. If a sense of order and purpose is to be other than occasional, noticeable only because of its usual absence, order must be established in one's life through discipline and practice. What moves only the mind does not move enough, and the random stirrings of emotion produce order only by chance. Concrete exemplifications of the good can move the whole man, can lay down dispositions of recognition and choice that inform the various moments of his life, that effect a rhythmic integration felt to be meaningful and right. Habits are the soul's foundation; patterns of habit are the architecture of the soul itself. Only a jejune rationalism could fail to see that if the moral life is to be other than a perpetual series of original and abortive beginnings without harmony or growth in wisdom, it must grow from dispositional grounds. And dispositions are not made by argument.

It is not too much to hope that the whole of experience can be given an inherent form which will satisfy the need for a sense of significance. This humane satisfaction can be obtained by a liberal expenditure of life, by intensity neither hoarded nor dissipated but fully spent within limits set by a just estimation of resources and hopes. But this hope must base itself on patterns of choice that seem almost instinctive and that are in fact dispositions acquired and perfected. Habit is for better and worse the great stabilizer of life, the force of inertia which can work for good or ill, in this depending on the direction of its exercise. The habits that shape us, or that are our shape, have been learned more through imitation than through theoretical teaching; their expression is selective attention, emphasis, and choice. To say that these conative-affective dispositions are the great conservatives of life is not to say that by the time we think to consider them our lives are too far gone in habit to be reformed. It is to say that conscious moral choice, whether to continue or to re-form, is itself a function (though it need not be an obvious or direct one) of given habits. This is true even when choice would be a first step toward a new life. When a new possibility of life seems most concrete and real the fruitful strain between what we are and what we would be is most intense. When the imitation of a model begins to feel natural and familiar, when exercise requires less effort of will and conscious choice, a new order is coming into our lives. When the manifestations of habit appear with the grace of instinct, when they bring with them that sense of fitting pleasure that Aristotle calls an added reward of the moral life, a new form has been attained.

The fundamental character of affective habits is important to both moral conduct and moral argumentation. The formation of disposition on a moral model is a continuing process. Although the effect of imitation is most intense in childhood, we are never beyond the reach of its efficacy. (Whoever else may have forgotten this, advertisers have not.) So far as our character is not determined by intellection alone, that far will affective models bear on our lives, and do so whether we know it or not. If there is a question to be asked about imitation, it is not whether we shall imitate, but whom. The educational importance of the question is obvious.

1. *Adjustment*

The question "Whom shall we imitate?" has both personal and social dimensions, and these can to some extent be distinguished. The social question can be translated "Who shall set the tone? What group or class shall set the standards for its environing society?" If this question is interpreted as a demand that there be a class to set the tone, it is misinterpreted: there always *is* such a class. The tawdriness of popular taste reflects the fact that its tone is set each moment by itself, by those who flatter it for money, and by the vulgar rich. There is influence or contagion, propagation like that of ripples in a pond, all on the same level.

There is no name for the doctrine that calls "valuable" anything that happens to be valued. As a vague, implicit premise of popular philosophy it probably represents a vulgarization of utilitarianism, of "descriptivism" or "naturalism" in the Mill-Dewey sense of the terms. In a wholly democratic measure of value, each of each person's values counts equally. The version of the good that emerges from this will comprehend all that is necessary to life and much that all men desire, but it is unlikely to go beyond what might be expressed by an articulate mole: warmth, comfort, security, "happiness" in the least demanding, the most fetal sense.

These animal goods *are* good; the best of men have added their desires for these things to the calculation of the mean. We may feel that no goods beyond these can be expected until these have been attained, and it is a mark of good sense to feel an obligation to provide them where they are lacking. But these necessities do not exhaust the human good, and this too has a social and moral bearing. Those who know that these goods leave much to be desired may at times need to summon a sense of resistance: to refuse to accept as complete what are in fact partial criteria; to reject the insinuations of the more articulate moles when they suggest that everyone is or ought to be like them, that there are no (normal or healthy) non-moles, that we are obliged to accept their mole's ideal of human nature, adjust to their values, and assent to the creation of a mole-centered world.

The claim that the mole's-eye view is omniscient may be comical or pathetic, but it can be an underground power move by a would-be super-mole. Beyond pointing to the impertinence of this and to its possible dangers, what is said here should not be construed as a social doctrine. Our view is based on a reasonable hope for the expression of a complex human nature, and it seems unlikely that such expression can be forwarded if we all simply imitate each other. If in a cultural democracy the group that sets standards is the majority, and if their norm forecloses on possibilities which they cannot or will not know, those who see further need neither accept nor condemn more limited views, unless the lowest common denominator constitutes itself a crusade, in which case its universal claims must be resisted. Full and coherent forms of life are not in principle the exclusive property of an elect. The patterns we shall describe and recommend are attainable by most of us, and in this sense what is said is democratic. Their achievement is natural in that they express the actualization of naturally human directions and potencies, but not "natural" in the sense of effortless and easy—not at first.

Everything nature does is natural, and nothing natural is easier than following the principle of least effort. What seems easiest for most people is imitation of the other people they happen to know. Happiness can be had this way, and it is always a question whether to disturb this little happiness on the chance that the person disturbed might achieve a greater. It is not a question that can be answered in general. It is possible to say that the conscious realization of human naturalness and the sense of meaning this accomplishment earns are not likely to be found along the path of least resistance. These achievements require discrimination and the selection that discrimination demands, discipline and the subordination of some interests for the sake of a more perfect whole. If it is asked "Why do this? Why consider the whole of life at all, or try to see and shape it in the light of some difficult and distant ideal model?" the first and approximate answer must be that the best chance of discovering a sense of meaning and of worth lies in this way of life. We feel that we have met the demands of our humanity, have approached our peculiarly human final cause, when our life has been formed in the light of a demanding and appropriate ideal form.

2. *Aristocracy*

It is easy to fall into a nostalgia for aristocratically oriented societies, especially since they have all disappeared. Since some group will always seem to exemplify the formal and final cause of its wider society, there are real advantages for all when this group is a privileged class—as long as the class knows how to pay for its privileges. In the heroic beginning, when Sarpedon made his speech to Glaukos, the payment was simple:

Glaukos, why is it you and I are honored before others
with pride of place, the choice meats and the filled
wine cups
in Lykia, and all men look on us as if we were immortals,
and we are appointed a great piece of land by the banks
of Xanthos,
good land, orchard and vineyard, and ploughland for the
planting of wheat?
Therefore it is our duty in the forefront of the Lykians
to take our stand, and bear our part of the blazing of
battle,
so that a man of the close-armoured Lykians may say of
us:
"Indeed, these are no ignoble men who are lords of Lykia,
these kings of ours, who feed upon the fat sheep
appointed
and drink the exquisite sweet wine, since indeed there is
strength
of valour in them, since they fight in the forefront
of the Lykians."
Man, supposing you and I, escaping this battle,
would be able to live on forever, ageless, immortal,
so neither would I myself go on fighting in the foremost
nor would I urge you into the fighting where men
win glory.
But now, seeing that the spirits of death stand close
about us

217

*in their thousands, no man can turn aside nor escape
    them,
let us go on and win glory for ourselves, or yield it
    to others.*[6]

Complexity does not change the principle. All have something all regard as worthy of high place; all have models accepted as deserving of imitation. A stable, self-perpetuating, privileged class is in the best position to fulfill this moral function. To do this it must deliberately accept the obligations of its role as repository of tradition and symbol of continuity and maintain its consciousness of place and duty by an almost familial discipline. The sense of continuity itself is one of the first products of this training, and it alone is a beneficent and informing influence. The more easily position changes, the more difficult it is to maintain this sense; where money is the sole determinant of social place, class memory disappears. It is not a value judgment but a historical or social fact that when membership in the only group taken as worth imitation is determined *wholly* in terms of cash momentarily on hand, that group does not play a morally responsible role in its society. This statement need not be supported by any mystique of landed property or old wealth: it is hard to find anything surprising in the fact that money in the bank is not a sufficient cause of social responsibility. The assumption of such responsibility by a class imposes difficult obligations, since it calls for an ordering of inclinations according to the form and function of the class, but when no group takes the role of paradigm as its moral vocation, a likely result is social and moral chaos.

Without fixed points of reference the people wander; within the ambience created by the sense of continuity, and difficult though not impossible without it, deliberate discipline can foster the Aristotelian ideal of good form. The individual in this context is most readily taught to see his task as the imitation of ideal humanity, as the achievement of a perfected human nature. It is not that direct apprehension of the ideal is here mysteriously possible, but here one begins by learning to imitate the defining characteristics of a class taken as closest to the ideal, a class that knows the educational advantage of having visible exemplars, members presumably valued in proportion to their manifestation of the ideal. When education by imitation of class ideals is practiced on the upper levels of a stable society, something of its sense animates the whole. To the generality it seems appropriate that one's models should be one's forebears, family, or class; at least this feels more natural and more graceful. Where these historical and visible groups embody respected traditions, they furnish a framework and support for the development of forms of life that rest on deliberately created habits and that have thus an inner assurance and order and an outer grace found satisfying by their exemplars and to their spectators.

It is in this sense that Aristotle means "to be a gentleman requires birth and breeding." "Breeding" is the establishment of affective forms so deep they are virtually instinctive, so intimate that their expression seems to be an instinctive sense of the proper importance of things. This is the source of that assurance which infuriates the envious. It is not in the blood, but in the training, in the fact that traditional forms have been as perfectly as possible impressed on the affections of those born to the tradition. While the matter of personality was most malleable, the patterns held essential to the class, its own conscious definition of ideal humanity, were set on it, gave it a universal stamp. Tradition thus becomes, to those who feel it, the word made flesh, their *logos:* what it says is humanly important, worth intensity, they accept and become.

a. THE INCARNATE UNIVERSAL

So far as it concerns the creation of character, aristocratic moral education is not a process of eliminating intensity, but of focusing or informing it. *Nil admirari* is too extreme a formulation; the basic lesson is more humane. It is that not everything is equally wonderful, that some events, situations, and crises are worth more intensity than others. To the vulgar the negative side may be more evident. Since their enthusiasm is indiscriminate, their devotion as given to the accidental as to the essential, any discrimination will strike them as artificial and cold. Compared with common affective slackness and sprawl, or with the gush and spontaneous overflow of feeling, attention to form may seem rigid and strained. But the refusal to give oneself indiscriminately to things as they come should be no more than the other side of affective concentration. The tradition singles out and celebrates actions, occasions, and objects that are fit for human concern. In the ways of its heroes it discovers the themes it holds to be worth attention, cultivation, intensity. Here custom is the most reassuring guide. Its followers feel that their order knows better than each new individual could the things that are important in human life, the things that repay devotion; this feeling tends to create its confirmation. Aristocratic discipline does not kill intensity, but forces passion back on itself and gives it deliberate direction. The sense of form itself becomes intense, and the form is felt to be that of ideal humanity.

Aristocratic discipline does all that deliberate moral training can do. It makes a second nature as strong as the first, a second nature supposed to be the perfection of the first, and it does this consciously and purposively. By regulating attention and concern, by directing intensity into ideal patterns, it creates a comprehensive affective form that is felt concretely as a universal. It may value the individual too little and despise the intellect too much, but it rightly sees that intellectual recognition of human likeness cannot be counted on for deep moral effects. That sense of humanity which those not formed on universal models may never find until their peculiar shape is broken by pain, the reconciliation with form which the purely critical can neither achieve nor forget except in madness

—the presence of that sense, informed, is the immanent justification and reward of the life that embodies a confident vision of what human life should be. Form itself is sensed as the contour of matter, the structure of feeling; if this shape is felt to be universal, if the force of intensity is sensed as filling out its ideal pattern, life itself will be experienced as intensity in its perfectly human form.

b. THE PAROCHIAL UNIVERSAL

The trouble is we know too much. We can see that the gentleman of tradition was deeply parochial in taking the ideals of a specific and historically conditioned class for the actual essence of the human genus. Perhaps unknown to him, and perhaps unfortunately for would-be inheritors, his local and historical limitations were a source of assurance and strength. This would not be so if education in form were intellectual; then, conditions of place and time might be transcended by pure reason and the achievement of form regulated by reference to an absolute metaphysical measure. The gentleman (or his more intellectual spokesmen) claimed this to be so. Tradition itself had its justification in a theological and metaphysical picture of reality, a teleological structure, tiered and hierarchical, of which society was an imitation.

There is no necessary connection between the cognitive utility of this vision and the affective benefits of the discipline it was used to justify. The world view was scientifically useless, the discipline of great use. In practice, metaphysical justification counted for little. The gentleman seldom had much regard for theory, and the modicum of assurance it might give the intellect was nothing compared with the emotional certitudes bred by local prejudice. Good form to him was the conative-affective pattern that felt properly, rightly human; his sufficient purpose was to fulfill that form by imitation. Whatever their rationalization, his judgments of form and sense of purpose were a function of cultural and personal familiarity, in fact reflected all the limitations of the training that produced them. The genuine aristocratic virtues—the absolute assurance, poise, and grace; the ordered, inner certitudes that show themselves with the appearance of instinctive tact; the confident sense of purpose in representing the highest form of humanity by living out its ideal pattern—are not independent of the certainties of the shire.

The gentleman as defined by tradition aspired to nothing less than becoming a concrete universal. Guided and sustained by his limitations, he took as his moral ideal the cultivation of humanity. His life was a work of art and its models those exemplars his class had created out of the matter of history and myth, incarnate archetypes of what a man should be. Theirs was the pattern to which he shaped himself. His conduct was judged by its appropriateness, a measure that took account of particular circumstances, but was always in conformity to the human ideal. Conduct regulated by this form felt congruous and fitting, hence purposeful. In the widest sense of "manners," the manners of the gentleman were the texture of his life, a texture isomorphic with the structure of his class. This relation of social macrocosm to microcosm did not need to be calculated or theoretically "known." It was tact and not cognition that judgment and conduct expressed; it was a socially supported sense of what humanity obliged that determined right conduct in a given situation. Not only the conduct but the sense itself often failed, but the standard by which man would judge himself was at once severe and humane.

Aristocratic societies tend to rot from the top. The less simple and military the tradition to be preserved, the more subtile become the ideal requirements for membership in the elite and (not necessarily, but generally) the more arbitrary, superficial, and fantastic its actual cachet. Not only is there no real possibility of an aristocratic organization of our society, but neither the myth of noble blood nor the theory of privileged natures bears on us. Our problem is scarcely the restora-

tion of aristocratic society, and it has little or nothing to do
with economic and political conservatism, at least as these are
understood in America. There is no American aristocracy to
conserve, and there can be nothing but confusion or disin-
genuousness in raising the lily banner over the ramparts of
Standard Oil and General Motors. These institutions may or
may not have sensible arguments in their favor, but a defense
in the mode of the Rockingham Whigs is somewhat beside the
point.

"The good man" and "the good life" have meant different
things in different climates; our situation and our problem start
from the recognition of relativity. But this recognition should
not lead us away from another of equal importance, that to
acknowledge the relativity of human ideals is not to deny all
existence to consensus. At least a degree of consensus exists in
those cultures which have grown out of Greece, Rome, and
medieval Europe, and among men whose affective lives have
been shaped by a similar past. If our problem is in part set by
the facts of personal and social relativity, the beginning of its
mitigation may be glimpsed in some deeper facts of affective
likeness, may be found in patterns of feeling that remain in
one sense local, but that can be consciously shared by all who
can trace their descent from sources in a common cultural past.

3. *Parvenu Virtue*

Nostalgia is not an adequate substitute for moral or political
philosophy. The sensible question to ask is whether we as individuals have anything to gain by becoming usufructuaries
of aristocratic tradition. Not living in an aristocratic society
and not frivolously pretending that we do, any use that we
might make of models from it will lack the grace of inheritance, and lessons learned will be less easily come by. But this
is a corollary of an autonomy we would not give up if we could,
and makes the affective nature of our possible gain clearer to
us than it could have been to our ancestors. Aristocratic societies

knew well enough the means of informing their members, but their view of the justification and end of their training tended toward the transcendental and fantastic. Our recognition of this limits the use we can make of traditional practice to whatever can be done without commitment to the myths that sustained the tradition. The limitation is severe, but its acknowledgment is a help in disentangling the traditional themes that are caught and lost in time from those that have a perennially human bearing.

Aristocratic education is moral education, deliberate modeling of affective matter to universal form. Its central insight is that discipline will be without fruitful affective significance either to those who administer it or to those who are formed by it unless it can be justified by mutually understood goals. This condition is most likely to be met when the discipline is a kind of imitation; imitation comes naturally to us all, filling a need that will always be answered in some way. Aristocratic training, classical and Christian, has from the beginning known the advantage of an orientation toward historical figures, exemplars that have all the charisma that time and custom can give them, and that are taken as paradigmatic of human nature. Whether expressed in an explicit ideology or not, it is "understood" that these archetypes at once exist in time and implicitly define the highest actualization of humanity. Their remembered real presence gives them emotional force, but it is equally important that they clearly define the ends of education. Acceptance of the definition of ideal humanity they manifest is what gives aristocratic education its rationale. Its material is the human being as given; its efficient cause is the discipline of imitation; its formal and final cause is *humanitas*. This humanity is a universal, most clearly and beautifully informing the lives of a few familiar paradigms, but potential and more or less actual in each particular man. It clearly sets the purpose of moral training: to make humanity more actual in each particular man.

There can be no doubt that aristocratic visions of ideal humanity were often fantastic and the education informed by them, except where it bore directly on the military virtues, was often grotesque or childish. But the first great point is that there *was* a definition of ideal humanity, that this definition *did* inform education, and that this education reached to the very roots of affective life and gave its shape to all subsequent moral growth. Looking away to its models, it set itself to the formation of human beings as to the creation of works of art, and succeeded in deliberately impressing a universal human form on particular affective matter.

If for our uses we ask what can be taught through imitation, the answer will not be found in the forms that shaped the gentleman of tradition. His ways are not without relevance to ours, but as a whole the model is obsolete. If we decide that certain aspects of it still apply (and hence that others do not), our choice will be made by reference to some broader or deeper standard. This more humane standard is implicit in aristocratic practice. It is a simple and traditional insight which the narrower training exemplifies. Stated without embellishment it is that some experiences are more important than others. All traditions through their models define a hierarchy of values, a structure of life determined by the relative emphasis given aspects of experience, the prominence attributed to themes, activities, and crises common to a favored class. Life is felt to have universal form and meaning when its affective force is given in the order ordained to moments that define humanity.

We may reject the judgment of relative importance embodied in the parochial paradigms, but the general moral of the stories transcends the particular heroes who live through them. What they knew and what we should know is that much in life does not deserve devotion, though it may demand passing and practical concern. Not everything we do or are is worth deliberate cultivation, and the indiscriminate sowing of attention or its scatter over the surface of accident leads to loss of concentration and failure of form. Without the sense that some themes in our lives are definitive, and without a structure of criteria to determine the experiences that manifest these themes and thus repay our full intensity, our hope for the feeling of meaning and purpose must be lost in barren distraction. It is when a variety of intense experience is ordered on an exemplary model of humanity that the whole of life is felt to be good and self-justified.

The recognition of the role of moral models may be more useful to us as parents than it is in the rest of our moral lives. We have already grown in the direction we were bent, and the strength of habit stands against re-formation. In the worst shape are those who were not knowingly bent at all but were allowed to grow like weeds, those ignorant of all the uses of conscious form including that clearly tyrannical use which permits open and clear rebellion. These spontaneous growths are no less warped because their directions are all accidental. It is easy to see that we can do more for our children than we can for ourselves, but even we, fixed as we may be in some senseless shape, are seldom perfectly set. If ever our dissatisfaction with the pattern of our life makes the first step to a perspective on other possible forms, there is a little hope for change. If this hope seizes the most efficacious means of re-formation, if a man can grasp the possible personal uses of the aristocratic tradition, its usufruct can be his. The rest is not easy. Few are heirs by right of birth, and if one were, he would still be without the support of appropriate social patterns. The modern man who would model himself on the form of the best in his background, who would achieve a conscious sense of meaningful human form, finds himself in an awkward and privileged position. His responsibility is both odd and great, and his autonomy is of a kind with a peculiar reputation: he must choose his ancestors.

B. THE HUMAN SHAPE

Aristocratic education succeeded in its purpose. It impressed on affective matter certain forms that were felt as the proper

shape of life itself. Our reservations will come with the question
of whether the intensities it took as definitive were rightly taken,
and whether its forms can engage and deserve our affections.
To say we doubt this, that we object to both the confusion of
genus with local species and the form of the species, is to say
that we feel differently. We can go a long way with Isocrates,
Quintilian, or Castiglione, but we feel that traditional cultivation was less generic than it felt itself, and may hope to find
an equally clear and more universal pattern. We must expect
some dilution, and the handicap of honesty can diminish affective appeal, but what cannot be absent in any order of life
if its actualization is to satisfy its purpose is a habitual sense
of the occasions worth human attention, of the universal aspects of our particular situations, of the moments whose emphasis creates the fulfillment of form. For this we must relearn
the lesson of relative value; we must gain the tact which tells us
the themes that deserve intensity.

And yet the saying that nothing human is alien at best
states an aspiration, and at its worst is humanistic cant. It may
be a way of stating the truth that what is alien can at length
be understood and even loved, but even in this truth one
must beware the note of condescension. Each of us finds what
is different strange, and none of us is free of local shape. If our
problem is to choose our ancestors, that wide provincialism
which reaches back to the roots of Western Europe sets the
kind of limit which is a source of strength. Except for the
doubtful and precarious chance of a permanently satisfying
exoticism—feeling perhaps the strangeness, excitement, and
theatrical unreality of a masquerade, but a masquerade in
which one's costume is badly fit—we have the best hope of
finding our exemplary past in our own historical culture. Here,
within a general unity, there is variety enough for every mood,
so much diversity that specific choice stands dazzled, but in
both themes and exemplifications our past is here. To know
this is to establish some claim as an heir. The conditions of

inheritance are unlike those which regulate a physical estate. One becomes a member of the family, is granted the sense of its continuity and the hope of preserving its forms, all through nothing more or less than openness, knowledge, and love.

1. *A Genealogy for Form*

To the attempt at goodness of life each of us brings himself, and no one else can know so well the burden each has brought. There is matter here that escapes generalization: the chance of achieving the satisfaction of form half depends on self-knowledge, and the self that each self knows is particular. Since each soul knows itself uniquely, only each is competent to estimate what is unique and given in its situation and in its potential; this means that each must judge for himself the distance and the consonance between himself and any paradigm.

But idiosyncrasy is only half the story, and a part too easy to exaggerate. We do not come formless to the hope of form. Being who we are and where we are, shaped by a local past, our sense of form is not so much absent as confused or overlaid, and our knowledge of it may be felt as recollection. Whether as an aspect of humanity as such or as a cultural inheritance, the patterns through which most of us would find it good to live are implicit if forgotten in the lives we cannot escape. Our past assures that the consonance is there; to understand what we are and can hope to be, to find those models suited to inform us, we can look to the very heart of our common tradition and take from it all that honesty can carry. Again, the limitation is severe. Honesty makes for diffidence in thieving, and the heart of the Western tradition is religious.

What we can hope to learn from traditional religion is not a means of escape to an immortal life in another world, but what is most meaningful in mortal life in this world, those human themes which determine our nature and repay intensity with the sense of human form. A list would sound presumptuous if it were original, but for the sake of plain statement an old list can be given: births and children; conscious commitment to some order that deserves loyalty; the sense of communion or of essential community; choice, pain, and the recognition that one's ways are corrigible; love; vocation; death and judgment; time and beauty. Wisdom is awareness of the ultimate importance of these things, these themes and crises which give structure to human life at its most human and deserve our celebration. The structure that we feel our lives to have will depend on the emphasis we give to these, will be our apprehension of the intensity that reaches out to them. (If the list seems too obvious or too inclusive, think of some objects of deep concern it leaves out: most of the newspaper and all of the advertisements; the rage for *things,* and money and status as ends; the single-minded dedication to diversion; the small change of social busy-work and gossip. None of these natural interests need be denied or condemned, but as objects of ultimate concern they tend to make an unrewarding religion.)

Traditional religion in its liturgical pattern vests in the language of celebration the universal meaning of each man's particular experience, junctures unique to the life of each and common to all. In the sacraments, in the great festivals and fasts, in the ecclesiastical year with the majestic and homely recurrence of its seasons, with perfect tact the Catholic tradition expresses its human wisdom. In two thousand years of brooding on the life of Western man, the Church has learned the themes that structure his life.

It requires a combination of historical near-sightedness and emotional insensitivity to deny all attractiveness to traditional religions. On the side of intellect there is the synthesis of classical and Christian thought created by St. Thomas, the systems of Maimonides and Calvin, the arguments of Luther, the educational theories of Melanchthon, the compromises of the Thirty-nine Articles. But religion engages more than the intellect; it probably engages the intellect least of all. Where its hold is least strong it gives way most obviously. We have seen that when naturalistic explanations of natural fact become possible, supernaturalistic "explanations" become at least cognitively superfluous. From its point of view the Church was right to condemn Galileo and to resist Darwin; God's position, to put it politically, is stronger when reference to Him seems necessary to explain the natural world. It misses the point to say that "God" thus becomes another name for ignorance; this is true as far as it goes, but it does not go far enough to feel the easement this title confers. We know that we could not live in a world in which nothing could be expected, and only a little better is a world in which the causes of the expected were unknown. They will never be perfectly known, and it takes an almost inhuman sophistication to regard the unknown as a field for further explanation rather than as an object of reverential acceptance. None of us is so consistently rational, and in times of emotional crisis any of us is likely to become as a little child. When we are frightened, and especially when we are confronted by what we feel as unknowable power, we are likely to seize on any means to restore the sense of familiarity, to throw ourselves into a context that allows for understanding, hope, and action.

But the same temptation is there when we find we have nothing to say—as to a parent whose child has died—and this signals a still closer approach to contemporary feeling and to the lesson it can learn from its ancestral religion. Perhaps because nature no longer feels as strange as it once did, perhaps because we live at an increasing distance from it, the crises which demand personal concern are more plainly crises in feeling. We have intelligently relinquished the understanding of nature to effective techniques of prediction, description, and control; what we now have to fear lies in ourselves. If the rest of nature seems always more systematic and less terrifying, we oscillate between a chaos that terrifies and a quietly killing disorder, between a hapless trusting to inner wind and weather and attempts to freeze life over; we would drown or walk on the water. These simple alternatives are hopeless and not exclusive. The world within need not be felt as terrible in its intensities and menacing or deadly in its calms; we need neither blindly fear nor worship the occasions when the power of affection strains the limits of the self. It is our affections that require order, the intensities of immediate experience that are the matter of our sense of form; the only appropriate information is that which allows them to fill their place in a pattern found good as a whole. The end is not description or prediction, although it requires knowledge enough to permit discipline. The end is the intrinsic satisfaction of a form fulfilled; not merely the *sine qua non* of a varied intensity somehow contained, but the sense of in-carnate, universal humanity.

If good moral sense presents itself too plainly, it is despised as simple-minded or rejected as insolent; for most of us to notice it, wisdom must come in fancy dress. The practice of the Catholic tradition has conduced to the sense of human order, but its human sensibility has taken on otherworldly disguise. The simple recognition is that life, like the year, has its lulls, its seasons, and its climaxes; that some definitive themes recur; and that there are decisive moments awful in their uniqueness. To recognize this requires training of attention, realization that some experiences are entitled to and repay all the intensity we bring them. The affective meaning of these essential figures is caught and impressed by the Church in their celebration, rhythmically and formally through the year. Small wonder that Catholics pity Protestants who seem conscious only of Christmas, Easter, and Mother's Day; shopping, eggs, and the-lines-are-all-busy. The lives of most of us must seem a form-less welter of events, a moil in which nothing is ever fully at-tended; ugly lives in which new birth can be less vital than baseball or crab grass, significance lost and choked in other concerns; where regrets amount to sentimental gloom and re-morse is a running sore; where love is sniggering back-seat groping and the only stars that cross are on a screen; where commitment is only slogan-deep and bridge substitutes for human understanding; where death means no more than life does and everyone's vocation is lost, all lost in the shuffle of wastepaper, status, and time.

Instead of this, in the lives of the fully conscious faithful there are the ceremonies of Baptism, Confirmation, Communion, Penance, Marriage, Holy Orders, and Extreme Unction. Here the immediate and ineffable experiences that determine all our lives are recognized, celebrated, magically held for a moment in the forms of ceremony: birth, love, renunciation, communion, time. How can it be denied that in the tumult or stagnation of our time the expression of these essential themes is seen as accidental, slurred over, blurred, peripheral, their central significance forgotten in the smothering press of things? How can it be denied that most of us muddle and drift through life without noticing that we have been born, without learning what we cannot have, without thinking that we must die? Our lives are popular songs structured only by repetition, the switch turned off in the middle of another meaningless measure.

And this we sense: we are not satisfied; we do not know where to turn for satisfaction; we feel as transitory and purposeless as comets, but not beautiful. How could it be otherwise when we fail to single out, fail to give ourselves, and only half-consciously celebrate the times that would respond to our devotion with the gift of conscious form, when we come to live, think, make love, and die with the radio on? Our hearts are where our treasure is, foolishly spent.

2. *Celebration and Form*

When religion is liturgical and ceremonial, it offers to imagination a visible pageant of the human world, a dramatic reconstruction in which the universal stands forth more clearly than it does in life itself, in which essential configurations and moments are colorfully marked and their human meaning justly symbolized. Consciously to live through the patterns it expresses, to give oneself to the concrete experiences it celebrates, is to become aware in one's particularity of a universal form of human life. But the efficacy of the sacraments is not magical. It is affective. Repetition and reward reinforce the growth of habit, and these ceremonies which are themselves satisfying express the themes and junctures, crises and concerns which we must attend to know our human form. Explicit and ordered celebration in this way is a means. Without a disposition to recognize what is humanly important, without the tendency to celebrate the experiences that define us, there is little hope for the realization of life. It is not enough to think one *knows* what is important. Our emotions must be disciplined; we must habitually give our attention to essential themes; concern will follow. To model affective life on the familiar pattern manifest in the sacraments, to be disposed to let one's heart go out to the experiences they represent, is to direct and shape the matter of intensity itself.

But training in imitation of humanity is not the only effect of celebration. For while it is true that immediate experience can be neither captured nor communicated, experience amounting almost to recapitulation can be had when a mythical or symbolic example of it is fixed in formal and repeatable ceremony. The intensities that are the contour of affective life are each of them passing and wordless: immediate experience is not a *thing* to be held or saved, and it is too close and too absorbing to be an object of knowledge. But imitation of an exemplary type of experience can serve as an indirect expression available again and again; it comes as close as we can come to knowing what cannot be known, to speaking what cannot be said. Where imitation is fixed in ritual formula, as in the Church's re-creation of the events that marked its temporal foundation, all who participate rehearse in common their common experience. It is participation in a nearly Platonic sense, each of the many reliving through one an aspect of the human situation. It is as if the flesh were made word, as if the close reality that must escape language had found an outward and public vocabulary. What cannot be kept in time seems rescued from time; what cannot be thought is made visible; what cannot be shared or given to others seems at once objectified and inner to each, commonly known and still immediate. The feeling of shared understanding follows the acceptance of celebration as a fitting correlate of the singular experience celebrated. Ritual can fulfill this condition, can serve as an objective recapitulation and reminder of our prerogative intensities.

Leaving aside supernatural sanctions and justifications, one danger in rehearsal of paradigms of experience is that the familiarity it brings can dull the awareness it should resurrect. When this happens it must count as perversion of a good. An extreme of habitual familiarity is more tolerable to the tired than full awareness of experience, and to some of the passionate and frightened it is a safe alternative to affective chaos. But the ideal result is not simply control; it is a familiarization sufficient to limit fear, with the preservation of respect appropriate to fearful occasions. The proper balance is fine. We must be neither terrified nor thoughtless when our heart would leave us to love what it finds beautiful and good, when it leads us toward experience in which we may be lost or broken: it is true that we must lose our lives to find them. It is also true that thoughtless giving is a kind of dissipation, that indiscriminate surrender to every immediacy follows ignorance to disintegration.

Intense experience is both attractive and frightening; to have approached its force and nature through enacted paradigms can qualify the fear of letting go and promote the sense that the touch of intensity is dreadful in its potency and import, finally determining the shape of our lives. Close enough to bring recognition, distant enough to teach without destroying, expressed through beautiful figures, larger than life, celebration of the human themes brings our nature home to us, shows us what we are, and teaches proper concern for what we are. The feeling of understanding rests on familiarity that is also respect, and the sense of purpose depends on acceptance of attainable ends as worth the cost of attainment.

Nothing beyond human nature determines the form of human life. When attention and intensity go out most fully to these universal concerns—a person loved, a family, a true vocation; a cause which earns well-confirmed loyalty; repentance and pain turned toward the uses of reformation; the knowledge of death—the whole configuration of experience is felt as oneness with the perfect type of humanity, as a communion which each self in its uniqueness senses as a realization of the meaning and purpose proper to its nature. Not every possible concern is comprehended in this pattern, but the various intensities it orders are those essential to the end of order, to the sense of human form. There may be no final reason why human beings are as they are; but as we are, with the matter we are given, without affective concentration we are not likely to find life good as a whole; we are likely to feel it as a meaningless waste. Any immediate and absorbing experience can be good in itself, but in each of our retrospections we discover that not all intensities are equally valuable in the composition of a satisfying whole. That ultimate and self-justifying experience depends not merely on intensity, diversity, and order, but on the further sense that the form that comprehends our intensity is essentially human.

While there is no honest, total, and permanent cure for aloneness, there is mitigation in the awareness that one's unique experience is an actualization of a distinctively human potential. The centrality Christianity gives to the Eucharist, the perennial reincarnation of the Word, can be taken to signal the hope or achievement of universal indwelling in the particular. Each of the other sacraments marks a narrower mode of common experience, and the pattern made by them all culminates in communion.

But if it is possible to take our knowledge of occasions from this source, recommendations of conduct do not automatically follow. Sometimes it is possible and helpful, but more often it is presumptuous and useless to state in general the particular actions particular people should take in their particular confrontations of universal themes. We can say that taking one's work as a vocation, giving the experience of it a due measure of true concern, is to find oneself living through a form-giving mode—but it would be foolish to tell the unknown reader exactly the work he should do. The needful sense of vocation can qualify any work; what is important is that the work be felt as a calling. Where it is not or cannot be, one aspect of experience is lost to the hope of satisfaction, however great or necessary its extrinsic compensations. There is no presumption in saying that life which owes no loyalty to an extra-personal cause, which has never known intense devotion to an idea or institution accepted and immediately felt to be worth living for, has missed one informing mode of experience—but in what commitment shall each be confirmed? We can take the negative conditions to be like the principles of Natural Law, simple to self-evidence and not very helpful: while any overriding loyalty can meet the need for commitment, one would not recommend a cause deficient in principles of humanity, decency, love, or honesty. To an individual one knows, one can say more; the only valid general point is made in stressing the importance of the theme. More particular recommendations made to more than one person at a time amount to party politics or dogma. If a greater degree of specificity is reasonable when talking about the closest of human relations, there are specific reasons for this, but even so the moralist can scarcely say to man in general whom in particular he should love and marry.

a. UNFAVORABLE AUSPICES

The full affective force of sacramental celebration depends on belief that the sacraments themselves were divinely instituted and that their justification and import transcend the merely human. Whatever may be left after this belief is gone has no fair title to the name of religion and will almost certainly not have the efficacy of whole-hearted religious belief.[7] Those who need the seamless whole will have it, and there will as often be cruelty as kindness in attempts to enforce clarity. Philosophic criticism embodies and tacitly urges one almost puritanical austerity: it attempts to limit the feeling of understanding to occasions on which a valid, true, or probable explanation has been given. When grown more latitudinarian, it tries to distinguish cases in which the feeling comes recommended by adequate cognitive grounds from those in which it does not, but does not insist that the latter be eliminated. (The present argument belongs to the broader persuasion.)

Even this distinction will encounter resistance. When criticism is sensed as a danger to cherished affective adjustments, even the most intelligent men will find ways to deflect it. It is not only ships at sea that depend on compartments for security. A man can hold almost any belief so long as he keeps it in a reliquary and sees it only through colored glass. Then "Consciousness accordingly, as it were, makes but a feint at thinking, and takes the form of adoration. Such thought as it has remains the mere formless tinkling of an altar bell, or the wreathing of warm incense smoke—a thinking in music, such as never reaches an organized notion, wherein alone an inner objectivity can be attained."[8] These obvious facts make obvious difficulties.

If we ask what contribution traditional religion can make to the moral life of a modern, areligious man, we are in effect undertaking to evaluate different parts of what has always and most forcefully come as a whole. Our attempt is to pick and choose, to criticize, to accept, to reject, and to dismember a body that some see as mystical and all should appreciate as organic. The prospects for this attempt are poor and dangerous. Honesty, piety, and history are against it. The first prescribes that we abstain from indulgence in emotional satisfaction when its cost is intellectual confusion; the second ensures that any attempt at evaluation and partial acceptance will meet resistance; and the third warns that the likeliest results of such an attempt are eccentricity, vulgarity, aesthetic and moral shallowness, and disorder.

Our question must be whether we can honestly claim any of the affective benefits of religious insight and spiritual discipline. Can anything of use be learned by those who will not take the transcendental step? Is it possible to accept the moral-affective insights at the foundation of theological superstructures, to accept and use the human wisdom while seeing through the otherworldly ambitions? In part, if only in part, the possibility is real and full of hope. The first step toward apprehension of a satisfying order in life is knowledge that such an order is universally potential, awareness of an ideal pattern that can be taken as a sensible model. It is true that ideal models are easily mistaken for literal descriptions of life in an earlier or later or better world, and too often true that the fictional description is taken as a necessary foundation of order itself. The full sense of purpose felt by the devout depends in part on a confusion of effects with causes, on a half-conscious effort to put and keep the cognitive cart before the affective horse. Fervor may depend on this, but for those who would be clear and sane and lead a human life, an appropriate degree of the same sense can follow a recognition of meaning and purpose, first as a human ideal and then as a possibility for feeling.

b· THE POSSIBILITY OF CHOICE

To know what is important is the first great thing. But knowledge is not sufficient: it is our emotional and volitional nature that requires training or re-formation. Our affections are far from entirely at our command, the shapes we have grown into are not easily changed, and yet the hope for satisfying form is not always unrealistic and the means are not recondite. Where discontent is followed by the will to change, the next requirements are for a means of change and a direction. It is not difficult to formulate what we can sensibly hope to find

or create in our affective lives: a diversity of intense or immediate experience ordered on a model of universal humanity.
The means to this will be imitation that informs; the end will
be a life sensed in itself as a fulfillment of human form and
purpose, as self-justifying. We know the direction and we know
the means, although neither will, means, nor direction can
have for us the potency, support, and sanction that many knew
when literal belief in supernatural truths was a live option for
all. For them an otherworldly end justified the practice of their
means; for us the means must be justified by their contribution
to the life of each who takes them. The means alter their
character with this change, and yet the ways that we can take
are recognizable descendants of those our fathers knew, and
retain more than a little share of their original force.

The technique of re-formation is simple. Its principle is
that belief and feeling follow action and then give rise to
action felt as right, good, and familiar. Practice leads to habits
of attention and feeling, but when the exercise of disposition
leads to a satisfaction that would not be had in its absence,
reward is intrinsic to action and education is complete. This
cannot be done deliberately unless there is a will to change;
dissatisfaction alone leads only to desperation. Even where
there is will enough to try for goodness of life, there is no
guarantee of its achievement, but with that necessary condition
present one can turn with justified hope to well-tried means.
For neither is will alone sufficient; without discipline and direction the will to change ends in anarchy or deformity. It is our
actions that are most subject to deliberate control; our affections are less so—they must be allowed to follow. They will
follow, and follow any lead, and that is a double reason why our
choice of models takes on controlling import for our lives.

What then shall we imitate, and how? Our need is for models
imitable in action, accepted as worth the tribute of imitation,
each exemplifying as nearly as can be the varied human form
of intensity. The problem of concrete exemplars is more acute

than that of defining the type: in our newspaper-wrapped society to live wisely is to live unknown. We have no culture-heroes worthy of either word, and yet it is hopelessly academic to think that imitation of abstract, universal humanity is an effective means to re-formation. Accidental models mislead, but principles without exemplars lack affective force. Starting as we do from our own responsibility and freedom, we do not inherit specific models we can accept without question. When we deliberately try to choose our ancestors we are exactly confronted with questions of abstract principles, questions concerning criteria of choice—but unless the principles can be concretely exemplified for our imitation, any determination of them is likely to remain merely intellectual and barren, to be without affective fruit.

This is not a paradox, but it is a difficulty. Its solution is to be found in a dictum we have heard before and that we can now interpret more fully. The saying is that good is what the good man does, and now we know what that is. Or, closer to our purpose, we can say that the good life is that in which the themes that define humanity are most intensely lived, and we know what these themes are. Aristotle based his definition of human nature and the proper happiness attendant on it on his theory of man's essential rationality. The goodness of anything with a function to perform was in performing that function well; man's unique and essential function was to reason, and thus his virtue and appropriate happiness were found in the exercise of rationality. Aristotle thus provides a criterion, dependent on a doctrine of essential natures, according to which we can recognize a good man or a good life when we find one. He says that with this much knowledge we can and must go the rest of the way ourselves. We can because we have a principle by reference to which we can assess possible models; we must, since the best pattern for each will be a compromise between his particular matter and the form of his species. The structure of essential humanity is, according to Aristotle, clear and fixed, but he knows that lives must differ in texture and that each must find paradigms appropriate to his station.

Aristotle's argument moves from presumed truths about man's rational essence to sensible recommendations concerning his moral posture. The good sense of his conclusions does not prove the truth of his premises, and a less pretentious argument can bring us to conclusions that are equally sensible and almost as strong. Our clues to man's nature come from diverse and empirical sources, from science, history, literature, and tradition. None of these nor all of them together adds up to a metaphysical theory of essential human nature, but there does emerge from our common past a thematic structure nearly universal in its bearing. These are the concerns of man as man. The pattern they make can be understood as familiar; the life that gives itself to them returns with the sense of human form and human satisfaction. We can say that our best chance for a life experienced not as unspeakably lonely and strange, but as one in form with the life of humanity, as full of a properly human meaning and purpose, lies in the disposition to recognize and emphasize the universal moments in their particular occurrence. With this much wisdom we can and must go the rest of the way ourselves. We can, because this gives us sufficient tact to reject unsuitable models; we must, since the best life for each will be a unique resolution of the tension between affective matter and ideal form. The universal structure of experience is buried in every life; it needs learning less than recollection, but lives differ in their various concreteness, and each, in the light of self-knowledge, must find exemplars appropriate to his particular situation.

3. *The Whole of Life*

To recognize that the benefits of sacramental religion are not supernatural but affective is to lose the affective benefits of sacramental religion. To continue to play the part after such recognition requires either accidental or deliberate confusion of mind. Both the honesty and the efficacy of the practice of religion demand acceptance of its supporting myths as true; anything else is a kind of cheating. The unbeliever cannot in good conscience expect to feel the full impact of religious practice; he has other advantages, and here he must settle for less. Clarity and autonomy can be hard to live with. They are demanding virtues, but they bring unique rewards. When a man knows that he is free and responsible, and knows that he must find his chief resource in himself, his mind and will are put to a strain that the thoughtless buyers of ready-made lives never know; out of that tension can grow the sense of self-creation. The true believer has all the props, and may be the more comfortable for that—those who must have illusions should have illusions—but once the illusions are gone and the props gone with them, it is the part of integrity and the way to goodness to accept the difficulties of self-determination, to set one's will on recognition and celebration of the informing themes. The initial dependence on will to attend to these is a human and imperfect reliance, but it is what can honestly be done, and it can succeed.

We know the ends and the conditions of our work. The affective characteristics of a life found good are, most generally, a complex variety of intense, immediate experience rhythmically ordered on the human form. Works of art can afford the most striking combination of intense immediacy and satisfying form; if their specific order does not directly illuminate the shape of human life, affective order is there to be apprehended, and appreciation of it can be a celebration of the idea of order itself. The magical and human events in *The Tempest*, the emotions evoked by a Beethoven quartet, the exact impression of tense power in a baroque façade are no more to our purpose than is the discipline that has made each richness into a whole. Our matter is the basic stuff of will and emotion itself, and the discipline appropriate to it is neither purely aesthetic nor arbitrary, but is founded in human nature and on the limits and conditions of human life. What is unique in the life of each, in the self and circumstances from which each new creation must begin, is enough to ensure that our work will not lack originality. The types of humanity we choose to set the directions of our growth, our incarnate universals, will also embody variations on the basic human themes. All that should be and all that can be set before us in general is the general human form. The events and emotions that give life to the form must be brought to it by the full particularity of each man's experience.

Each particular life has come to be what it is through causes both unique and general. It is a kind of insanity to suppose that re-formation can start except from the forms into which we have grown, or that reasonable reconstruction can ignore historical data. We have done what we have done, things have happened to us, we have made terrible mistakes and accomplished a little good, and none of this can be undone. But it is also true that our felt lives are a constant reconstruction and projection built out of these data, a never-ending reinterpretation of the significance of events, of the past, the present, and the future which we see in hope or fear. Within limits set by fact and temperament we create our affective lives. The form that life is felt to have is a function of our attention when we meet it and when we survey it. There may be features of the prospect irrevocably fixed, and we must recognize these, but the view out over past and future is always present, always changing, and to some extent at least the perspective depends on us. It depends on the points we have especially marked as we passed them, and it may be dark where we have gone in ignorance, but the life that at any time we feel ourselves to be living, the form that is seen by the eye of the soul, is our doing. It is we who have made it.

This can be conscious creation. We can practice to make attention our celebrant and memory and hope our ritual. Our minds in any case work in imitative and ritualistic ways; we rehearse and almost relive events that have struck us as significant, and the more we think of them the greater they grow. The judgment of significance is most often left to accident, but it need not be. The brooding of thought over the face of experience can be given deliberate focus if we will. The outward and visible machinery of celebration is a help we do not have; we lack the dramatic and public scaffolding of form, and so we must act out in ourselves the observances that determine our lives. The particular and immediate presence of these structuring themes—new births, commitment, communion, corrigibility, vocation, love, and death—can be especially greeted, especially kept. No rites of memory or hope can wholly recapture their immediacy, but regular and constant recollection of them comes as close as can be, and it makes them the points around which the composition of affective life is arranged. This unillusioned recourse is personal and uncertain; that is the price we pay for awareness of individuality and autonomy. The other possibilities are return to illusion or loss of hope for satisfying form.

Our situation in the creation of life is as similar to that of the artist as it is to that of the believer. We have gained some but not all the freedom of the former, and lost some but not all the fixity of the latter. In any case, neither freedom nor fixity is ever absolute. If a humane religion recognizes and allows for individuality, the artist works within or against the discipline of his tradition. He brings to his material not only his personal past and original genius, but also the history and ritual of his art. Of course the artist qua artist is more freely related to his tradition, his material, and his work than we are when our work is no less than our lives, and this is only one of the points at which the analogy shows itself to be no more than an analogy. The matter we have to work with is at any time given, and the traditional forms that invite us are in their most general structure fixed in our nature and in our situation. Perhaps ours is the advantage here. The artist has no better ritual for celebration than we have, the materials he has to work with are never wholly tractable, and he has no surer discipline for the creation of affective patterns that will be found good; the forms we would find satisfying are already potential if unrealized in each of our lives, and their realization comes with the sense of familiar recognition and consequent rightness.

Even where this analogy is most suggestive it is not perfect, for the making of life must take together complexities that the making of works of art can take separately. Dewey was right when he said that each brush stroke summed up and consummated all that had gone before, held for a moment the whole meaning of the work, and looked to the future; Eliot was right when he said that each new work not only followed from but gave a fresh perspective on its past. But the making of life is a continuing creation, we are never done with it while we live. It is a work that exists only in its creation and re-creation, complete at every moment and never finished. The insights of the pragmatist and the poet both apply: each experience newly encountered and encompassed is qualified by, qualifies, and sums up the past, and this meeting in the present reaches forward in an imagined future to apprehend the whole. Each life follows the history of the species, and each shows through its differences what the species is. Life, like art, or when it is like art, can seem almost to capture time in form, to keep or celebrate the patterns of flow itself; but here there is no creation independent of the creator's experience, no static product that can be saved, and only one performance. Its whole being is comprised in the vision that is always re-formation and revision, in the whole that at any time lives only in the memory, apprehension, and hope of its author.

We do not and cannot live only in the present. We live in the whole of our lives. But our lives are complete at every moment, every moment is the end of all that has gone before, and only in the present can we know the whole of our lives. The rest of the structure is a constant reconstruction, a doing and undoing in imagination, each recollection a new creation out of old material, each projection a reworking of past and present in the light of hope and fear. This is the whole which is our total affective environment, the felt structure in which we live, and even if it changes with each new perspective, it is not an environment wholly beyond our control. We must respect what is given and cannot be changed—"I would remind you that there are impossibilities in this world"—and properly appreciate our uniqueness, but we have traditions that can guide our will to form, and can find exemplars to show that form is attainable. Our traditions, our discipline, our points of reference are neither fatalities nor are they arbitrary. The human structure they afford for our realization, the directions to which they bend our concern and our intensity are justified not only by their universality, but by the satisfaction that comes when this universal humanity is felt to live in the particular man. This is the sense of completeness, atonement, communion, that can be made to environ each singular moment and to lend the meaning of its wholeness to each event.

Resolution of the problems of the meaning and purpose of life, of aloneness, responsibility, and pain, must be found in our affections, if they are to be found at all. The answers come only to the man who becomes the answer. When the whole of life is apprehended as a fulfillment of human form, when its intensities have gone out to live through and almost to break the pattern of human life, then, as we sense it in a perfect work of art, we find in ourselves the awareness of completion, of immanent meaning, and of satisfied purpose. This awareness is still the sense of each who knows it, and each who knows it is still finally alone, but when a man intensely feels that the very form of humanity lives in him, his particular life becomes a perpetual communion with the life of humankind.

VII

THE SENSE OF REALITY

"The great secret of morals is Love," Shelley writes, "or a going out of our own nature, and an identification of ourselves with the beautiful which exists in thought, action or person not our own. A man to be greatly good must imagine intensively and comprehensively. . . . the pain and pleasure of the species must become his own." Shakespeare is even more "greatly good" than Shelley suggests is possible; for he can identify himself with what he thought ugly and detestable, knocking all the time at our heart for pity and awe.[1]

DOVER WILSON, *The Essential Shakespeare*

None of us will ever have to face a moral problem no human has faced before—there are no moral problems without precedents. It is also true that circumstances alter cases. Moral philosophy must find its way between platitudes and presumption, and either lapse or both together are most likely when the moralist tries to say in general what particular people should do in their particular situations. What can be said in general should be said in general; the trouble with platitudes is that they are generally true, and often so obviously true that once we hear them we suppose that everyone must not only take them for granted, but act on them concretely. In this supposition we are wrong. It is not always easy to act on the obvious, and hardest when its verbal formulation is taken for granted and its application to particular cases unthought of or crude. What is needed is not merely new bottles for old wine, but renewed touch with the affective ground beneath the obvious and often forgotten general truths. Insight is not sufficient. One must be disposed to act on his insight, and have an acquired sense for appropriate occasions of action. It is not enough to know the last word in inter-personal relations. It cannot be enough since so many have heard it to such little avail:

Though I speak with the tongues of men and of angels, and have not charity, I am become as sounding brass, or a tinkling cymbal.

And though I have the gift of prophecy, and understand all mysteries, and all knowledge; and though I have all faith, so that I could remove mountains, and have not charity, I am nothing.

And though I bestow all my goods to feed the poor, and though I give my body to be burned, and have not charity, it profiteth me nothing.

Charity suffereth long, and is kind; charity envieth not; charity vaunteth not itself, is not puffed up,

Doth not behave itself unseemly, seeketh not her own, is not easily provoked, thinketh no evil;

Rejoiceth not in iniquity, but rejoiceth in the truth;

Beareth all things, believeth all things, hopeth all things, endureth all things. . . .

And now abideth faith, hope, charity, these three; but the greatest of these is charity.

But we need to reach the natural ground of *caritas*, and to learn its affective meaning well enough to practice our wisdom.

The opposite danger to useless generality is misplaced or impertinent specificity. It is one thing to call attention to the importance of concern with essential themes, but something else again to prescribe exactly what an unknown person should do in living out the moment to which he has given his particular heart. The closest approach that can reasonably be made still leaves us on a middling level of generality, and even this degree of specificity depends on likenesses at once generic and culturally conditioned. Where we have reason to suppose such similarity it is possible to discuss not only the structure of well-spent intensity, but the finer texture of specific spending.

Fortunately this is true of the theme of love. No aspect of our emotional lives is more central or more pervasive than this, but not because romance is the whole meaning of life or its experience the only immediacy worth living for. It is rather that the love of men and women, and the love that can inform a family, are the original type and can be the paradigm of all objective relations. Our mistakes and failures here perfectly represent the various ways in which we fail of a satisfying relation to the whole of reality.

A. ON LOVE

Truly hopeful ways of life always appear more attractive when set off against unreasonable extremes. This is one reason why we usually learn our moral lessons too late. When it comes to talk about love, all the dangers lie on one side. We scarcely have to fear an excess of rationalism; our troubles are likely to have their ground in two species of the romantic attitude, one hot and one lukewarm. The era of marriages arranged on dynastic or financial calculations is over and done, and the time of eugenic calculation has not yet arrived. Whether things were better once or will be in the future is not our question: we are virtually without ideas of love and marriage other than those inherited from European romanticism. Too much cultural inertia carries this on to permit hope of major change, even if that were clearly desirable; but it may be useful to display the bent of a tradition that has shaped us all, and to show how it can be deflected to greater goods than those toward which it generally tends. In both its wild and domestic varieties the romantic attitude toward love remains an affair of the solitary self and never reaches out to embrace the concrete otherness of another human being.

1. *Darby and Joan*

As a caricature of comfortably habitual domesticity, Darby and Joan are not really out of date. The physical and social setting of their snug little world has changed, and the surface of their relationship reflects different colors; togetherness in the suburbs has a different look from jogging along together in the village or on the farm. The happy old couple whose picture appears in the weekly newspaper—"Married fifty years and never a quarrel"—are at any rate old and were married in a different world. What is most visible in their lives seems so different from what meets the eye in ours that it is easy to overlook the deeper respects in which we are they. It is not that every cottage held or every split-level holds a Darby and Joan, but that the situation suggested by the name is, except in its accidents, as common as ever. Since its essence is the death of love, it is not uncommon.

Darby and Joan are the couple who take each other so much for granted that neither realizes the full and concrete existence of the other. Domestic habit, arrested only by minor irritations, has smothered or narrowed awareness, and each good partner feels the other as a reliable feature of the environment or an adjunct or extension of his own life. What is gained by losing the sense of otherness is a level of comfort not to be despised: it is on the surface of life that most of its troubles appear, and it is tempting and often sensible to live on the surface in confidence that nature will manage the rest. Sometimes there will be little

else to manage, and a tepidly happy life can be spun out in conversation on minor domestic concerns. When a man's deepest
devotion is given to golf and the daily paper, or a woman's heart
to shopping and to gossip, there may be little hidden to know or
to love. It is easy to think that such usual objects of ultimate concern would not be so if there were any deep or complex life
behind them, but distraction can also serve as a mask for discontent. The sparkling or flat domestic routine—the cocktail party,
the company picnic, the camping trip, the P.T.A., the coupon
books, the meeting in bed—may cover and may be known to
cover a terrible, mutual absence. Confinement, and knowledge
of the absence of love—this is the prototype of hell.

Few varieties of domestic damnation are spectacular. Commonly, its desperation is invisible and quiet, seldom intense,
deriving its character in part from lack of intensity. But sometimes we come to feel we have lost a good that might be found
in isolation and have not gained the advantage of company; we
are pressed by an alien presence without knowing another self;
we have foregone what we valued in aloneness, and yet remain
alone. When it comes to awareness that our situation joins the
faults of desert island life with those of life with a stranger, then
from apathy can grow a dull and steady sense of resentment, an
uneasy dislike that sinks with relief into hatred. The happy old
couple who saw no way out may have resigned themselves to the
death of the heart; we are likely to cherish the feeling that we
have been cheated, or to go to court.

Any generalization will miss the varied detail of its cases, and
some situations are beyond the reach of anything that could be
said to normally reasonable people. But when so many sensible
men and women seem in the same way mutually, secretly bitter,
no longer able to love and forbidden to hate, we must hope to
find a common cause. One cause can be found in an attitude
that commonly shapes the relations of men and women, warps
us so easily that alternatives may seem unnatural. Coming care-
lessly from different directions we fall into the same trap, and

learning to live there we think it must be home: to the wife her husband exists as the functions he performs, and to her husband the wife is the sum of her services.

It is true that the relation of marriage has moved from status to contract, and true that in our kind of world the cash nexus tends to replace every other, but the unthought notion of marriage as an exchange of commodities is a product of neither the industrial nor the romantic revolution. Its contemporary form owes much to romanticism, but the type of the relation must be as old as society. Through historical and personal time the details of function change, but for Darby the reality of Joan is exhausted in her various roles, and for Joan her Darby is a social place, a good provider, a reliable father, and nothing more. The husband and wife who exist to each other as functions and fixtures have almost forgotten that a human being can be more; each has lost the other except as a habit; each feels the other only as an extension of or an accommodation for the self. Under an excess of familiarity the sense of loss lies buried and poisons life. Feeling oneself valued for proficiency alone, knowing no other way to value another self, the deeper intensities fade and die into calculation, sympathy contracts to prediction, and love becomes convenience.

The relation of Darby and Joan is an abstract relation. Each has lost awareness of the other as a concrete and independent being. Each can need and value and praise what the other provides, but these will be helps or uses for the self, and all sense for the other self who performs the service has disappeared, except as an occasional and mysterious source of disturbance when some part is ill-performed. When we think we value a person for performances that money could buy, we are valuing only the performances. When attention seems directed only to our various roles, we feel left out of account, feel the absence of care. This feeling is neither wholly reasonable nor wholly unjust. The notion that we can be known or can know another as we "know" our own immediate experience is a romantic illusion, but there is a kind of concern for concreteness that we *can* reasonably hope, and that will be missed in a relation at heart contractual. Neither Darby nor Joan lives with an individual wholly real in his own right: each has abstracted a set of functions from the other and put this set of functions to the service of a self. Without rising far enough to see and respect universal humanity, each has lost in abstraction the presence and care of an individual and objective life.

This is one kind of emptiness that underlies habitual domesticity. It need not, but it so usually does that many take it as an ideal. Our standards for "successful" marriage are so unimaginative and low that an absence of visible strain—visible to the neighbors—can count as happiness, and emotional atrophy as satisfaction. The mutual loss of the feeling of mutual care, the belief that one is valued as a commodity would be (however high that value may be set), leads to a relation neither personal nor intolerable, neither respectful, intense, nor without compensations. Communication of sorts there will be, a conventional system of taps heard through a wall, but the affective vocabulary will be kept safely thin, the syntax necessarily crude and narrow. Such a useful social arrangement, marked by absence of communion and failure of love, has an excellent chance to pass as ideal marriage. It may be that little is lost by this in most cases and that many of us present little purchase for knowledge or love, but it is an unnecessary contraction of hope to think that this is always true. Nor would resentment lie so visibly across the institutional air of marriage if it were not often a two-celled prison for two lost souls.

Even from society's impersonal point of view, this attenuation of affection carries penalties. The habitual unawareness of the happy old couple was scarcely disturbed by the notion that things could be otherwise, and their relation was supported by a moral and social structure that felt inevitable to them and stable to their children. When awareness of individuality was rare, loss of individuality could seldom count as loss. When Darby and

Joan, married fifty years ago, saw in their little world no relation unlike their own, or none felt as an appropriate model for
them, their standards of domestic felicity suffered no strain by
comparison, and their family unconsciously grew into their
shape.

That institution was sometimes felt as a prison by the young,
and sometimes the young were right; right or wrong the domestic
world they broke away from is itself now broken. The new Darby
and Joan are neither oppressed nor supported by inbred custom and ignorance, and in supposed freedom and half-knowl-
edge have discovered new bitterness. Each is apt to feel he had
once owned himself concretely, perhaps most valued himself for
what was felt as most individual, but that this uniqueness had
been written off in arriving at their common balance. The suspicion of abstraction will be most bitter if the new Darby and
Joan are disillusioned romantics. Our great-grandparents could
seldom resent the loss of a dream most never had, but the happy
young couple whose picture appeared in yesterday's newspaper
have absorbed their attitudes toward love from a tragic couple
whose story they have never heard to the end, a pair whose influence, diluted and vulgarized, has made them a common,
unconscious paradigm. The secret poison at the heart of the
modern Darby and Joan has been distilled in their descent from
Tristan and Isolde.

2. *Tristan and Isolde*[2]

Not every Darby and Joan trace this descent. Many still begin
as they end, concerned not with individuals, but with goods and
services. This is far from the best satisfaction our nature can rise
to, but it is anything but unnatural. We are among other things
social animals, and it is an old observation that most marriages
are made at cross-purposes, the man's being animal and the
woman's social. Nothing in this is newer than society itself; the
protest against it is less authentically antique, depending in

general on the value given individuality, but often more particularly on a romantic attitude toward the self and the world. What is modern about these attitudes is less their existence than their incidence. Ranges of thought and feeling that were once the exclusive preserve of a privileged class, and subject to whatever discipline that class could impose, have come to be common property in disordered societies. Tristan was a knight, the most accomplished figure in his world, and his story was sung to men who shared his code and knew his worth; Isolde was a beautiful lady, once upon a time, when there were few human females who pretended to be either. It is not possible that the rumor of their affair should come to us undistorted. Our little comedies end in marriage, their tragedy ended in death, but up to the limit of our trifling potential for tragedy we unknowingly do our best to imitate them. Like them we take an impossibility for an ideal, but we do not follow our ideal to their death. We quietly die into Darby and Joan.

In our ignorant and sprawling sentimentality we have so far forgotten how to read the figures of Tristan and Isolde in their context that we take from them as our good what leads to death, and miss what can lead to life. What they knew was the relation between concreteness and intensity; each, by magic, recognized the other as unique, and took an individual as the focus of concern. Their realization was tragically flawed, but their fiercely contracted vision saw truly what it saw: that fullness of love depends on intense awareness of otherness; that love becomes a transforming power only when it strains the limits of the self in reaching toward a particular, separate self. Here the romantic insight is deep and narrow. They see that if love and life itself are to have any content at all, are to be sensed as more than empty gestures, particular moments must be apprehended without abstraction. Further, they see that the most intense of these moments depend on a sensed relation of the self to something not itself, a movement toward a reality at once objectively other and as concretely particular as the given self. Beyond this their vision blurs. The tragedy of Tristan and Isolde lies in a misunderstanding of limits, an inability or unwillingness to look beyond one range of intensity, a failure that makes it finally impossible to love the wholeness of another life.

Paradox marks the way to the romantic catastrophe. At first each of the lovers seems intensely aware of the other as a more than natural echo of the heart's unique desire and as a separate self, indefeasibly other—different from all the rest of the world, miraculously discovered, and hopelessly out of reach. The contrary aspects of this awareness feed and strengthen each other, and its intensity increases with the ambivalence. The pain of this can be a pleasure so keen that "pleasure" will seem too low a word; compared with the exquisite strain of what is felt as a relation between pure spirits, pleasure and happiness will seem merely sensible and crude. The immediate rewards may be worth their cost, but the tension on which they rest is precarious, and its intensity must grow or die. The attempt to preserve and increase the ambivalence on which intensity depends may take the form of exaggerating all that separates, of brooding on all that reminds of otherness, so that the heaven of oneness may be felt as impossible of attainment and hence the only worthy consummation. For Tristan and Isolde this tension becomes the meaning and purpose of their relation; the intensity of the relation becomes its whole good.

When romantic lovers go this far they have left behind the possibility of objective relation to another self. It is not merely that the tension they love is impossible to sustain, but that the narrow focus of their intensity, its one-pointed concentration on what is unique, concrete, and confined to the moment of having, limits their concern to a kind that can comprehend no reality beyond immediate experience. They are adepts in one intensity; its immediate quality exhausts the good of their relation, but this given like all others is given to each alone. The goodness they would know without distinction, the intensity they would possess in perfect oneness, is necessarily individual. Their mistake is not so simple as supposing that particular immediate experiences alone are valuable. Beyond this error lies another more dangerous, and to this the lovers in their fanaticism press as to salvation. Each wants to know and to have the other self at once totally and in all concreteness, to know and to have the other with all the intensity and finality that can belong to immediate experience itself.

A certain pedantry may be useful in speaking of things so close. There are good reasons for saying that one does not "know" even his own immediacies. One undergoes them, enjoys them, suffers them, appreciates them, has them; immediate experience is too near, too wordless to be known. There cannot be shared knowledge of the incommunicable—but the sharing of given experience itself is virtually inconceivable. Virtually, because in a world constituted differently from this one we might be able to speak sensibly of an experience at once numerically self-identical and common to several selves. But in our world, as far as we can tell, each immediate experience is unique to each who has it. When we look together at the evening star, or when you feel sad on Monday and I on Friday, in both cases our immediate experiences may have qualitative likenesses, but your experience is an event in your life and mine an event in mine; they may be similar events, but the two are not one. This is one ground on which we distinguish one self from another. But it is precisely distinction and separateness that Tristan and Isolde would overcome. It is as if they felt that knowledge of another self could not come until each had the other's identical experience. Since their love seems to demand that each know the other wholly, the ideal of final knowledge fuses with that of perfect possession. Love becomes a desperate attempt to have the other with the finality of immediate experience, to "know" the other as one is acquainted with his own givens of sense and feeling, but as nothing at all can be known. The intensity of apparent concern with otherness tends through a typical romantic inversion backward toward the self.

There are other and better senses of knowledge and love, ends whose achievement does not depend on a despairing fling toward impossibility. But the romantic lovers are fanatics, and desperate. They cannot abide that the intensities of each are not the one intensity of both; the otherness that had been a source of sweet painfulness becomes a torment; separateness is felt as cause for despair. When the felt problem is set this way, there will seem to be only two escapes, and no solutions. The usual romantic way is to regard the other as an aspect of the self's own consciousness, to reduce otherness to an occasion for immediate experience. Each such lover ends by living in a hall of mirrors, encountering reflections of himself at every turn; to the passionate solopsist his love is his own experience, there is no other. Then, in time, as novelty fails, loneliness settles in, emptiness growing ever more deadly as each new love lets slip its mask and shows the most familiar face of all. To start with a seeming awareness of another person, then to try in seeming love to know and to have the other as one's own intensity is to be aware of images and projections of the self, to know and to have and to be in love with nothing beyond the self. This is the course of the lesser romantics, and in it objectivity and otherness are lost.

Except in the dignity he borrows from Mozart, Don Juan is a pathetic or comical character. But Tristan and Isolde are heroic figures, and if we sense a certain ludicrousness in their exaggerations, this is itself a genuine aspect of their tragedy. Their high ideal is mutual transcendence of individuality. Neither would meanly regard the other merely as an occasion, as an excuse for experience or escape, or as a part of the self. The distinction from which they suffer is characterized by conviction of the absolute worth of the other, and if the conviction heightens their suffering, it lifts them beyond desire for the little solution. They would know nothing less than perfect mutuality: not reduction of one self to another's satisfaction, but absolute freedom from selfhood so that both selves might merge into one partless, boundless whole. The way to this paradoxical end lies through the dissolution of all that individuates and separates one self from another, but Tristan and Isolde feel the only loss will be a loss of unwanted limits. And so they concentrate all intensity at one point of love, burningly focus all concern on the uniqueness, concreteness, and otherness they would overcome; the strain is increased and increased until it seems that the self must break or dissolve, resolve itself into one intensity.

Romantic lovers in the old heroic mold try to shatter the limits of the self, to strain toward otherness past endurance, to become one infinite experience. To this impossibility all that is possible is sacrificed. Misapprehending the truths that fullness of life requires intensity, and that love depends on the double presence of concreteness and mutuality, the romantic lovers despise all hope for wholeness of life, reject the human situation, and in the rage to disappear as distinct and separate selves rush on to death. The abandonment of hope for more diverse and inclusive patterns of satisfaction is not accidental: that promise depends on acceptance of the conditions and forms of human life, and Tristan and Isolde are not reconciled to humanity. Life limits them. Death seems the only opening to the only mutuality in which they could rest. For the romantic love always leads to death, or is scarcely distinguishable from it. Tristan and Isolde literally, or at least dramatically, die—as they had to do. The error that guides them is on the heroic scale, almost achieving a perfect inversion of wisdom. Their end is to fuse past all distinction that which is ineluctably individual and distinct, to become one in the matter of immediacy itself. The varied form of human life, its sharable patterns of experience, they disregard or destroy.

The one-pointed romantics would crack all form, go beneath all order to formless intensity, to pain, to death. You will scarcely find their like today. But the impossible ideal of oneness in matter affects us still, as a confused or disavowed dream, although the rhetoric of perfect passion has given way to talk of togetherness. At unheroic altitudes the romantic becomes a sentimentalist and keeps too much sense or too little courage to follow his false premises to their truly deadly conclusions. The common little romantics do not go all the way to physical death; they stop at marriage. Their ideal was to have each other wholly and, necessarily failing that, they lose each other altogether. Despairing of the impossible, but not very fervently, they turn away from hope of understanding the affections of the other and learn to live with a reliable abstraction. This too is a kind of common death, and Darby and Joan sometimes know it. They may not be fully aware of what has happened, but in their prosaic way they illustrate again the old romantic falling of love into death.

The special bitterness in this is that love *should* lead to life. There is a soberly meaningful sense in which we can take love to be our chief relation to the objective world, or even to give us that world. The going out of affection to otherness, the re-creation of concreteness, and the recognition of form—our sense of reality is a function of these. (Our knowledge of truth is something else again. It is not only possible, it is not unusual to have one without the other.) But this tact is impossible without discipline. It is exactly when intensity is at greatest strain that there is greatest danger of losing touch with otherness and finding oneself not enlarged, but isolated. The control that is necessary —necessary to one's own felicity, required if we would retain felt relation to objective reality, and due to the reality we feel—is most rewarding when most difficult. Those who know how to love know this, or rather they sense it; their wisdom wordlessly tells them that love requires both oneness and the restraint of respect for difference.

The sense that expresses itself as intense and other-regarding tenderness, as true concern, as loving kindness, has no words; it belongs to the life of the affections. But a rationale can be found for it, one which shows where the great and the small romantics go astray. It is as true as such things can be that the self must be lost to be found, and it is in love that the self is best for-

gotten, in the furthest reach of this affection that we come closest
at once to transcendence of self, to communion with otherness,
and to self-fulfillment. But the romantic lovers cannot understand or accept the conditions of human love, the natural limits
that give it form and value, or the way these conditions and
limits must be respected if they are to support a redeeming tension of oneness and difference. We have seen that the living person can be understood as matter informed, as at once unique and
a human being. In these terms we can understand that the romantic lovers die to be one as they cannot be, and scorn to
meet as they can. But it is less than the whole truth to say that
we can be one only as we are universal, and must be isolated in
our uniqueness. Tristan and Isolde truly felt one part of wisdom,
but they mistook the romantic part for the whole. We must see
how close to communion, to substantial affective oneness structured by human form, the mutuality of true love can be.

B. *Caritas* AND REALITY

Not all romantic lovers end operatically, or as Darby and
Joan, or in the courts. If their appreciation of intensity can
become more complex and catholic, if respect for what is not
the self is commanded, there is better hope for them than for
the many who begin less intensely. It is hard to be reconciled
to the fact that a purely passionate love is self-destroying, that
love which will not alter cannot live, that all human love is
ephemeral; those who have had to learn this, and learn it in
time, are deeper in love than those who were never deluded.
Falling in and out of love is easy and accidental; love for another
person is an achievement, and rare, but one can begin by loving
his impossible dream of love, and end by loving the other who
was its occasion. Such love requires appreciation of all the concreteness, intensity, and idiosyncrasy that individuates the other,

but at least equally it requires ability to cherish as if it were one's own most cherished experience the life of an irreducibly separate self.

The saving grace is that the life of another need be little further from us than is the whole of our own. Our view of the whole of our lives is an interpretation of the absent. Only in imagination do we see ourselves complete, and the self we see is a constant re-creation; our present is the changing center from which the shapes of memory and hope are seen anew, a vanishing point that takes its meaning from the figure as a whole. But the same imagination that gives this perspective to each can imitate the immediacies and patterns of another's experience. That other life re-created in our own is an imaginative reading of time-bound and passing impressions, a constructed concreteness at once less and more than an abstract hypothesis about human behavior. It is an experiential configuration we know to be our own, but can only believe or hope to be like that of another person. The distinction of selves is not lost in this; it remains true that each can have only his own experience. If this truism still feels tragic, without its acceptance there is neither under-standing nor love, only the genuine loss that follows attempted assimilation. The awareness that there *is* another to know and love, a being like us and yet apart from ourselves, is an appre-ciation of given signs, intimations which seem to show that we are not unique in our sense of uniqueness, isolation, and pe-culiar reality.

Each of us will always sense some mystery at the heart of other-ness, a final opacity or reticence which we do well to respect. The understanding we can reasonably hope to have is still wonderfully worth having. Our understanding is like a trans-lation of a poem from a language we can never really know. We recognize that no translation gives us all that its original means and suggests, we know that there must be losses, distor-tions, false colors, but we can hope for a re-creation in which our language imitates as nearly as its nature allows the idiom and meaning of another. If the other language is inaccessible, we can only guess at the closeness of our version to its original, guided by our own sense of how such a thing should be done. Beyond this hoped-for faithfulness, itself a function of respect and willingness to love, if the translation is to live in its second setting it must be intelligible there. If the new words bring no feeling of understanding, if their form and import when most openly entertained remain so foreign and unfamiliar that our native language cannot comprehend their significance, then the effort of understanding will seem greater than its product justifies, and will—perhaps too soon—be given up. Last of all, and living at the very edge of hope, there is the possibility that the re-created concreteness will be a good and beautiful work in itself. The difficulty of achieving this marks the aptness of translation as a metaphor of human understanding. Faithfulness, intelligibility, and beauty; justice, comprehension, and love are what we can hope for in personal relations. The understanding involved is not the same as knowledge. It is at once concrete and finally unconfirmable, first-personal and seemingly self-transcendent, immediate and immediately giving the sense of objective otherness. It is imagination that can reconstruct and feel and cherish the life of a separate and independent self. It is through an act of imagination, intense and disciplined, that the human world can be ours.

Just understanding is unusual, but to understand with loving kindness is so rare it may seem a gift of grace; for most of us it can be only a hope and an ideal. And yet the understanding of another, even a willingness to try to reconstruct his experience of life, is already a fair beginning toward the ends of *caritas* and communion. Appreciation of the other neither as passion alone, nor as opportunity, role, or problem, but as matter informed, is an interpretation that necessarily touches one's own affections. The shapes of feelings we take on become ours, their familiarity qualified by strangeness and the knowledge that we merely imitate. Unless we are deadened by ignorance and hate of ourselves, the life we have tried to understand will capture our concern. So far as our intepretation is deeply felt—and such interpretation is a rehearsal of life—that far will the translated experience become real as our own. If perfect human understanding must remain an ideal, at least we can say what its perfection would be. It would be to realize in imagination the distinct life of another, to respect its native reality knowing it not to be overcome, and to feel the interpreted experience with all the intensity given our original immediacies. It is in the same direction that we find that sense of charity in which all need charity—and the perfection of charity is love.

Where the imagination of otherness is wanting, the names of love and charity have turned from their best uses and sound operatic or empty. In the sensible fullness of love one feels with the other so closely that the harmony seems to be sharing. If this "understanding" is not "knowing" it is something better: it is as close to communion as we can ever come. If this communion still falls short of love, the something more that love requires is a care for the concreteness of the imagined life, a concern that differs only in direction from our interest in ourselves.

The experience of love cannot be put into words, but self-esteem and self-love are allowed to be common, and the person who has felt these must only imagine them as attached to another to gain a first insight into the nature of love. The trouble is that this first insight is often the last, since equally common are the failure of imagination to reach out to otherness and failure to give oneself in trust to the life of another. These are the bonds of selfishness that tie a man to himself, and if the selfish man is frightened it may do no good to tell him he must give his life to gain it. Yet in the exposure that comes with openness, in the vulnerability we feel when the whole of another's experience is more dear to us than our own, we find the most intense realization of life, and the most transforming conviction of our relation to an objective world. To be without love in this sense is almost to lose everything, and all the knowledge in the world cannot make up for this loss. To care more for another than for the self—to love and cherish the concreteness we can imagine but can never really share, and to love and respect the forms we have in common—not only gives us back ourselves enlarged, but is the obvious best answer to isolation. The sense that there is a real world with men and women in it, the feeling of their reality and of our real relation to it, is a consequence of charity, a function of love.

1. *Mutuality*

There is nothing in the nature of love which ensures that it will be returned in kind, and love at its best will not endeavor that this be otherwise. When a person fully realized as other is one's care, the understanding and love of that person and his happiness are a sufficient enlargement and reward. But if the demand to be loved as one loves is an imperfection, the wish is almost unavoidable. The demand is vicious; the wish casts forward to the *summum bonum* of love. This highest good is not impossible, although its achievement is rare, and humanity should keep us from scorn when humans mourn its usual loss. Nor will it do to say that the informed life as a whole can afford to laugh at this one of its desiderata. Every life will in some degree feel itself incomplete, but the absence of this completion is the saddest of all. It need not cancel out the rest, but it leaves a space in our lives and hopes that nothing else ever quite fills. It might be better for us if love were enough and we had no need to be loved; we might be better people if we did not wish that a love like our own be returned by those we love, but most of us cannot be as selfless as this, and we can never keep ourselves from hoping.

Our hope is that the other will understand us with the same loving kindness with which we have tried to respect and re-create his or her affective life. We want to feel that our experience has been imaginatively taken up, lived through, and cherished. We dream that the other will try to appreciate both our uniqueness and our common likeness, our concreteness and our universality. We do not want tolerance; we want a sense that our affections have been realized in another life, entertained there with tenderness, cared for, and forgiven. We want a place where ourselves—understood—will be accepted, a home and a refuge in the heart of another, a love that makes no conditions. Such a love we will seldom find in this world, but we cannot infer from our need that we must find it in another. The *summum bonum* may set our direction, and we may hope to approach it more and more closely, but it is not reasonable to expect perfection, and should that near-miracle occur, we could never finally know that it had. The sense of mutual care is created by an exchange of signs, varied and subtle but outward and visible; the giving of rings is open to all the world and all the world can read it, but both before and after that the language of affection requires a kind of interpretation less easy, less public, and less conventional.

Nevertheless, the signals must continue to be given and received. Our sense of the regard in which another holds us will be an interpretation of his bearing; our clues may be as tenuous as a tone of voice, a shift of the eyes, the touch of a hand or its withdrawal from our touch, but these are the signs we have to read, and if our vision has any ground at all, from these it rises and to them it returns for confirmation. The matter is often too subtle for the spirit of geometry, depending as it partly does on a sensitivity to the unique and calling on an affective tact that goes below the possibility of words. The metaphor of machine translation may illuminate the human understanding of wholly unimaginative and narrow people, but only theirs. Whatever we may say of knowledge, the imaginative exercise that is our understanding of another depends on interpretation of gesture, tone, and color. If no action is given us to interpret, or if our reading has no relation to what should be its text, then what we think or feel will be fantastic or perverse. Either can happen: from indifference, dullness, or inarticulateness no signs may come; through constriction of imagination or too peculiar a warp we can misread or fail to catch the word we are given. Worst of all, and perhaps the only such sadness that deserves the name "tragedy," is the situation of those who would love with all their hearts, but who can neither one translate the heart's language of the other. All marriages are mixed marriages, but those most sadly mixed enmesh a man and a woman who would love each other to the limits of what each understands as love, except that each understands something different by love. Each would signal to the other the signs that to him meant concern and tenderness, but the gestures seem not to be understood, the most important words pass without notice, and all the significant silences are empty. Then love may end in bewilderment or worse, for love apparently refused can breed its opposite.

Breadth and depth of sympathy are never infinite; try as we may there will be some things we can never understand. We come to each encounter with affections already formed, and when affective backgrounds and vocabulary are terribly disparate, the translation we must try to make will be too much for us. If there is to be a sense of mutuality in understanding and love, understanding and love must be understandably evidenced. Each must try to learn the affective language of the other, must with patience, honesty, and tact try to feel the affection expressed in modes originally foreign and express his own love with a care that it be felt as such by the other. Our need is not exactly to be loved in our own terms, but for a love whose meaning does not escape us in translation. If a man is to believe his dream that he is loved, he must on some awakenings find a real flower in his hand. And if, having learned our lessons, we understand that our life is the care of a life for which we care, then we can ask nothing further of human relations; we have already been given far more than most.

a. MAN AND WIFE

No association can ensure a thing so rare, although practice can confirm it. It is in the context of a family that the opportunities for learning to understand are greatest, are not only thorough but uniquely so; there too the chance for charity is equal to its need. Among strangers the sign language of affection is most often necessarily shallow and crude, and the social imagination when honest must be different. The understanding that can exist between a man and wife or between dear friends depends on familiarity to feed the imagination; on a tried sensitivity to changing manifestations of mood, memory, and hope; on an ability and willingness to read from one look the life looking out from the eyes of the other. Our view of the facts of our own lives must at once respect those facts and see them in a succession of changing perspectives; in the same way, but with less certain charts—fixed readings all conjectural, great areas marked as unknown, fantastic monsters ready to rise from fantastic depths—we try to follow another changing life. It can never be done once for all, and to think it has been is a deadly mistake. The reading need not be conscious, and often it cannot be, but it must be constantly responsive if one would not lose touch with the other, perhaps in time to find his devotion given to a being long dead.

If the sense of mutual understanding and love depends on the chance that each of the two who make a marriage has the ability to comprehend the other's experience, it is not surprising that most marriages amount to little more than a social convenience. And yet the institution does embody a unique opportunity for learning the touch of objective relatedness, the awareness of an understandable life close to but plainly different from one's own. To this learning and this rightly imperfect closeness marriage can contribute more than the fact of propinquity: there are the questions and answers posed by sex and the best of chances for sharing whole patterns of life.

The significance of sex when confined to the satisfaction of random urgencies has little constructive force in life as a whole, though its relief can be legitimately wanted, and its isolated intensities most potent in their time. But it is when through practice two people learn not merely proficiency—though that is much—but a pervasive responsiveness to experience at once very foreign and very like, when generosity learns to combine with selfishness, that we can say with the least exaggeration that two feel as one. We are likeliest to find our most intense immediacies in sex, perhaps because in sex as in pain we come closest to the material and merely organic ground of our lives. We seem to lose ourselves wholly, in coincidence of function all thought of form and separateness is forgotten, and for a moment the dream of oneness is real.

If random encounters are seldom as happy as this, the practice of sex in marriage can have rewards that go still further. We often feel gratitude where we have been given pleasure, but casual satisfactions, however intense, seldom earn for their giver a permanent sense of thanksgiving; grudged favors often earn the opposite. When sexual contact is all at hazard, the only fixed point is one's own sensation. For two people living faithfully together the outgoing of gratitude grows constant in direction, and what was only passion takes on tenderness. Neither simply the possession of another, nor blind self-forgetfulness, but an intensity for which we thank a being we understand—understand as concretely real, imperfect, and lovable— is the best consequence of conjugal love. To find the ground of one great satisfaction in one objective reality is to fix a deep affection beyond the self; and if constancy is matched by familiar understanding, then a home has been made in the world.

The tact of loving kindness may be learned in other ways, but no way we would willingly seek can teach so well as this, and not the least of what we learn is that we are bound to what we understand and love. Around the paradigmatic act of love memory and imagination create a thousand ties of affection, its familiar intensity is felt as understanding, and the mutuality of sex comes to be a central figure for all participation. A tie to the objective, created by love, is not a guarantee of happiness; what it brings is a sense of communion with reality, but this sense is marked by fear as well as hope, is felt in the annoyances that qualify devotion, in its hurts and restrictions as in its completion. Love finds itself in the hostages it gives, in the vulnerability that comes with awareness that its good is bound to a being in the world, and is surprised when the movement away from the self, the intensity given another, returns increased and with the gift of intensely realized objectivity. Otherness in such love becomes affectively real in us, and by it we are given our full reality.

A satisfactory sexual relation may be neither necessary nor sufficient to a satisfactory marriage, but common sense knows that it betters the chances for every other form of goodness. Here, at least, is a contour of intensity clearly and closely manifested: two outgoings which two people find it natural to take as one in form. The centrality of sex may owe as much to the obviousness of this isomorphism as to the intensity of its experience; oneness in matter and oneness in form seem realized here and can serve as a model or ideal for the whole of life together. But in the interpretation which is the whole, the relation of parts to total pattern is reciprocal, and the meaning of sexual love itself is shaped by its place in a wider affective context. All of life's concerns can be shared in marriage, and when they are, the man and wife share nothing less than the structure of human life. Though sex may long remain the cynosure, almost any common concern can tend toward communion; a joint interest in stamp-collecting or neighborhood gossip is better than the absence of any ground to meet on.

Each of us so seldom feels rightly understood that the slightest indication that some other cares about what we care about, that he or she imaginatively shares the direction of our interest and moves with us in sympathy along some private way will strike us with startled gratitude. (Walking late at night, tired and lost in an unknown city, we hear at our side the sound of a voice from home.) We know that there can be illusion in this, but we will take the signs of another's concern with our concerns as cause for hope that the other might care for us. Such shared textures are generally trivial, but however limited their extent or depth they are almost always welcome. In marriage, however, there is a chance that the themes lived through together will be those which most repay the deepest intensity— the varied themes which structure human life.

We are likeliest to find a sense of meaning and purpose when our affections to go out to fulfill a universal form, and although we may know that the order it defines is universal only within parochial limits, our past is a parish very old and wide, and the models it gives each man for his measure are as little arbitrary as any ideals can be. It might be possible to argue that the junctures and moments celebrated in the traditional religion of the West are common to human life in every climate, but this argument would add no normative force and is unnecessary. There are themes that have long been taken to define human life in our familiar world, and as we grow into this inheritance we feel them as definitive. When a man and wife so feel them, when each understands that the intensities of both are spent in the same human pattern, marriage is an ideal type of objective relation. Oneness of form guides and sustains the imagination of otherness, and interpretation constantly refreshed intensifies the sense that two separate beings are sharing the whole of life.

If this is less than the romantic dream of perfect identity it is also more, being an attainable ideal and meeting at once the need for a sense of communication, of community, and of communion. These affective factors combine when the isomorphism of two lives is evidenced in tenderness and mutual understanding. When the like experience of life intensely realizes the universal concerns, meaning and purpose are felt together, are shared. Man and wife in vision and revision imagine the same shapes of memory and hope, and moving together see from every vantage the intense and varied form of humanity. When we consider marriage as a relation between two selves, this is its highest good, an achievement in understanding to which every other understanding can look for light. But when we further consider that man and wife are also father and mother, we see to the end of human love and beyond it to the charity that returns to us the sense of reality.

b. THE FAMILY

We take our first and lasting model of the world from the family. When we are most open, it is our universe; our parents are the sun and moon and climate, and they can make the first world their children know into a model of what the world should be. Or the parents are like artists whose material is the stuff of life itself, not only their experience together, but life at its most malleable in their children. No other world can be so much a creation, no age so golden, but the touch of such a time can live in us through our later worlds of brass and iron.

However it may have been with us, the hope that our children will have this help is largely in our hands. If in their first world they learn what goodness of life can be, if without the need for thought they sense in their lives the possibility of order for which we stand as present patterns, then they and perhaps their children in turn will grow in grace and beauty and realize ever more perfectly in each particular life the form of humanity. The mother and father may find in this a hope for a kind of unremembered immortality, but that hope is not their motive: their ground is love. The perennial wonder, here as everywhere, is that most is given to the love which asks least for itself.

The human matter we are given is never perfectly plastic, but in the family as nowhere else we can create an island of order that goes beyond the boundaries of the single self. Very few of us can contribute largely to a general reform of society, but it is open to each of us to make of his own family a small society as exempt as can be from the pressures of public formlessness and vulgarity and perhaps a beacon for those who see its light. A family cannot be exempt from the social atmosphere that surrounds it, nor can it withdraw from the world, but when it is conscious and confident of its values it can, out of its own resources, withstand the worst of the drab disorder that afflicts society at large. More often than not the family succumbs to being the vulgar world in miniature.

It might be easy to blame too much the man who resigns the task of reshaping an entire society; it would be difficult to blame too much the man who in weariness or indifference gives over to society at large those lives which are his unique responsibility, those few lives it is his unique opportunity to inform. Nothing is simpler than to decry democratic society and its agents, the schools, for failure in moral education, but the schools cannot usefully offer images of goodness that are not popular compromises adapted to the varying capacities of those who come to be taught and of those who teach. The schools as they are must be broad and loose and shallow in their impact if they are to have any impact at all. What is good in their democracy restricts their influence to re-enforcement of the lowest demands of their setting, and their only gift to the individual child is a common touch of common worldliness. The uniqueness of each child is forgotten in school, and the child himself is in danger of forgetting it there. In the family uniqueness can be recognized and remembered, but tempered with a sense of membership far deeper than any other he is likely ever to know.

In the past the enforced intimacy of family life was often felt as a prison. Its goods were taken for granted as belonging to the natural order of things or as an independent aspect of human nature, and its evils convincingly emphasized by the disaffected and articulate. But the Victorian family or the patriarchal group set neither opportunities nor problems for us. If some badness has disappeared from the world with them, our gain has been less than entire, for we stand in some danger of forgetting the good that can still come from family solidarity and close family life. If in most families in our time and place blood seems thinner than gasoline, this is through a weakening of will which surrenders the family to all it should resist. It need not be so. Economic bases change and social grounds erode, but the living together of parents and children necessarily retains the primitive organic roots from which it originally grew and from which in each particular case goodness can grow again. One must not only cultivate his garden, he must be prepared for the extra difficulties that come to the defender who knows that walls will not accomplish his purpose, that his final dependence must rest on openness and in the strength of those whose growth he has informed. To the end of conscious information it is not enough for parents to be objects of love; they must also be the pattern of love. Our children will imitate us in any case; their picture of what things ought to be will form around us as we are and grow in the light of our relation to them and to each other.

What counts is not what we tell our children, but what they overhear. If the affective meanness and commercial obsessions of the great world invade the family through our life and conversation, we are not entitled to surprise when our children fall into ugly ways or drift into an existence as meaningless, harried, and finally dull as the glittering life that surrounds them. It may be inevitable that all of us to some extent succumb and that our children will be drawn into the richly baited trap of distraction, but if our children have no bearings likelier to lead to satisfaction than those they take up from gossip and television, that will at least in part be our fault and mean that a genuine opportunity has been lost or thrown away. Of course, it is easier for parents to complain and do nothing, comforting themselves with the reflection that the world will sooner or later have its way, and forgetting that later is much better than sooner. The complaint is designed to prove a general superiority to the ordinary lot, while through forgetting parents avoid the trouble of holding their children back from the downward drag of things and evade the responsibility of mediating between the child and the ideal.

It is the order of love that children can learn in the family. The patterns our present world is most likely to offer them are coercive, lifeless and brittle, precarious. We know they will of necessity learn the force of authority they cannot or should not respect, will discover that to most of the world they are no more than instances of some easy category, will be taken as mirrors in which strangers see only themselves, or as mines to be exploited and abandoned. This is the way of the world and it always has been, but the form of our first familiar world can be the fruit of natural tenderness, and in its ambience affection creates its own best discipline. Our actions are the models for our children, and in the signs we give them they should sense a love that gives itself without making conditions, a love that draws its force from levels below the animal, grows toward understanding, and bears in its season the gift of human freedom. We will be imitated, and if the relation of husband and wife is loving, intense, and in the best sense objective, our children will at least have the chance to assimilate our patterns. Even more, our relation to them will first focus their general vision and sense of reality and impress the first outlines— vague, forgotten, persistent—of a satisfactory structure of life in that setting. Unless we force to our children's attention that we will not or cannot play this part in their lives, they will accept our authority as natural. In the exercise of government that they expect from us lives the best hope they will ever have of feeling together qualities that could be perfectly combined only under a mythical ruler: justice and mercy, service and freedom, fear in the aspect of a love given past possibility of comprehension or thanks.

These figures are larger than life; it is our own lives and discipline that are the educators of our children. The affective forms they take from us will not be exactly our own, but the humanely ordered emotion our lives exemplify can shape their bent toward an experience of life found good. This is true of all the combinations or tensions on whose resolution the sense of communion, of human meaning, purpose, and satisfaction depend. Children can understand their membership in the family—the most intimate and primitive of groups, the association in which oneness arises from communion of flesh—and each child can be made to feel that he is unique, an individual singular and irreplaceable, and in these divergent and inseparable aspects an object of love. One would scarcely speak to a child of universality and concreteness, of the one and the many and their union, but in the family the child can feel the meaning of these too-intellectual terms. So it is with freedom and discipline, intensity and restraint. The child's is the discipline of imitation, the parent's the discipline of love; through our practice we can show—more perfectly and believably than any precepts can—that order is not incompatible with emotion, that the restrictions of equity and respect for otherness need not be the cold impositions of some alien justice but can be the perfecting forms of affection. Some lessons come hard to the parents and late to the children. The child you love is the child you want to hold, to make one with you, but your love is not complete unless you can let him go. He is the life of your life, and having given life and form your love must prove itself by further giving, by the restraint that gives your other life its freedom from your love. And you know that this last lesson will not be wholly understood by your child until he has children of his own.

To say to parents in general "Just now is the time to hold, now to accept otherness and let go; now punish, now kiss, now rage" would be impertinent, banal, or both. The generalizations that can be made are too old not to be obvious, but their application cannot be reduced to the letter; even if there were always rules, there cannot always be rules for interpreting rules. The disposition to guiltless and happy reconciliation of singularity and humanity, immediacy and order, matter and form will be the more useful as it is general and flexible. What we can say is that affection trained to appreciate the varied intensities most specifically human, habits of concern informed by imitation of a loved and exemplary type of humanity, tend to a life that feels itself as an intrinsic realization of meaning and purpose. We know that we must give our children into the world, and we know that the world will take their innocence as its price, but their good beginning is our responsibility and strength. We can create for our children one little world in which the right things are important. We can do this if we will, and we will if our love is strong enough to stand against the seductions and sanctions of a civilization that mistrusts or scorns simplicity, that has tried to forget all forms that are not commercial, and that fears any distinction that cannot be bought for money.

To hate the world for this would undo our purpose, but we must go our own way. Without the support of popular social forms, without belief in the supernatural benefits of sacramental religion, we must celebrate the essential themes through the life of the family. Our children will feel what concerns us, and their imitation of the concerns they see and hear and guess will bend their attention to the shape of ours. If our life centers on the indiscriminate appetite for sensation, money and status, things and spite, our family will reflect this and our children— blasé in kindergarten—will discover even sooner than we the symptoms of affective meaninglessness.

Every family has its rituals, and if most of these recognized regularities are happily trivial, all of them need not be trivial. It would be absurd to propose specific domestic substitutes for the sacraments, but the context given by familial unity and difference does conduce to recognition of essential themes. The unafraid expression of affection, the experiences we fear or go out to meet, the respect we manifest with gladness—these are the original grounds of celebration, and when their objects and rhythms are as evident as they can be in the close communion of family life they will be felt as celebration still. It is not simply by the occasions we keep, but by the constancy or recurrence of our chief concerns and their expression that we give measure to the lives of our children. We cannot wholly arrange our life together as if it were a single and various ritual or work of art, but if we know the pattern and have the will that which we would have accustomed, ceremonious, will be so and will seem to be so rightly. The affective habits that are the structure of the moral life can be made to seem fitting, proper, and humane; the intensity of immediate experience finds here a discipline sanctioned by the sense of appropriately human naturalness. The child who has grown to form in a family that manifestly observes in its life the affective disposition of human life at its best has been given the best gift in human power to give. Perhaps it will be obvious that the parents who direct and dispose their hearts to this end may find themselves leading a more meaningful life than any they could have achieved with only their own good in mind. It is easy to love your family better than yourself, and this greater love and care can have a proportionately greater power for re-formation.

But even this is not the final reward. The last gift to the parents combines the promise of joy and sorrow, as did the gifts presented at the most human of all epiphanies. There is no real love unacquainted with willing sacrifice, no real love unmixed with fear, no real love where there is no vulnerability. We know that our children will not love us as we have loved them; that love they will give to their children. We know that our children will leave us for a world we cannot but fear for their sake, that we must make it seem right to them that they should go, that we must not insist on the truth that they have taken our hearts with them. If in them we have been born again to a beginning more precious and more full of hope than we ourselves remember or have realized, we will suffer with them more than all our past pain had led us to think possible and imagine their happiness with an intensity more deep and constant than any felt in self-concerned experience. The person who must leave us is the child we have come to understand so well that we know his reality goes beyond our understanding; nothing beyond the self so naturally holds the devotion of our imagination. Our participation in his being is increased by love, but that light is shadowed by knowledge that its object must go from us into a world that will not see as we do; in the light and darkness of love and loss we recognize the face of otherness and feel the depths of our involvement in objective reality. The child carries with him our love, understanding, and fear, and we feel the world in which he moves with all its burden of independent life, with all its potencies for happiness and pain.

When the world beyond the family is felt as the situation in which the child who has left us must find goodness of life or fail, an affective tie to that alien world has been formed, an imaginative outgoing that can grow toward comprehension of all that is not the self. The imagination of what is wholly other can come in other ways, but for many the sense of reality follows a child into the world. At least this is an opening of communication that can be made naturally and without sophisticated thought, a commitment to the objective that is neither arbitrary nor waits on demonstration. The loving family is the model and the matrix of all affective relations: what we learn there—parents and children alike—are the affective patterns that lead to goodness of life; but with this we learn that by giving our imagination and charity to otherness we feel its real existence, and our own.

2. *The World Regained*

Protagoras can have only the next-to-last word. Reality in itself, if that phrase has any meaning, may not be a suitable object for human knowledge; yet we do have knowledge, for if anything is entitled to the name, what science tells us can be called knowledge. We have no better examples of rationality than can be found in its methods, no meanings of "explanation" and "truth" so clear as those applied to its confirmable results. If we dislike the term "objective truth," then "inter-subjective" will do as well, for the words that emerge from the laboratory present only technical difficulties of interpretation and communication. It is not a question of whether we like the methods, results, or tendencies: we will not be clear about any of these until we appreciate the criteria and the end of the endeavor, respect its autonomy, and reject the temptation to see scientific knowledge as identical with human understanding. Some are tempted to sentimentalize science or condemn it on the grounds of inhumanity, while others suppose that understanding and wisdom must be nothing because they are not physics or chemistry. Both kinds of partisanship, the obscurantist and the *lumpen*-scientific, confuse distinct and complementary approaches to the world, and do this to the confusion of both ways. It would exaggerate little to say "knowledge is physics" and necessary to the success of our work in the world. Knowing is always finally the servant of doing, and our doings stand a good chance of failure unless in a scientific spirit we have learned what we are about. When we set our hearts on a course in which we must for goodness and safety take account of truth, or if we would confine our beliefs to what it is warranted and sensible to believe, we must be guided by empirical and scientific lights. The world may not be as we wish it were, but it is the world we have to live in, and to learn the truth about it our only prudent and honest recourse is to the cognitive criteria used in the scientific enterprise and to the confirmable truths of fact that its practice increasingly refines. One may be unwilling to look to science for wisdom, but wisdom without knowledge is precarious, wisdom that affects to scorn knowledge can be dangerous, and for knowledge we must look to science.

Wisdom, human understanding, affective tact are richest and most reliable when disciplined by knowledge, though the knowledge may be no more than the good observer's description and prediction of the ways of the world. But wisdom is not equivalent to knowledge. We would not call a man wise or understanding if events more often than not turned out other than he expected, if his judgments of people were most frequently overturned by their behavior, or if his advice when taken consistently led to disaster. We may refuse him the title on no grounds other than our feeling that his life and advice show an insufficient awareness of things as they are, as science or common sense say they are, or as we feel them to be. This neither exalts nor reduces understanding to knowledge.

Understanding, as that word is used here, is imaginative re-creation, an attempt to reproduce the guessed concreteness of another being, and its justice is in principle unconfirmable; it is sustained by observation and can be revised by the pressure of knowledge, but it is finally a matter of feeling. Affection and imagination go out together to meet otherness; in immediate experience, itself below knowledge and incommunicable, new patterns form; then there is the hope of likeness, the hope that our wordless translation has not missed the life of the other. It is ourselves we try to shape in such interpretation; when we try in imagination to re-create a concreteness recognized as foreign, we are increased, our affections have learned a new language. Of course the world and all the creatures in it are strange and foreign; the world is not like home and we must live among strangers; but to let our own nature go out to identify itself with the beautiful and the ugly, to imagine so intensively and comprehensively that the concrete being of things becomes our own, is to invest the alien world with as great a sense of familiarity as we in our time are able to feel.

If not reality itself, the sense of reality is in the heart of the beholder, but there is much that hearts can have in common. Sometimes imagination leads, sometimes love, and the fullness of each requires the other. There is no true charity without the re-creation of otherness, and loving kindness completes our understanding, gives us a world felt in all its concreteness, puts an end to the worst of our isolation. The movement of the self from self-concern to care for another to the love of a family and then out to the world is not inevitable, but when made it has the strength and virtue of natural growth. The poses of those who would jump from the first to the last are generally strained and self-conscious even when genuine. The best of charity begins at home; the clue or model found there remains our most satisfactory and moving paradigm for all affective relations. In the family community loving translation can be so close to its texts that understanding is felt as identification, and communication has no need for words that cannot be spoken. The self in its immediacy apprehends a reality more precious than its own, yet a reality it must finally accept as independent. Perhaps the self can never be forgotten for very long, and talk of self-transcendence is always hyperbolic, but when the life of a separate being feels not only as real as our own but more valuable, then we have come to that giving of self which saves our lives. It is almost as simple as this: that which we love in this way is real to us, and our relation to it takes us out of isolation and into communion with the real. If our intensities have gone out to fulfill the human order, our life will seem to us an incarnate universal, good in itself, self-justifying. But just as communion is the central sacrament, so charity is ingredient in our most meaningful relations to the world.

It is charity that makes things most real to us, a habit of loving kindness that tries to create their distinct concreteness in our affective lives and to cherish their being as our own; charity is the essence of our sense of reality, and the essence of charity is incarnation. We need not and should not abandon our human shape, and we can and should respect what is not the self, but we can imaginatively take otherness into the established structure of our affections and entertain it there, and what we accept with respect and love is redeemed from unreality. But by this love we also are redeemed: the felt reality that lives in us is the reality in which we feel we live. In this we become vulnerable as one always does in love, subject to limitation and exposed to humiliation, pain, and death that might not otherwise be felt in such full measure; but this is the price that seems demanded if we would have the sense of significant membership in the world. When we try with loving kindness to realize things in terms of their own objectivity, our transactions with them carry the affection we invest, and the relation rises to the sense of communion, a giving and return in which the self takes its place in the real.

This is the way that *caritas* gives us the world, and the world it gives us is one in which our particular part is essential. It is in the light of our lives that we understand the life of the world, and in love we can find a new relation to almost everything. Imagination, knowingly pathetic or fanciful, still can feel its sympathies as re-creations of every reality under the sun, and giving ourselves in this understanding we seem to regain a shared life wonderfully familiar. This is not to know the truth about things; it is to feel the burden of their mystery. But our concern has not been with knowledge; it has been to rediscover ways that lead to goodness of life. The last of these is the obvious and difficult way of love, yet it would be truer to say that charity fills and animates the whole form of a life found good. We earn the sense of human meaning and purpose by giving ourselves to the various themes that determine human life, but each of our true concerns is finally a work of love and an act of communion. Although we cannot reasonably expect one perfect and universal answer to all our affective problems— our discontents depend too much on selves and a world warped beyond hope of perfect re-formation—when it is homelessness that has hollowed our lives, we discover that the devotion which informs the heart has ended its estrangement. It is still possible to be at home in the world. Its new foundation must be laid in our affections, and all that we welcome with charity will live and find understanding there. Our world will be the place we have made with love.

NOTES

INTRODUCTION

1. David Hume, *An Inquiry Concerning the Principles of Morals* (Indianapolis: Bobbs-Merrill, 1957), p. 5.

2. Aristotle was right to call ethics a branch of politics; in the Greek city-state it was. Western man is still a citizen, and his political role is not unimportant, but it would be implausible to claim that the whole of his moral concern could now be encompassed in that part. We take for granted a degree of separation of public from private life that goes beyond anything Aristotle knew.

3. Thomas Mann, *Doctor Faustus*, H. T. Lowe-Porter, trans. (New York: Alfred A. Knopf, 1948), p. 485.

CHAPTER I

1. William Butler Yeats, Letter to Lady Elizabeth Pelham [1939], From *The Letters of W. B. Yeats*, Allan Wade, ed. (New York: Macmillan, 1955).

2. The following illustrative definition is from Ambrose Bierce, *The Devil's Dictionary* (New York: Dover Publications, 1958), p. 95: "*Ostrich*, n. a large bird to which (for its sins, doubtless) nature has denied that hinder toe in which so many pious naturalists have seen a conspicuous evidence of design. The absence of a good working pair of wings is no defect, for, as has been ingeniously pointed out, the ostrich does not fly."

3. There would be precedent for the dismissal of such problems as merely psychological and thus philosophically uninteresting or

unreal. This kind of banishment from proper philosophy is associated with the program of logical positivism. (The best popular statement of the program is found in A. J. Ayer, *Language, Truth and Logic,* originally published in 1936.) Positivism in the last thirty years has abated most of its strictness, and in its most intolerant and dismissive form is scarcely alive today.

4. If the question "Why is there anything rather than nothing" is meant as a demand for some justification of all existence, it is literally absurd.

5. David Hume, *A Treatise of Human Nature,* L. A. Selby-Bigge, ed. (Oxford: Clarendon Press, 1888), p. 415.

6. We need not become involved in the so-called "problem of free-will." It is foolish to ignore the causal conditions of human choice, but for now let the reader refer to Book II, Part III, of Hume's *Treatise of Human Nature,* where the confusions about free-will are untangled. Very briefly, Hume shows that there is no incompatibility between an action's being caused and being free. A "cause" is simply an event that gives some grounds for predicting a subsequent event; it is not an occult power or connection that necessitates its effects. It is annoying to have one's behavior predicted, especially by parents, wives, husbands, and polls, but to say that behavior is predictable does not mean that it is compelled. If I correctly predict that you will have chocolate rather than vanilla, it does not follow that you have no choice.

7. John Dewey is right in saying that this distinction of means and ends is far from rigid. Ends can become means and means come to be taken as ends. One may start to take walks on doctor's orders, and continue them for their own sake long after health has returned.

CHAPTER II

1. Aristotle, *Metaphysics,* Book 11, Chapter 6 (1062b), in *The Basic Works of Aristotle,* R. McKeon, ed. (New York: Random House, 1941), p. 858.

2. Thomas Wolfe, *Look Homeward, Angel* (New York: Scribner's, 1952), p. 1.

3. Of course there are other ways to approach our moral situation; to come at it by considering how and what we think we know is not to suggest the illegitimacy of other attacks. The epistemological way

does have some peculiar advantages for our peculiar purpose. Its individual bearing is more immediate than are results in the social sciences, while psychological findings are themselves subject to epistemological criteria (of meaning, evidence, and truth). Religiously based discussions tend to be attended only by those who already believe. The philosophers who have caught the public ear seem more concerned with dramatizing their problems than with solving them. The way of epistemology is straight and narrow and does not lend itself to the melodramatic diversions with which a Kierkegaard or a Sartre beguiles our attention away from his lack of cogency, from the absence of argument. The approach through theory of knowledge may be dry, but it is clear, and its final justification must be the illumination achieved by taking it.

4. In one sense it is a trivial truth that I cannot be you. The present point is that this truism can feel like a tragedy.

5. Protagoras, Fragment No. 1, from *Ancilla to the Pre-Socratic Philosophers,* Kathleen Freeman, ed. (Cambridge: Harvard Univ. Press, 1957), p. 125.

6. Accept, say, the pragmatic theory of knowledge of C. I. Lewis's *Mind and the World-Order,* or what purports to be the universal solvent contained in Ayer's *Language, Truth and Logic,* or Gilbert Ryle's analysis (in *The Concept of Mind*) of the uses of "mind" and like words. Read any one or all of these classics in paper covers, take to mind the arguments and resolutions, and you may well agree that the egocentric predicament is a pseudo-problem, and feel it more deeply than ever.

7. The rejection of metaphysical statements as cognitively meaningless, as being neither possibly true nor possibly false, has been directed against the claim that metaphysics gives substantive knowledge, akin to that found in science but far deeper, consisting of information about the *really* real. This is a sensible rejection. Drawing a clear line and hewing to it has cleared some areas of philosophy and science of confusions that come of mixing categories, and can eliminate pseudo-explanations that arise from affective needs. Whatever it is we get in metaphysical speculation, it is sufficiently different from scientific information to make it a virtual condition of clear-headedness to distinguish between them; it is not a question of legislating an activity out of existence, but of refusing to assimilate disciplines

unlike enough to be usefully distinguished. (The case for distinction is strongest when compounding solves the real problems of neither area, but generates spurious perplexities and their answers out of the uneasy and unstable compound.) If we mean by "metaphysics" just the attempt to define categories and criteria that will be useful for organizing and anticipating our various experience, and to make more clear and responsive the categories we use, then "metaphysics" names one of the most useful pursuits a philosopher can follow. Cf. C. I. Lewis, *Mind and the World-Order*, Introduction.

8. There are possibilities of evasion here and some of them are highly successful in concealing the individual's responsibility, at least from himself. What seems nearest to release from the pain of self-determination is the sense of an almost coerced abandonment of one's own will to the will of God. It seems to be easy to forget one's decision that such surrender is a moral good, to ignore one's judgment that it is indeed God's will to which one's own is given, to assume that the knowing of His will requires no interpretation, and to overlook the fact that one morally judges in accepting God's will as the guide to right action. Yet each of these is a kind of decision, and could be called correct or incorrect, right or wrong, only by reference to independent criteria. We may say that following God's will is good because He has said so; this means that we have somehow decided to take His word for this, and take it that the word we have heard is His word, perhaps because the word includes the claim that it is His word. We may say that God's will determines the good simply by being God's will; this is a tautology, at best a decision to add the word "good" to whatever God happens to will.

To speak of the goodness of God sensibly it is necessary to judge God good. The statement that God is good is the conclusion of a moral judgment, and we are responsible for the criteria by which we judge.

9. Aristotle could be discussed here, too, but at too high a cost in complication. He will make his appearance later, as he did.

10. David Hume, *A Treatise of Human Nature*, p. 252.

11. We may think the unlikeliest of arrangements to be a compromise between Platonism and that phenomenalism which translates all being into appearance, between the vision of forms transcendentally real and providing an escape from the self and the doctrine

that to be is to be an appearance. And yet it is just such a compromise that is suggested by the work of Virginia Woolf. Her phenomenalism, her focus on appearance, is what first strikes one's attention. It is a critical platitude to call *To the Lighthouse* a Berkeleian novel and *Mrs. Dalloway* a Berkeleian novel without Berkeley's God. Everything in these novels exists in the mind of someone, exists as a concrete image, or perhaps as something more abstract in the mind of Mr. Ramsay. But at least a complementary and perhaps a redeeming sense of reality is conveyed in *To the Lighthouse;* in the complementarity of what must at first appear irreconcilable emphases—the Platonic love of formal order and the Berkeleian concentration on immediate experience—a hint of potential affective structure can be seen.

There is a sense of "real" seldom separated from metaphysics, a sense in which "real" is reserved for what is most valuable. It is plain that for Plato the real is the valuable, but for him forms or universals are valuable because they are real. For Virginia Woolf it may be that what is real is real because it is valuable. For her it is the seen and felt embodiments of form that are real; what is real, what stands out from the flux of time, is the manifestation in sense of formal beauty. In this Virginia Woolf stands partly in a classical tradition; for Plato, Aristotle, and Plotinus, forms have both a moral and an aesthetic function, and these are scarcely to be distinguished. That joint function is first to be eternal and extra-spatial standards of perfection and beauty, and then so far as possible to make perfection manifest in the world of sense. Forms themselves are principles of organization; the Platonic Idea is the source and final point of rationality. The imitation of these paradigms by the changing things of sense is inevitably, even tragically, imperfect, but it is in this way that beauty lies.

So far as Virginia Woolf supposes reality to be found in the immediacies of sense, she is a Berkeleian. So far as she finds the highest reality in beauty of form, beauty of order manifest in sense, she is in the tradition of Plato. When she finds the real in the momentary appearance, she is a phenomenalist, and would seem to promise no escape to a transcendental ground. When she almost tells us that it is the beauty of things that gives them meaning, that the beauty of order is eternal, and form eternally valuable, she comes close to

Platonism. Her metaphysics and theory of knowledge are Berkeleian, almost Protagorean, and her theory of value Platonic.

Without pretending that we can in this way account for the complexity and loveliness of her work, we can at least say that in the tension between these extremes, between the emphasis on the realities of immediate perception and the longing for order and eternal form, lies much of the strained beauty of her style. She offers no visions of escape from sense and self, unless the ordered perfection of sense should count as an escape. To think that immanent in the flux of life itself, obscured there but able to be elicited and felt as form, are patterns of almost Platonic beauty—to sense that sense itself and life itself can take on form and find the values of form—this artist's thought we can hold to in all that follows.

12. The same divergence in doctrine and convergence in popular effect can be seen in the case of "pragmatism," "logical positivism," and most lately "linguistic analysis."

13. The political application of this distinction has been most useful. For one thing, the individual who stands outside the State as defined by itself—although of course it speaks for the Absolute—has no metaphysical-political reality, and therefore can be liquidated without real loss.

14. If in Sartre it sometimes seems that the *En-soi* with which the *Pour-soi* longs to combine is a natural object as natural objects are understood by common sense and science, this is an illusion. To be at once in-and-for-oneself is to be a moment in the Hegelian Dialectic; the paradigm of the *En-soi–pour-soi* is the Absolute.

15. A first principle of conduct is a *general* normative statement; in theory particular statements or actions can be deduced from it. Here, for example, is a random sample of first principles:

"The true end of man is the actualization of his essential rationality." That is, "To be a good human being or a real human being is to try always to be more and more rational."

"So act that you could consistently will the basic intention of your action to be the efficacious motive of all men in similar circumstances."

"Always burn with a hard, gemlike flame."

"Always be kind to dumb animals."

"Take to be important in life its universal themes: those patterns of experience at once uniquely yours and common to all men."

16. *Cf.* Jean-Paul Sartre, *Being and Nothingness* (New York: Philosophical Library, 1956), pp. 553–554, 589.

17. In 1793, Collot d'Herbois, member of the Committee of Public Safety, said "Some wish to moderate the revolutionary movement. What! Can a tempest be steered? The Revolution is one. We cannot and must not check its motion. Citizens, patriotism must always be at the same height! If it drops for an instant it is no longer patriotism. . . ." From R. R. Palmer, *Twelve Who Ruled* (Princeton: Princeton Univ. Press, 1951 [1958]) , p. 129.

18. One could illustrate this point by following the development of the idealistic philosophy of J. G. Fichte, which moves from pure theoretical egoism to oratorical assertion of the moral primacy of the nation.

19. Any story more complex than a fable of Aesop will illustrate any number of moral points or none at all. This means that one always selects and hypothesizes in using stories to illustrate moral lessons, but the same processes are involved in the use of history and biography and in reviewing one's own life. We all think the life of Charles XII instructive, but would hesitate to say that he intended our instruction. We would often go wrong were we to suppose an author concerned to preach through his story the lessons we take from it, but no such assumption need be made. The didactic use of works of art need presuppose nothing about an artist's intention, and certainly is not committed to the view that the intended purpose of art is moral instruction.

20. Conrad calls Heyst a "stoic," but while stoicism does preach emotional isolation, it does not advocate Heyst's practical, literal isolation from society. Epicureanism does argue for the garden life, affective invulnerability, and above all the avoidance of pain. Epicurus and Lucretius saw the relation of vulnerability to pain so vividly that it frightened them.

21. Nathanael West, *Miss Lonelyhearts* (New York: New Directions, 1933) , p. 79.

22. Joseph Conrad, *Victory* (New York: Modern Library, n.d.) , p. 206.

23. *Ibid.,* p. 164.

24. *Ibid.*, p. 76.

25. *Ibid.*, p. 209.

26. *Ibid.*, p. 188.

27. *Ibid.*, p. 383.

28. It is not inevitable, but it is not unusual for antinomianism to lead to crime. This is because a mind limited to knowledge of its immediate cultural environment takes the breaking of a law or custom of that environment to be an adequate proof of freedom. If one resolves to ignore the laws completely, there is a good chance he will break them; but to break a law scarcely shows that one is ignoring it; it may show that one can think of nothing else.

At the same time it is dangerously wrong to infer the practice of crime from the holding of a theory that would permit it.

To punish a man because he has committed a crime, or because he is believed, though unjustly, to have committed a crime, is not persecution. To punish a man, because we infer from the nature of some doctrine he holds, or from the conduct of other persons who hold the same doctrines with him, that he will commit a crime, is persecution, and is, in every case, foolish and wicked. . . . If, indeed, all men reasoned in the same manner on the same data, and always did what they thought it their duty to do, [the latter] mode of dispensing punishment might be extremely judicious. But as people who agree about premises often disagree about conclusions, and as no man in the world acts up to his own standard of right, there are two enormous gaps in the logic by which alone penalties for opinions can be defended. . . . Man, in short, is so inconsistent a creature that it is impossible to reason from his belief to his conduct, or from one part of his belief to another.

T. B. Macaulay, "Hallam's History," in *Critical and Historical Essays,* Vol. I (London: J. M. Dent & Sons, 1907 [1951]) , pp. 7–8.

CHAPTER III

1. William Blake, "Annotations to Sir Joshua Reynolds's Discourses, in *The Complete Writings of William Blake,* G. Keynes, ed. (London: Nonesuch Press, 1957; New York: Random House, 1957) , pp. 451–466. "The three volumes of the second edition of Reynolds's

Discourses which belonged to Blake are now in the British Museum. Blake's marginalia are written in the first volume only. . . ." [G. K.]

2. See Irving Babbitt, *Rousseau and Romanticism* (New York: Meridian Books, 1955). There is a family resemblance between the present views and those of Irving Babbitt, but this essay is much further removed from the parent stock. Babbitt would disown it on the same grounds on which we should reject "humanism" as a label for it. He does not recognize or will not accept the primacy of emotion in the moral life, and his humanism rests on an implicit metaphysical or quasi-religious foundation; its normative sentences, like those of Aristotelian ethics, are taken as descriptive, as reports of the real essence of human nature.

The belief or supposition that some prerogative qualities metaphysically determine the essence of a species is not supported with arguments by Babbitt, partly because such arguments would be too technical for his context, and partly because none of the old arguments is valid. To reject this piece of metaphysics is to be, in Babbitt's terms, a naturalist. Add to this renunciation, which has been more or less cheerfully made by most contemporary philosophy, the consequent views that the use of ethical terms is commendatory, the last word in ethical discourse persuasive, and the ground of morals affective, and one has a position that Babbitt would consider naturalistic in a thoroughly reprehensible way. If pragmatism upset him, there is no important philosophic movement today that would not send him into shock.

3. C. I. Lewis, *Mind and the World-Order* (New York: Scribner's, 1929), pp. 52–53.

4. *Ibid.*, pp. 75–76.

5. Thomas Wolfe, *The Web and the Rock* (New York: Sun Dial Press, 1940), p. 682.

6. Babbitt, *loc. cit.*

7. Samuel Johnson, *The Lives of the Most Eminent English Poets* (London: J. Rivington & Sons, 1790), p. 29.

8. "Imitation," in Aristotle's sense, implies the following of a rule, a rule not discovered by special metaphysical noesis, but based on the immanent nature of the matter to be formed.

The question of how far the use of Aristotle's language of universals commits one to (what some commentators consider) Aristotle's reification of universals is too complex a problem to enter here; it is not even clear whether and where Aristotle is committed to the doctrine that the essence of a species is a subsistent entity. Whatever Aristotle meant by "universal" and its cognates, we need mean no more than "recurrent quality or pattern of experience." Our use of "universal" can be more modest than Aristotle's; since we claim to prove less than he claims to prove, we need not suppose universals to be subsistent metaphysical entities.

9. *Cf.* John Dewey, *Art as Experience* (New York: Minton, Balch & Co., 1934), pp. 40–41.

For in much of our experience we are not concerned with the connection of one incident with what went before and what comes after. There is no interest that controls attentive rejection or selection of what shall be organized into the developing experience. Things happen, but they are neither definitely included nor decisively excluded; we drift. We yield according to external pressure or evade and compromise. There are beginnings and cessations, but no genuine initiations and concludings. One thing replaces another, but does not absorb it and carry it on. There is experience, but so slack and discursive that it is not an experience. Needless to say, such experiences are anesthetic.

Thus, the non-aesthetic lies within two limits. At one pole is the loose succession that does not begin at any particular place and that ends—in the sense of ceasing—at no particular place. At the other pole is arrest, constriction, proceeding from parts having only mechanical connection with one another. There exists so much of one and the other of these two kinds of experience that unconsciously they come to be taken as norms of all experience. Then, when the aesthetic appears, it so sharply contrasts with the picture that has been formed of experience, that it is impossible to combine its special qualities with the features of the picture and the aesthetic is given an outside place and status. . . .

The account that has been given of experience dominantly intellectual and practical is intended to show that there is no such contrast involved in having an experience; that, on the contrary, no experience of whatever sort is a unity unless it has aesthetic quality.

The enemies of the aesthetic are neither the practical nor the intellectual. They are the humdrum; slackness of loose ends; submission to convention in practice and intellectual procedure. Rigid abstinence, coerced submission, tightness on one side and dissipation, incoherence and aimless indulgence on the other, are deviations in opposite directions from the unity of an experience. Some such considerations perhaps induced Aristotle to invoke the "mean proportional" as the proper designation of what is distinctive of both virtue and the aesthetic. He was formally correct. "Means" and "proportion" are, however, not self-explanatory, nor to be taken over in a prior mathematical sense, but are properties belonging to an experience that has a developing movement toward its own consummation.

Dewey is cited at this length because he could scarcely be classed as an "aesthete," and his support is useful as a defense against the possible charge that this book represents a late flowering of Wilde-Pater-Moore "aestheticism." Aestheticism is a view of life in which appreciation of the fine arts is the most important value; the experiences held to be most worth having are those found in the presence of paintings, poetry, music, and architecture. Beyond question the importance of these *is* great, but to claim that such moments alone are important is either vicious or pretentious, and in either case absurd. When aestheticism was preached as a philosophy of life, its one-sidedness resulted in the recommendation of a way of living that was as impressionistic as the painting that the aesthetes admired. It is all very well to catch bright experience on the wing, but exclusive attention to bright or lurid patches and to their pursuit could scarcely fail to foster a life of perpetual flights and hoppings, a life rendered finally trivial by its lack of continuity and form.

10. George Santayana, *The Life of Reason: Reason in Science* (New York: Scribner's, 1948), p. 253.

CHAPTER IV

1. Fyodor Dostoyevsky, *The Brothers Karamazov* (New York: Modern Library, n.d.), pp. 289–291.

2. *Cf.* Bertrand Russell, *A History of Western Philosophy* (New York: Simon & Schuster, 1945), pp. 173, 184. It is, for instance, the apparent lukewarmness of Aristotle that stirs to wrath a passionate soul like Bertrand Russell:

He [Aristotle] shows no sign of having had any of the experiences which make it difficult to preserve sanity; all the more profound aspects of the moral life are apparently unknown to him. He leaves out, one may say, the whole sphere of human experience with which religion is concerned. What he has to say is what will be useful to comfortable men of weak passions; but he has nothing to say to those who are possessed by a God or a devil, or whom outward misfortune drives to despair. For these reasons, in my judgment, his Ethics, in spite of its fame, is lacking in intrinsic importance.

With all respect to Lord Russell, this polemic misses half the point. Aristotle could scarcely have found it necessary to recommend passion to the Greeks. If he emphasizes temperance, control, and the golden mean, it is because he had good cause to suspect their absence in those who might read his works or attend his public lectures. He is not recommending passionlessness, but rather the comprehension of the intensities man is given: without matter there is nothing to be formed.

It should also be remembered that it is to man as *citizen,* and specifically citizen of the city-state, that the *Nicomachean Ethics* is addressed. Any Greek would have considered those passions that Russell censures Aristotle for ignoring to be apolitical, "idiotic," and to have no necessary place in the *Ethics.*

3. Dostoyevsky, *op. cit.,* pp. 279–280.

4. *Ibid.,* p. 287. *Cf.* pp. 283 ff.

5. It is reasonable and proper to study the affective lives of famous men, and these slogans can give excellent clues to the attitudes of those who use them. We can learn something about human nature by trying to fathom a Robespierre or a de Maistre, Marx or Calvin, Dewey or Niebuhr—not to mention Rousseau and Augustine—but what we learn is about *them,* the species of human nature they represent. It will always be a mistake to take their vision of the genus literally.

6. Werner Jaeger, *Paideia: The Ideals of Greek Culture* (New York: Oxford Univ. Press, 1945), p. 21.

7. When in 1774 the House of Commons was debating the taxes that were finally to precipitate the American Revolution, C. W. Cornwall was brash enough to say that the only subject of inquiry

ought to be "not how we got into this difficulty, but how we are to get out of it."

It was inevitable that Burke should reply to this. "In other words, we are, according to him, to consult our invention, and to reject our experience. The mode of deliberation he recommends is diametrically opposite to every rule of reason and every principle of good sense established amongst mankind. For that sense and that reason I have always understood absolutely to prescribe, whenever we are involved in difficulties from the measures we have pursued, that we should take a strict review of those measures, in order to correct our errors, if they should be corrigible; or at least to avoid a dull uniformity in mischief, and the unpitied calamity of being repeatedly caught in the same snare." Edmund Burke, "American Taxation," in *Speeches and Letters on American Affairs* (London: J. M. Dent & Sons, 1908 [1956]), p. 3.

8. Charles Baudelaire, *Intimate Journals* (Boston: Beacon Press, 1957), pp. 11–12.

9. T. S. Eliot, "The Hollow Men," in *Complete Poems and Plays* (New York: Harcourt, Brace & Co., 1952), p. 56.

10. We can try to attend to the way we are beneath all distinctions, and then try to describe what we have found, but to the extent that we have been successful in the former, we lose our gain in the latter: to think and to talk is to make distinctions. We *can* go a little way with metaphor, and hope to evoke in our hearers something like the immediate experience we have had. The mistake of philosophers of Will and Intuition is in thinking their metaphors to be descriptions, and that described to have prerogative reality or value. It is playing with loaded words to call the supposed objects of sub-cognitive apprehension "real," and everything else "illusory" or "unreal"; this may reflect a judgment of relative value (we do tend to give the honorific "real" to what we cherish) but there is no reason beyond this for using these particular names. (*Cf.* Lewis, *Mind and the World-Order*, pp. 147–148.) When we leave evaluation and metaphysics aside and consider Schopenhauer or Bergson as descriptive artists of the romantic school, artists who take as their subject the more primitive levels of natural human experience, we most clearly see what they have to show us.

11. Having argued against Plato that form is adjectival, that it has

no real being apart from matter (except perhaps in the mind of the thinker who knows it), that reality consists in substances which are always inseparably compounded of form and matter, that the soul is the form of a natural substance that possesses the possibility of life— after all this Aristotle says that God is pure form without matter (although he also says that God is not a natural object), that the forms of species may exist on their own, and that man's active intellect, the highest actualization of his unique and prerogative form, can eternally exist without its matter (though there is nothing personal about this immortality). It is doubtful that Aristotle need have said any of these things to maintain his systematic position. On the contrary, they seem to be the views of his teacher creeping in, and they sort very badly with the rest of what he says.

CHAPTER V

1. Thomas Mann, *Doctor Faustus*, pp. 236–237.

2. Recently Donald Williams said "some such contrast as that of form and matter would be common intellectual property, no doubt, even if Aristotle and Kant had not made such relentless metaphysics of it. As things are, the Aristotelian notion in particular has probably affected more human beings than has any other philosophic concept. Few doctrines are easier to explain in a textbook paragraph; almost none is harder to understand in detail and in principle." ("Form and Matter," *The Philosophical Review*, LXVII [1958], 291.)

This is true in the present case, but the exigencies of our practical use of Aristotle's language do not include a close analysis of his theoretical use of it. Aristotle would probably disapprove of our unmetaphysical use of his terms and the consequent shift in the basis for judging "more or less formed," a shift from an intellectual to an affective ground of judgment. Our care is not fidelity to Aristotle's meanings—which are in any case vexed—but to use "universal," "form," and "matter" only in those senses that the absence of metaphysics allows.

3. Descriptions take on perspective import when they are *used* as rules, or when the thing described is used as a model. As we shall see, this is not a "deduction" of normative from descriptive statements; the process is more like that in which descriptions are trans-

formed into definitions. See C. Douglas McGee, "Explicit Definitions and Ethical Rules," *Ethics,* LXXIII (April, 1963), 198–207.

4. Those who hold metaphysical beliefs emotionally consonant with the moral recommendations to be made here will probably find those recommendations congenial, but feel that they would have greater stability and strength if they were supported by speculation on the essential nature of things. Those whose beliefs on the ultimately real chime better with some other moral view will probably think their metaphysics an argument against our evaluations. Except as an adjunct to rhetoric—and the semblance of cognitive ground in metaphysics *can* have persuasive force—the support and attack alike are spurious, and false in pretending to a kind of meaning they do not have.

5. "Similarly in all other things which involve production for an end; the product cannot come to be without things which have a necessary nature, but it is not due to these (except as its material) ; it came to be for an end. For instance, why is a saw such as it is? To affect so-and-so and for the sake of so-and-so. This end, however, cannot be realized unless the saw is made of iron. It is, therefore, necessary for it to be made of iron, *if* we are to have a saw and perform the operation of sawing. What is necessary, then, is necessary on a hypothesis; it is not a result necessarily determined by antecedents. Necessity is in the matter, while 'that for the sake of which' is in the definition [the form]." Aristotle, *Physics,* R. McKeon, ed., pp. 251–252. *Cf. Metaphysics, loc. cit.,* pp. 756–757.

6. Aristotle, *Nichomachean Ethics,* R. McKeon, ed., pp. 991, 999.

7. Mann, *op. cit.,* p. 134.

8. *Ibid.,* p. 182.

9. *Ibid.,* pp. 240, 241.

10. Contempt for the perfectors of a tradition is most often absent in those we should least hesitate to call great artists. This is true even of the best romantics: the early Goethe, Shelley, Géricault, Mendelssohn, Schumann. Of course good men will always look down on hacks, especially when the hacks win all the prizes, but great men generally recognize their own sort—think of the relation of Delacroix to Poussin. When they revile academicism it is the vulgarization or trivialization of a tradition against which they complain; perhaps they know what will in time become of their new departures.

CHAPTER VI

1. William Butler Yeats, "A Prayer for My Daughter," in *Collected Poems* (New York: Macmillan, 1956), p. 186.

2. Aristotle, *Nicomachean Ethics*, M. Ostwald, ed. and trans. (Indianapolis: Bobbs-Merrill, 1962), p. 35.

3. This is quoted by Sir Kenneth Clark in *The Nude: A Study in Ideal Form* (Garden City: Doubleday Anchor Books, 1959), p. 33.

4. Jaeger, *Paideia*, pp. 36–37.

5. George Santayana, *The Library of Living Philosophers: The Philosophy of George Santayana*, P. A. Schilpp, ed. (Evanston: Library of Living Philosophers, 1940), p. 563.

6. Homer, *The Iliad*, R. Lattimore, trans. (Chicago: University of Chicago Press, 1951 [1957]), pp. 266–267. To most ages before ours this whole speech was almost a cliché, its moral obvious to all those likely to read Homer. As one would expect, Pope's translation points the lesson more sharply than does the original:

Why on those shores are we with joy surveyed,
Admired as heroes, and as gods obeyed,
Unless great acts superior merit prove,
And vindicate the bounteous powers above.
Tis ours, the dignity they give to grace;
The first in valour, as the first in place
That when with wondering eyes our martial band
Behold our deeds transcending our commands,
Such, they may cry, deserve the sovereign state,
When those that envy, dare not imitate!

7. The life that spends its intensity on the concerns celebrated in the sacraments stands well on its way to the pervasive sense of significant form. But, from a religious point of view, to interpret the sacraments as we have done is to make the step poor Christian made when he followed Worldly Wiseman from the Slough of Despond. In the Western tradition every religion worthy of the name has mistaken its mythical reconstruction of human destiny for a set of literal truths, has taken its vision of man's end for an essay in history and physics. This mistake is the essence of supernatural religion: do away with the mistake and you do away with religion itself.

Here is one way to put the dilemma that undercuts much of the wisdom in George Santayana's *Reason in Religion,* and that embarrasses or should embarrass advocates of the New Theology: Religion is best understood as a mythical version of man's natural and moral situation, having its whole significance as a poetic paradigm or archetype of affective life; to accept religion as an edifying myth is not to accept religion at all, but to steal the emotional force of its name and associations as a cover for some system of worldly wisdom. There is worse than semantic dishonesty in the attempt to appropriate the traditional dignity and affective power of "religion" while evading all historical and cognitive obligations; there is a refusal to think through to the grounds and sanctions of wisdom and conduct. Such slipperiness is particularly unbecoming to theologians, but it is understandable when we see that honesty would force them either to a straightforward supernaturalism or out of business.

Those of us who are not theologians can say that traditional religions have often been right about means and always wrong about ends, wrong about the final "why" but right about the "how," about the discipline of attention and its proper objects. In abandoning the supernatural "why" one gives up religion and is left with something thinner and more pallid, less rhetorical, less able to take strong hold on the affections—but also honest, less fantastic, and able to command at once clarity and assent.

8. G. W. F. Hegel, *The Phenomenology of Mind:* "The Contrite Consciousness," J. Royce, trans., *Modern Classical Philosophers,* B. Rand, ed. (New York: Houghton Mifflin, 1908 [1952]), p. 620.

CHAPTER VII

1. Dover Wilson, *The Essential Shakespeare* (Cambridge: The University Press, 1933), p. 82.

2. To take Tristan and Isolde as figures of romantic love is not to accept the sweeping use of their story made by Denis de Rougemont. *Love in the Western World* is an immensely suggestive book, but the further its author goes from human wisdom expressed (and distorted) by the sacrament of marriage, whether his flights be into theology, metaphysics, history or description of the modern world, the less we can depend on his intuitions. It is characteristic of quasi-theological speculation to start from natural facts as difficult to deny as to

explain and to take the latter difficulty as reason or excuse for interpretation that escapes into mystification. This being said it must also be said that despite de Rougemont's distortions and exaggerations—perhaps even aided by them—we can, through his work, see afresh some finally simple and natural facts about men and women in love.

BIBLIOGRAPHY

In addition to editions actually cited in the text, this bibliography lists the most available or least expensive editions of works cited or mentioned in the text.

Aristotle, *The Basic Works of Aristotle* (R. McKeon, ed.), New York: Random House, 1941.

———, *Nicomachean Ethics* (M. Ostwald, ed. and trans.), Indianapolis: Bobbs-Merrill, 1962.

Ayer, A. J., *Language, Truth and Logic,* London: Gollancz, 1936; New York: Dover Publications, 1952.

Babbitt, Irving, *Rousseau and Romanticism,* New York: Meridian Books, 1955.

Baudelaire, Charles, *Intimate Journals,* Boston: Beacon Press, 1957.

Beardsley, Monroe C., *Aesthetics: Problems in the Philosophy of Criticism,* New York: Harcourt, Brace & Co., 1958.

Bergson, Henri, *Creative Evolution* (A. Mitchell, trans.), New York: Modern Library, 1944.

Berkeley, George, *The Principles of Human Knowledge,* La Salle: Open Court, 1940.

———, *Three Dialogues Between Hylas and Philonous,* La Salle: Open Court, 1947.

Bierce, Ambrose, *The Devil's Dictionary,* New York: Dover Publications, 1958.

Blake, William, *The Complete Writings of William Blake* (G. Keynes, ed.), London: Nonesuch Press, 1957; New York: Random House, 1957.

Bunyan, John, *The Pilgrim's Progress from this world to that which is to come,* London: J. M. Dent & Co., 1909.

Burke, Edmund, *Speeches and Letters on American Affairs,* London: J. M. Dent & Sons, 1908 (1956).

Clark, Kenneth, *The Nude: A Study in Ideal Form,* Garden City: Doubleday Anchor Books, 1959.

Conrad, Joseph, *Victory,* New York: Modern Library, n.d.

Descartes, René, *Meditations* and *Selections from the Principles of Philosophy,* La Salle: Open Court, 1937.

Dewey, John, *Art as Experience,* New York: Minton, Balch & Co., 1934.

Dostoyevsky, Fyodor, *The Brothers Karamazov,* New York: Modern Library, n.d.

Eliot, T. S., *Complete Poems and Plays,* New York: Harcourt, Brace & Co., 1952.

——, *The Sacred Wood,* London: Methuen & Co., 1920; New York: University Paperbacks, Barnes & Noble, 1960.

Fichte, Johann Gottlieb, *The Vocation of Man* (W. Smith, trans.), Indianapolis: Bobbs-Merrill, 1940.

Goethe, Johann Wolfgang v., *Leiden des jungen Werthers,* Leipzig: G. J. Goschen, 1787.

Hegel, G. W. F., *Logic* (translated from *The Encyclopaedia of the Philosophical Sciences* by W. Wallace), Oxford: Clarendon Press, 1874.

——, *The Phenomenology of Mind* (J. B. Baillie, trans.), New York: The Macmillan Co., 1931 (1955).

——, *The Phenomenology of Mind:* "The Contrite Consciousness" (J. Royce, trans.), *Modern Classical Philosophers* (B. Rand, ed.), New York: Houghton Mifflin, 1908 (1952).

——, *The Philosophy of Hegel* (C. J. Friedrich, ed.), New York: Modern Library, 1954.

BIBLIOGRAPHY

Homer, *The Iliad* (R. Lattimore, trans.), Chicago: University of Chicago Press, 1951 (1957).

Hume, David, *A Treatise of Human Nature* (L. A. Selby-Bigge, ed.), Oxford: Clarendon Press, 1888; Garden City: Dolphin Books, Doubleday & Co., 1961.

———, *An Inquiry Concerning the Principles of Morals,* Indianapolis: Bobbs-Merrill, 1957.

Jaeger, Werner, *Paideia: The Ideals of Greek Culture,* New York: Oxford University Press, 1945.

Johnson, Samuel, *The Lives of the Most Eminent English Poets,* London: J. Rivington & Sons, etc., 1790; Chicago: Gateway Editions, Henry Regnery Co., 1955.

Joyce, James, *Portrait of the Artist as a Young Man,* New York: Modern Library, 1928.

Kerouac, Jack, *On The Road,* New York: Compass Books, Viking Press, 1959.

Kierkegaard, S., *Fear and Trembling, The Sickness Unto Death,* New York: Anchor Books, Doubleday & Co., 1954.

Lewis, C. I., *Mind and the World-Order,* New York: Scribner's, 1929; New York: Dover Publications, 1956.

Locke, John, *Essay Concerning Human Understanding,* La Salle: Open Court, 1933.

Macaulay, T. B., *Critical and Historical Essays,* London: J. M. Dent & Sons, 1907 (1951).

McGee, C. Douglas, "Explicit Definitions and Ethical Rules," *Ethics,* LXXIII (1963), 198–207.

Machado de Assis, J. M., *Epitaph of a Small Winner,* New York: Noonday Press, 1952.

Mann, Thomas, *Doctor Faustus* (H. T. Lowe-Porter, trans.), New York: Alfred A. Knopf, 1948.

Mills, C. Wright, *The Power Elite,* New York: Galaxy Books, Oxford University Press, 1956.

Palmer, R. R., *Twelve Who Ruled,* Princeton: Princeton University Press, 1951 (1958); New York: Atheneum Publishers, 1965.

Plato, *The Dialogues of Plato* (B. Jowett, trans.), New York: Random House, 1937.

Protagoras, *Ancilla to the Pre-Socratic Philosophers* (K. Freeman, ed.), Cambridge: Harvard University Press, 1957.

Rechey, J., *City of Night*, New York: Grove Press, 1963.

Riesman, David, *The Lonely Crowd*, Garden City: Anchor Books, Doubleday & Co., n.d.

Rougemont, Denis de, *Love in the Western World*, New York: Harcourt, Brace & Co., 1940.

Rousseau, Jean-Jacques, *The Confessions* (J. M. Cohen, trans.), Baltimore: Penguin Books, 1953.

Russell, Bertrand, *A History of Western Philosophy*, New York: Simon & Schuster, 1945.

Ryle, Gilbert, *The Concept of Mind*, New York: Barnes & Noble, 1949.

Santayana, George, *The Library of Living Philosophers: The Philosophy of George Santayana* (P. A. Schilpp, ed.), Evanston: Library of Living Philosophers, 1940.

Santayana, George, *The Life of Reason: Reason in Religion*, New York: Scribner's, 1905 (1948); New York: Collier Books, 1962.

——, *The Life of Reason: Reason in Science*, New York: Scribner's, 1905 (1948); New York: Collier Books, 1962.

Sartre, Jean-Paul, *Being and Nothingness* (Hazel Barnes, trans.), New York: Philosophical Library, 1956; New York: Citadel Press, 1964.

Schopenhauer, Arthur, *The Will to Live: Selected Writings* (R. Taylor, ed.), New York: Anchor Books, Doubleday & Co., 1962.

West, Nathanael, *Miss Lonelyhearts*, New York: New Directions, 1933; New York: Avon Books, The Hearst Corp., 1964.

Whyte, William H., Jr., *The Organization Man*, New York: Simon & Schuster, 1956; New York: Anchor Books, Doubleday & Co., 1957.

Williams, Donald C., "Form and Matter," *The Philosophical Review*, LXVII (1958), 291–312, 499–521.

Wilson, Dover, *The Essential Shakespeare,* Cambridge: The University Press, 1933.

Wolfe, Thomas, *Look Homeward, Angel*, New York: Scribner's, 1952.

——, *The Web and the Rock*, New York: Sun Dial Press, 1940; New York: Dell Publishing Co., 1960.

Woolf, Virginia, *Mrs. Dalloway*, New York: Modern Library, 1928.

BIBLIOGRAPHY

————, *To the Lighthouse,* New York: Harcourt, Brace & Co., 1927.

Yeats, William Butler, *The Collected Poems of W. B. Yeats,* New York: The Macmillan Co., 1956.

————, *The Letters of W. B. Yeats* (Allan Wade, ed.), New York: The Macmillan Co., 1955.

ABOUT THE AUTHOR

C. DOUGLAS MCGEE *was born in New York City in 1926. He received his B.S. and M.A. from Northwestern University and his Ph.D. from Harvard University. Mr. McGee is Chairman of the Department of Philosophy at Bowdoin College, where he has taught since 1963. He has also taught philosophy at Harvard, Vassar, and Northwestern and spent 1961 in England on a Vassar Faculty Fellowship. His articles have appeared in* The Journal of Philosophy, Philosophical Quarterly, Mind, Inquiry, The Chicago Review, *and other periodicals. At present he is working on another book that will develop further the themes introduced in the last chapter of* The Recovery of Meaning. *Mr. McGee, his wife, and two children live in South Freeport, Maine.*

TYPE NOTE

The text of this book has been set on the Linotype in a type face called Baskerville. The face is a facsimile reproduction of type cast from molds made for JOHN BASKERVILLE *(1706–75) from his designs. The punches for the revived Linotype Baskerville were cut under the supervision of the English printer George W. Jones.*

John Baskerville's original face was one of the forerunners of the type-style known as "modern face" to printers: a "modern" of the period A.D. *1800.*

The book was composed, printed, and bound by The Hadden Craftsmen, Inc., Scranton, Pa.